CHICAGO CERAMICS & GLASS

an illustrated history from 1871 to 1933

by Sharon S. Darling

artifacts photographed by Walter W. Krutz

Chicago Historical Society, Chicago, Illinois, 1979

Frontispiece: Polychrome terra cotta block designed
by Louis H. Sullivan for the Henry B. Babson
residence, Riverside, Illinois. Executed by the
Northwestern Terra Cotta Company, Chicago, 1909.
(h: 25½"). *David Norris*

Published by the Chicago Historical Society
Clark Street at North Avenue, Chicago, Illinois 60614

Distributed by the University of Chicago Press
5801 S. Ellis Avenue, Chicago, Illinois 60637

Publication made possible by support from
the National Endowment for the Arts and
the Philip K. Wrigley Special Publication Fund

Library of Congress Card Catalog Number 79-91566
ISBN 0-913820-10-5

Editor: Fannia Weingartner
Design: Staples & Charles Ltd

Typeset by Publication Composition Corporation
Printed in the U.S.A. by Congress Printing Company

iv

ACKNOWLEDGMENTS

▼▼

The research that became the basis for *Chicago Ceramics & Glass* and the exhibition it accompanies began in 1972, when two Teco vases acquired by the Chicago Historical Society first sparked my interest in Chicago-made ceramics. I soon discovered that some of the leading producers of ceramics were primarily engaged in manufacturing architectural terra cotta. Almost simultaneously I learned that many of Chicago's most beautiful stained glass windows and mosaics had also been made in local workshops and this prompted me to seek information about the people who had created them.

While the contributions of many individuals are reflected in both the exhibition and publication, a special thanks must go to George A. Berry III, Kendall Bird, Frank J. Drehobl, Jr., Trygve Kristiansen, Paul F. Larson, Edgar Miller, Donald and Russell Parsche, R. J. Pyne, John Sand, William Scudella, Thomas S. Snyder, and Lubomyr Wandzura who shared with me their experiences in the glass and terra cotta industries. Descendants of artisans who willingly located objects, biographical information, photographs, and tools include: Elizabeth F. Cheney, Mrs. John T. Cochrane, Jr., Richard J. Donath, Valentine Moreau Epstein, Ora Gates, Mary Claire Hersh, David Miller, Joseph O'Shaughnessy, Dorothy Pickard Platt, Edward R. Schauble, Elsa B. and Walter E. Seidel, Carlyn L. Whitehand, Robert Williamson, and Marianne Flanagan Zeman.

As the exhibition developed, Rosalie Berberian, Robert A. Furhoff, Linda Kriegel, Annette Krum, David Norris, Timothy Samuelson, Charles R. Steers, and Irma Strauss enthusiastically assisted in locating suitable objects in private collections. Beatrice Swartchild and Frances Spence checked city directories and compiled exhibition records, while Susan Morris devoted countless hours to the unglamorous tasks of processing loans, locating photos, and cleaning objects.

Fannia Weingartner, the Society's editor, gave invaluable help in all aspects of this project. Gail F. Casterline, Paul Evans, Erne R. and Florence Frueh, Glen E. Holt, Walker Johnson, Trygve Kristiansen, Timothy Samuelson, John Sand, Mel Skvarla, Carl John Sterner, and John Vinci all read the manuscript and contributed constructive criticism. Sylvia Landsman cheerfully and expertly undertook the burdensome task of typing the manuscript and labels. Marcia Beales and Grant T. Dean proofread and Patricia Brennan prepared the index. The talents of designers Barbara Charles and Robert Staples are reflected in both the exhibition and publication.

The expertise of Walter W. Krutz, who photographed the objects, is evident throughout the book. Eleanor Gordon, Donald G. Kalec, Jean Nerenberg, and Roberta Stadler generously shared their slides of terra cotta buildings, while William R. Boles provided excellent architectural photographs.

Staff members of various museums, libraries, and business establishments who proved particularly helpful include: Donald Magner, American Arts & Crafts, Brooklyn; Cecelia Chin, Deborah Ezzio, Milo M. Naeve, Daphne Roloff, and John Zukowsky, The Art Institute of Chicago; Rev. Patrick Mullins, St. Vincent's Church, Chicago; Jethro M. Hurt III, The Chicago Architecture Foundation; Mikell C. Darling, Evanston Historical Society; Thomas M. Tomc, Fly-By-Nite Gallery, Chicago; Bruce Pfeiffer, The Frank Lloyd Wright Memorial Foundation; Donald G. Kalec, The Frank Lloyd Wright Home & Studio Foundation, Oak Park; Donald P. Hallmark, The Richard W. Bock Museum, Greenville College, Greenville; Joel Cohen, Joel Cohen Antiques, Chicago; Todd Volpe, Jordan-Volpe Gallery, New York City; Mary Dawson, Loyola University; Yvonne Spiegal, Marshall Field & Company, Chicago; Thomas M. Sersha, Milwaukee County Historical Society; Pat H. Johnson, *Pottery Collectors Newsletter;* Marilyn Hasbrouck, Prairie Avenue Bookshop; Shirley Mann and Faye Spiro, The Red Bandana, Chicago; Richard Hartung and Maurice Montgomery, Rock County Historical Society, Janesville, Wisconsin; Daniel Perlman, Roosevelt University; Joseph Francis, Second Presbyterian Church of Chicago; J. Jefferson Miller II, National Museum of History & Technology, Smithsonian Institution; A. Christian Revi, *Spinning Wheel;* Norman Temme, *Stained Glass;* Joan Severa and Anne Woodhouse, State Historical Society of Wisconsin; Joseph Duci Bella, Theatre Historical Society, Chicago; Mary Ann Johnson and Mary Lynn McCree, Jane Addams Memorial Collection, University of Illinois at Chicago Circle; Alan K. Lathrop Northwest Architectural Archives, University of Minnesota; Jairus Barnes, The Western Reserve Historical Society, Cleveland.

Sharon S. Darling
Curator of Decorative Arts

LENDERS TO THE EXHIBITION

Michael and Fern Abrahams, Brooklyn, New York
Jane Addams Memorial Collection, University of Illinois at Chicago Circle
Adrian Alexander
The Art Institute of Chicago
Bruce Baker
Collection of Florence I. Balasny-Barnes
Frances B. Barbera
Mrs. George A. Basta
Rosalie Berberian
George A. Berry III, TC Industries, Inc.
George and Judith Blucker
Collection of Sonia and Walter Bob
The Richard W. Bock Sculpture Collection, Greenville College, Illinois
Mrs. LeRoy T. Carlson
Mr. and Mrs. Jeffrey L. Casterline
The Center for Research Libraries
Robert and Margaret Chainski
Elizabeth F. Cheney
The Chicago Architecture Foundation
Joel Cohen
Robert and Kathy Coleman
Tari Costan
Mikell C. Darling
DePaul University
Mr. and Mrs. Edward De Young
Mr. and Mrs. Alan Dobry
Richard J. Donath
Drehobl Bros. Art Glass Co. Inc.
Joseph R. Duci Bella
Beatrice Fortner
Theodore N. Foss

Research Center, The Frank Lloyd Wright Home and Studio Foundation
Florence Frueh
Robert A. Furhoff
Gallerie Areta, Miami, Florida
Family of William Day Gates
Marcia and William Goodman
Mr. and Mrs. Joseph A. Guyer
Mr. and Mrs. Ronald Handler
Wilbert and Marilyn Hasbrouck
Roger and Jean Helm
M. Epstein Hersh, Inc.
Glenn C. Hjort
Mrs. Chauncey G. Hobart
Jordan-Volpe Gallery, New York
Trygve Kristiansen
Walter and Teresa Krutz
Mr. and Mrs. W. C. Kummerow
Harriet Wesley Lanyon
Richard Lanyon
Frank L. Linden, Jr.
Hedwig L. Loeb
Andrew Lopez
Mr. and Mrs. Terry Lutz
D. Magner, American Arts and Crafts, Brooklyn, New York
Marshall Field & Company
Dickinson Martin
James Mattucci
James and Louisa McPharlin
Edward and Allen Mertes
David and Ruth Michael
David Miller
Frank Milligan, Milligan Antique Galleries
Milwaukee County Historical Society

National Museum of History and Technology, Smithsonian Institution
Thomas J. Neniskis
Walter and Dawn Clark Netsch
The Newberry Library
David Norris
Joseph O'Shaughnessy
Amanda Palmer
Parsche Studios
Dorothy Pickard Platt
Mr. and Mrs. Daniel Potochniak
Lenore Pressman
R. J. Pyne, Western Sandblast Mfg. Co.
Gertrude E. Rangel
Marvin and Eileen Reingold
A. Christian Revi
Rock County Historical Society
Roosevelt University
Mr. and Mrs. Timothy Samuelson
Mr. and Mrs. Howard E. Schauble
Second Presbyterian Church of Chicago
Elsa B. Seidel and Walter E. Seidel
Thomas S. Snyder
Paul Sprague
State Historical Society of Wisconsin
Charles R. Steers, Anaheim, California
Mr. and Mrs. Helmut Strauss
Thomas M. Tomc, Fly-By-Night Gallery
The University of Chicago
John Vinci
Todd M. Volpe Collection
The Western Reserve Historical Society
Dora Williamson White
Mr. and Mrs. Frank H. Whitehand
Terry and Nancy Young
Marianne Flanagan Zemen
Mr. and Mrs. Charles O. Zollar

CONTENTS

PREFACE   xi

AUTHOR'S NOTE   xiii

DECORATIVE ARTS   1

  INTRODUCTION TO DECORATIVE ARTS   3

  HANDPAINTED CHINA   7

  ART POTTERY   47

  CUT & ENGRAVED GLASS   83

ARCHITECTURAL ARTS   95

  INTRODUCTION TO ARCHITECTURAL ARTS   97

  STAINED & ORNAMENTAL GLASS   101

  ARCHITECTURAL TERRA COTTA   161

OTHER SHOPS & CRAFTWORKERS   205

SOURCES   211

INDEX   215

PREFACE

This book, *Chicago Ceramics & Glass*, is the second in a series of publications related to exhibits which explore important aspects of Chicago's rich tradition in the decorative arts. The Chicago Historical Society has very special resources to bring to such a project. As a major repository of original historical materials it is an especially appropriate center for such research. Its staff, including curators, librarians, and others of many talents, can use the society's collections and related research materials to perceive the city's history in new ways. And its exhibits and publications serve to bring this information before a broad public audience.

That is the function of this book, which, like the earlier *Chicago Metalsmiths* (1977), is a pioneering effort. In *Chicago Ceramics & Glass,* Sharon S. Darling has studied several groups of objects representative of the decorative and architectural arts. But she has done more than study the objects themselves, she has placed them in their larger historical context. In doing so she has created not only an important work of original research, but has provided a model for other historical studies of the decorative arts in America.

Harold K. Skramstad, Jr.
Director

AUTHOR'S NOTE

Between 1871, when the Great Fire destroyed the city's business district, and 1933, when Chicago hosted its Century of Progress Exposition, the city's artists, craftsmen, and architects were responsible for some remarkable innovations in the decorative arts and architecture. Some of the men responsible for these innovations—Louis H. Sullivan and Frank Lloyd Wright, for example—have become legends; most, however, are known to only a few specialists or have been forgotten altogether.

Chicago Ceramics & Glass focuses on two groups of art products and on those who designed and created them. Section I, Decorative Arts, discusses the smaller scale, primarily decorative objects: hand-painted china, art pottery, and cut and engraved glass. Section II, Architectural Arts, deals with the products whose design and manufacture were closely tied to architectural trends—stained and ornamental glass and architectural terra cotta.

While this study has not attempted to encompass all aspects of the history of these diverse art industries, it has tried to set the course for further exploration.

DECO ◆
RATIVE
◆ ARTS

INTRODUCTION TO DECORATIVE ARTS

The development of china painting and art pottery in Chicago shared a number of common elements. To begin with, the practice of these arts evolved, thrived, and declined during the same period—from after the Fire of 1871 to the onset of the Great Depression at the end of 1929. Second, many of the same people were drawn into the design and manufacture of both kinds of products. Eventually, both changed from being primarily female domestic crafts to what were known as art industries, carried on in sizeable manufactories which advertised nationwide. Both were stimulated by the preparations for the 1893 World's Columbian Exposition in Chicago and by the subsequent opportunity to see examples of arts and crafts from all over the world.

The third art industry, the production of cut glass tablewares, was in fact an outgrowth of the 1893 Fair. Like handpainted china and art pottery, cut glass offered a touch of elegance within the means of a growing middle class. And like the producers of ceramics, the artisans who created cut glass drew inspiration from geometric and botanical forms as they attempted to turn utilitarian objects into works of art.

The local evolution of all three paralleled what was happening in the major urban centers of America, England, and the Continent. As in the case of other arts, styles and techniques crossed the Atlantic and traveled to Chicago with remarkable rapidity. Equally important, the stream of immigrants drawn to Chicago in the late nineteenth and early twentieth centuries brought to the area craftsmen with a high degree of skill in various fields, including those of china painting, the making and decorating of ceramics, and glass cutting and engraving. But all was not merely a matter of imitation. In two cases—the innovations of the Atlan Ceramic Art Club in china painting and the experiments of William Day Gates in developing Teco art pottery—departures from the conventional resulted in unique contributions to design.

At the turn of the century Chicago's decorative arts reflected the influence of the Arts and Crafts Movement. Having spurred the development of similiar art industries in England since the 1860s, this movement reached Chicago by the 1880s. Essentially a protest against some of the alarming social consequences perceived as byproducts of industrialization—dehumanization of the worker by the machine and a decline in the quality of the goods produced by machines—the Arts and Crafts Movement stressed simplicity in design, respect for natural materials, and the use of handmade objects which embodied the skill and the spirit of the craftsman. Calling for a return of art to the people, Arts and Crafts advocates hoped that reverting to small scale craft production would accomplish two objectives: restore dignity to the workman and improve the design of everyday household objects.

Although William Morris and other proponents of the Arts and Crafts philosophy in England were initially criticized both there and abroad, their ideas gradually gained acceptance. By the 1880s "art" furnishings had become profitable as well as fashionable, and their production was considered a respectable livelihood and a morally regenerative force in cities as far away from England as Chicago. Here, by the end of the century, organizations such as the Chicago Arts and Crafts Society, the School of the Art Institute of Chicago, and individuals as diverse as social worker Jane Addams and architect Frank Lloyd Wright were promoting fresh approaches in all aspects of decorative design—in ceramics and glass as well as architecture.

By 1929 all three industries, along with the Arts and Crafts Movement itself, had reached their peaks of popularity and were beginning to decline. World War I had brought material shortages while the postwar era brought changes in taste and a public no longer willing or able to pay for handcrafted objects. But, in the meantime, numerous designers and artisans had enriched Chicago's private homes and public buildings with the products of their skillful hands and lofty aspirations.

1. The tools of the china painter.
*CHS; Milwaukee County
Historical Society*

2. *Old Japan* plaque with blue
chrysanthemums, painted by
Helen F. Frazee, 1898. (d: 12").
*CHS, gift of Mrs. Clifford Nolan,
Sr.*

HANDPAINTED CHINA

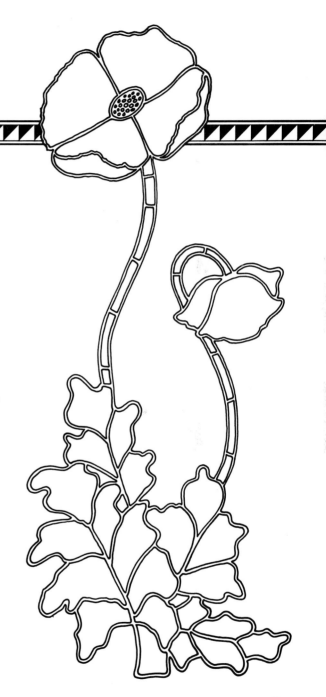

At the very time that enthusiastic British entrepreneurs were hailing the technologies introduced by the Industrial Revolution as harbingers of a better life for all, some nineteenth century social critics like Thomas Carlyle, John Ruskin, and later, William Morris, were raising their voices in dissent. These critics feared that the widespread use of machinery would produce uncreative and unhappy workers on the one hand and debased and poorly made objects on the other. In their view, the advantages of cheap and abundant household goods were outweighed by the long-range corrosive effects of mechanical production on the skills and spirit of the craftsmen and on the taste and judgment of the consumers.

By introducing such techniques as the use of molds, transfer printing, and what was essentially assembly-line production, British ceramic factories had begun to produce large quantities of inexpensive, elaborately ornamented tableware for the mass market. However, designers such as William Morris and Charles Eastlake viewed these heavily ornamented pieces as ill-proportioned and gaudy and called for simplicity in line and decoration. By the 1860s such criticisms had stimulated a revival of the handpainting of porcelain tablewares not only in England but in other industrialized countries like France, Austria, and Germany.

It was craftsmen from these countries who brought the art of china painting to the United States in the years following the Civil War and carried it to the major American cities. Many of them opened small china-decorating establishments, where they not only produced handpainted tableware for sale but also offered lessons in china painting and sold the necessary paints and porcelain blanks.

The first establishment of this kind in Chicago was the Western Decorating Works on Randolph Street, owned by Frederick L. Grunewald and Frederick J. Schmidt, two Germans who had come to Chicago in the late 1860s. The Western Decorating Works provided instruction in "artistic decorating and lettering on china and earthenware" and carried a complete line of German and English mineral colors along with undecorated porcelains, earthenwares, tiles, and plaques.

3. Trade card from Burley & Tyrrell, one of Chicago's largest crockery and glass importers, 1837–1919. *Staples & Charles*

4. Advertisement for the Western Decorating Works appearing in Mary Louise McLaughlin's instruction manual, *China Painting*, 1877. *CHS*

By 1878 local interest in china painting was sufficient to encourage the Western Decorating Works to install its first professional kiln to fire the overglaze decorations executed by its customers. Until then amateur painters had had to fire their work at home one piece at a time using small muffle kilns resembling ovens. The large kiln permitted the simultaneous firing of many pieces and reduced breakage due to improper temperature, thus saving both time and material. This encouraged beginners to attempt additional pieces, while offering advanced painters the opportunity to fire multi-piece projects like an entire tea set in a single firing.

Other classes in china painting had been taught since 1873 by L. T. Starring, a Mrs. Goodell, and Olivia Olsen, soon followed by Roxanna B. Preuszner, Mrs. John W. Marsh, and Adelaide Lyster. Professor Adolf Jann and his wife, talented artists from Dresden, and Mrs. Susan H. Clark, who established the South Side School of Art on 22nd Street in 1879, also offered instruction during this period.

Those who could not attend classes could teach themselves at home by using handbooks such as Mary Louise McLaughlin's *China Painting: A Manual for the Use of Amateurs in the Decoration of Hard Porcelain* (first issued in 1877) and *Suggestions to China Painters*, both published in Cincinnati.

In china or mineral painting, as it was sometimes called, the paint was applied over the glazed surface of a plain porcelain form or "blank" which had first been rubbed with turpentine. The design was then drawn on the surface with a lead pencil. Soft brushes and light, delicate strokes similar to those employed in watercolor painting were used to apply the mineral colors, which were composed of coloring oxides mixed with a flux of ground glass that permitted the colors to melt into the glaze during firing. When the decoration was complete, the piece was placed in a kiln and fired at a low temperature to permanently fuse the decoration onto the surface.

Since American porcelain factories were still in their infancy, most of the blanks used by china painters were imported from France or Germany, where they were turned out in huge quantities by manufactories in Limoges or Berlin. Of high quality, these imported wares came in intricate and fashionable shapes. Chicago's oldest and largest importer of china and glass, Burley & Tyrrell (renamed Burley & Company in 1884) carried so many of these porcelain blanks that it published an annual catalog for the convenience of its clients.

Access to firing facilities and the relatively inexpensive nature of the materials used made china painting an attractive hobby for Victorian women with some experience in oil and watercolor painting. In the hands of the truly talented it became a form of artistic expression. And for many it would become a genteel means of earning a living.

5. Tea set decorated with naturalistic violets, painted by Effie Dawes, 1900. (h: 6¾″).
CHS, gift of Mrs. Raymond Dawes

A Respected Profession and a Profitable Business

By the 1870s Chicago could boast a substantial number of prosperous families with wives and daughters who had time to give to good works and the pursuit of culture. Like embroidery and sketching, china painting was considered a suitable accomplishment for middle-class ladies. While many remained dabblers, a large number became highly skilled and serious about their work, and several earned acclaim as artists. That many considered china painting an art can be deduced from the fact that china painters signed their pieces with their names or initials.

The uncertain economic climate of the latter part of the nineteenth century—which brought inflation and recessions as well as periods of boom—gave some women an economic incentive to become china painters. Middle-class women in reduced circumstances, especially widows and unmarried women, found that they could turn this skill into a respectable source of income, and thus crossed the boundary that separated the amateur from the professional.

It was in response to the plight of such "gentlewomen thrown upon their own resources" that the Chicago Society of Decorative Art was founded in 1877, on the model of a New York organization established a year earlier. The Society sponsored classes in embroidery, drawing, woodcarving, and china painting and filled orders from clubs, businesses, and private individuals in an attempt to provide training and honorable employment for women. In its salesroom at The Art Institute of Chicago, the Society displayed and sold the work of its students.

During the following decade china painting became a staple course in young ladies' seminaries and art schools and its popularity continued to spread rapidly as articles giving instructions in the craft were printed in the *Ladies Home Journal*, the *Art Amateur*, and other magazines. Beginning in 1887 the art acquired its own voice, the *China Decorator*, a magazine which printed designs, suggested color schemes, and gave advice about choosing suitable china blanks. A successor, *Keramic Studio*, subtitled "a monthly magazine for the china painter and potter," was published in Syracuse, New York, by ceramist Adelaide Alsop Robineau from 1899 until her death in 1929. Reinforcing the growing popularity of handpainted china was the spreading influence of the Arts and Crafts Movement, which encouraged people to make art a part of their daily lives and to surround themselves with household objects that combined beauty and utility.

Teacups, plates, and tiles were the staples of beginning china painters while the more difficult fish or game sets, tea sets, and dresser sets were also much in vogue with the more ambitious painters. Decoration was usually keyed to the use for which the object was intended. Many followed the lead of Mary Louise McLaughlin, who, in her china painting manuals, indicated that while flowers were appropriate and pleasing on any surface, the use of heads and figures should be confined to objects not intended for table use—vases, plates or plaques to be hung as pictures, or tiles to be inset in a piece of furniture. For table or dresser use, she recommended flowers or conventional motifs inspired by Japanese designs or nature.

Flowers were universally favored and were applied to every type of object. Roses, violets, sweet peas, forget-me-nots, and daisies led the garden in popularity, with sunflowers and orchids becoming more abundant as the century progressed. The large china table services were decorated with themes symbolizing their function: fish sets featured various types of fish and shells; game sets displayed wild birds; punch bowls were encircled by grapes and spiraling vines. Delicate pastel shades were favored, as were maroon and brown tones, all highlighted with bands of gold or rococo touches of raised paste ornament.

As long as china painting remained popular, women taught classes in their homes and relied upon exhibitions and studio receptions to sell their work. By 1892, however, some of the more adventurous and talented painters had moved out of their homes and rented studios in the "china painting district" which encompassed the Auditorium tower, the Venetian Building, and the Marshall Field Building in the downtown business and cultural district. Noting this activity, the *Clay Record* of August 12, 1892, reported that "out of the 1,000 in and about Chicago whose taste and ambition have led them to make an effort in this direction, there are seventy teachers and several studios where orders are filled for customers, many coming from outside cities and towns." The article also noted that several ceramic organizations had recently been formed in preparation for the upcoming 1893 Fair.

Organizing and Elevating Ceramic Art

Early in 1892, as the great white city of the World's Columbian Exposition began to take shape on Chicago's southern lakefront, the city's women started to organize into various groups, clubs, and associations with the common goal of preparing exhibitions for the Woman's Building at the 1893 World's Fair. At the same time ceramic workers began organizing locally and nationally to try to secure a comprehensive representation of their achievements at the Fair.

The first attempt to unite Chicago's ceramic workers resulted in the formation on January 15, 1892, of the Chicago Ceramic Association. Its membership of 260 included both professionals and socialites. All of its officers, however, were leaders in the local ceramic field. They included Mrs. John W. Marsh, long one of the most popular teachers; Roxanna B. Preuszner and Mrs. Victorine B. Jenkins, experienced china painters as well as early experimenters in art pottery and underglaze decoration; and Annie Pratt Harrison,

6. Porcelain plaque depicting Chicago's lakefront, by Helen F. Frazee, 1891. Entitled *Chicago in '91*, it was exhibited at the 1893 World's Columbian Exposition. (6" x 12"). *CHS, gift of Mrs. Clifford Nolan, Sr.*

Mrs. F. A. Crittenden, and Mabel C. Dibble, three of the city's best-known china decorators.

On a national level, Susan S. Frackelton of Milwaukee, known for her many contributions to the field of china painting, was at work organizing the National League of Mineral Painters in an attempt to bring the mineral painters of the United States into closer association and assist in the elevation of the standards and status of ceramic art. Many Chicago china painters joined the League, creating a strong local chapter, and exhibited their work with the association at the World's Columbian Exposition. Afterwards, Chicago chapter members assumed leadership roles in the League, preparing its study courses and organizing its annual exhibitions.

Under the umbrella of these two large organizations, small china-painting clubs were formed by women who shared instruction from the same teacher or lived in the same neighborhood. The most influential of these small clubs was the Atlan Ceramic Art Club, organized in January 1893 by fifteen of the city's most talented china painters. Many of these lived on the city's South Side, primarily in the fashionable Hyde Park-Kenwood neighborhoods.

The club's name, Atlan, was inspired by a suggestion in a translation of an old Egyptian papyrus which claimed that the use of clay had been taught to the ancient Egyptians by their forebears, the inhabitants of Atlantis, before that island disappeared into the sea. *Patience, Persistence, and Progress*—all necessary for success in ceramics—became the motto of the club and a logo incorporating three P's was stamped on the bottom of all pieces decorated by its members. Formed only sixty days before the opening of the World's Fair, the club allied itself with the National League of Mineral Painters and made a creditable showing in the Woman's Building by winning eighteen medals, more than any other club in the country.

While planning for the World's Columbian Exposition had resulted in the formation of important ceramic associations, the closing of the Fair also had lasting repercussions in the city's china-painting community: after 1893, males replaced females as the foremost ceramic decorators and teachers. The World's Fair had drawn artists who worked in various media to Chicago from many foreign countries as well as from various parts of the United States. When the Fair closed, many of them remained in the city. Among these were several china painters. Trained as ceramic decorators or artists in Europe, the men tended to be highly skilled technicians who could paint the most intricate figures or portraits. Though few in number, they quickly overshadowed most of the self-trained local painters and drew large classes to their studios.

One such china decorator was F. Bertram Aulich, acknowledged by *Arts for America* in 1895 as "without a doubt the best china decorator in the West." A native of Prussia, Aulich had been trained as a

7. Platter decorated with blue, white, and deep pink morning glories, by Franz B. Aulich, c. 1900. (d: 13½″). *Roger and Jean Helm*

glass painter, but after arriving in the United States in 1879 he tried the wholesale lamp business. In 1891 he sold this business and toured Europe for a year before deciding to attend the Chicago World's Fair. When a bank failure tied up his funds and left him stranded during this visit to Chicago, he opened a class in china painting. This proved so successful that he was able to establish a permanent studio in the city. From time to time he gave courses in Boston, New York, and San Francisco, setting up temporary studios there for that purpose.

Aulich usually painted fruit and flowers and became famous for his beautiful roses and feathery chrysanthemums. "He is one of the few artists who can paint roses with the dew and moisture of life clinging to their petals without loss of their decorative value," *Arts for America* noted in October 1896, adding, "He has learned to interpret not only the form but the secret of nature." By 1902 one critic reviewing the local ceramic exhibitions wrote that the work of Chicago ceramic artists "inclined toward the influence of Mr. Aulich," with an abundance of roses executed with varying degrees of skill.

Other talented male china decorators with studios in Chicago by 1900 included H. O. Punsch, who specialized in portraits; Franz J. Schwartz, who taught figure and miniature painting on porcelain and ivory; and John W. Hasburg, an expert ceramist who operated a laboratory where he prepared mineral colors including his Hasburg Roman Gold. Special blends of mineral colors, glass paints, and gold were also marketed by F. Bertram Aulich and Edward Donath, while Sleeper's Crucible Gold was prepared by chemist Fred L. Sleeper, who had gained experience at the company established by Hasburg.

Aulich, Punsch, Schwartz, and Hasburg joined with the ladies of the Atlan Ceramic Art Club, the employees of several china-painting studios, and dozens of amateur decorators to show their work and compete for prizes at the exhibitions which were sponsored each year by the Western Decorating Works, the National League of Mineral Painters, the Chicago Ceramic Association, the Chicago Arts and Crafts Society, and two large ceramic supply houses, Thayer & Chandler and Burley & Company.

The first exhibition of locally hand-decorated ceramics had been held at the Western Decorating Works prior to 1890. It had been organized by owner Frederick Grunewald, one of Chicago's most ardent promoters of overglaze decoration and later responsible for organizing the Columbian Ceramic Association's exhibit at the 1893 Fair. The following year—encouraged by the popularity of the exhibits at the Western Decorating Works and the highly favorable reception given their own displays at the 1893 Exposition—the Atlan Ceramic Art Club, the Chicago Ceramic Association, and the National League of Mineral Painters began to sponsor annual exhibitions and sales of their members' work.

Ceramics with overglaze decoration were displayed by the National

8. The ceramic laboratory of John W. Hasburg, a leading manufacturer of mineral paints and gold, as illustrated in the November 1898 *Arts for America*.

League of Mineral Painters and the Atlan Club each fall at The Art Institute of Chicago; the Chicago Ceramic Association's work was exhibited there in the spring. Later, members of all three organizations joined with those from the Chicago Arts and Crafts Society each December in entering ceramics in the annual Exhibition of Designs for Decorations and Examples of Art-Crafts Having Distinctive Merit, later called the Annual Exhibit of Applied Arts, sponsored by the Art Institute from 1902 through 1921.

These exhibitions rewarded individual talent through prizes and proceeds from sales. At the same time they provided a showcase for local china decorators to display their work, attract attention, establish their reputations, and sell their wares. To encourage entrants, the Atlan Club and the Alumni Association of the Art Institute's Department of Decorative Design awarded prizes for well-executed objects, and local suppliers such as Burley & Company, A. H. Abbott & Co., and John Hasburg offered awards for the most appropriate tableware designs, best individual exhibit, and best use of gold, respectively. Increasing attendance at exhibitions and the sale of large quantities of hand-painted china at jewelry, department, and art stores reflected a growing appreciation for handcrafted objects on the part of the general public as well as the serious efforts made by many painters to improve the quality of their work.

The leaders of both the Chicago Ceramic Association and the Central Art Association saw that the creation of a ceramic art that was original and distinctly American depended on improving and encouraging the skill of individual china painters and thus raising the standard of ceramic art in general. To further this end both groups began to offer their members instruction in the basics of design, drawing, and color. In 1895 the Chicago Ceramic Association adopted a study course in American ceramics outlined by art historian Edwin Atlee Barber in *The Arts,* the organ of the Central Art Association, and made the recommended books available in their rooms in the Auditorium Building. During the winter a parallel course in color was conducted by Frederick Grunewald of the Western Decorating Works.

The following year the Central Art Association introduced a practical course in china painting for clubs, schools, and home study, intended "to elevate the standard of the art by cultivating good taste among the people." Organized by a multi-talented Art Institute graduate, Christia M. Reade, the lessons featured the painting of a different flower each month and offered instructions for drawing it both in a naturalistic manner and as a conventionalized motif, and for applying the designs to some special form of china. While study courses had long been popular, Reade's course was important because it exemplified a new approach to ceramic decoration which developed in Chicago—the use of "conventionalized" designs derived from nature.

In explaining the distinction between the terms naturalistic and

9. Exhibit of the Atlan Ceramic Art Club which won a gold medal at the Paris Exposition of 1900. *CHS, gift of Mrs. Clifford Nolan, Sr.*

15

conventional as used in ceramic decoration, ceramist Adelaide Alsop Robineau, editor of *Keramic Studio,* made clear that in this context "conventional" had a meaning quite different from its daily usage.

> *To make a conventionalization of any naturalistic form one examines several specimens, selects the points on which the majority agree, eliminates any details which are mere individual characteristics or accidents, and from these points constructs a type of generalization which is the conventional form, ready for design.*
>
> *For instance, take several wild roses; most of them have five equal petals, a few have but four, some have six or seven; some, abortive, some larger than others. The majority having five, the conventional flower will have but five equal petals. The majority of the roses having heart-shaped perfect petals, and so on through all the points of the flower. A conventional person is one who reflects all the accepted ideas of the community. A conventional flower or other form bears a general resemblance to all of its kind. This makes a safe citizen and a safe form for design, but not an interesting one. As people and roses vary considerably in color, that quality is left out and a conventional flower as well as a conventional person is colorless. Color is necessarily individual, not general. Here is where the artist comes in and lends the personal, individual touch which is so necessary to good design; but it is the individuality of the artist, not the flower. To be strictly correct one should speak of a conventional design as a decorative conventional design if one refers to anything out of the ordinary, but most of us are lazy and we use conventional alone or decorative alone, taking for granted that every one understands.* [Keramic Studio 7, no. 6 (October 1905): 119]

Thus the conventional decorative approach was basically an exercise in abstraction: it reduced nature to its basic forms and relied upon the artist's training in design and color to guide him or her in creating an appropriate and beautiful design. A naturalistic treatment, on the other hand, relied on the artist's skill as a copyist to replicate the beauties of nature.

Followers of the conventional school believed that studies of nature were important, but primarily to be copied (as one copied an old master in the Art Institute) to gain technique, or used as sources from which conventionalized designs could be derived. Naturalistically painted fruits, flowers, and figures belonged on plaques, panels, tiles, or other flat surfaces that could be framed like oil or watercolor paintings and not on three-dimensional objects like vases, teapots, cups, and saucers. Conventional decoration was carefully planned to fit the shape of the object, with as much thought going into the ornamentation of an item of everyday use, such as a dessert plate or hatpin holder,

10. Plant analysis from the 1912 *Keramic Studio* showing conventionalized motifs based on the dogwood blossom. *CHS*

16

as into a work on canvas or paper. Emphasis was placed on using simple and original designs derived from nature, particularly the flowers and plants of the prairie woodlands, or from preindustrial cultures such as those of Japan, China, Persia, or the American Indian. Colors were flat and unshaded, with harmonious, earthy colors preferred. Backgrounds were usually left white.

The conventional approach to ceramic decorating was first practiced in Chicago by graduates of the Art Institute who had studied decorative design under Louis J. Millet. A partner in the decorating firm of Healy & Millet and an artist, Millet had begun to teach an evening course in design in January 1886, in which he stressed the "conventionalization of natural forms" and the derivation of designs from nature and historical ornament, as well as freehand drawing and watercolor skills. The course was specially recommended for ladies, many of whom took this opportunity to receive instruction from Chicago's most celebrated interior designer. Millet's course formed the nucleus of the Art Institute's Department of Decorative Design established in 1891, and by the mid-1890s some of his students were applying his principles of design to ceramic decoration. Of these, Christia M. Reade, Bessie Bennett, Helen Fenton Frazee, and Florence Pratt Steward were directly responsible for spreading the techniques of conventional design throughout the city via the Central Art Association, the School of the Art Institute, and the Atlan Ceramic Art Club.

The Atlan Ceramic Art Club

The conventional style was fervently adopted by the Atlan Ceramic Art Club. Since its organization in 1893, club members had devoted their winters to the serious study of antique ceramics. In January 1898, seeking professional guidance in design, they engaged Mrs. Florence Koehler, a talented local china painter, to lead them in a systematic course of study. Mrs. Koehler showed them how to use enamel paints on porcelain and introduced the club to her philosophy of Historic Ornament, which, like Millet's, advocated deriving conventionalized designs from the different cultural traditions—Egyptian, Persian, Arabic, Moorish, East Indian, Japanese, and Chinese. This course offered by the Atlan Club was later credited by Mira Carr Edson in a May 1911 article in *Arts and Decoration* as "the first of its kind in the United States aiming to bring the decoration of china into the field of recognized art."

In 1898 an invitation from the Chicago Arts and Crafts Society to participate in their first exhibition provided the Atlans with an opportunity to test public reaction to their departure from the customary floral and figural decoration. This experience, followed by an exhibit with the Western Mineral Painters a few months later, demonstrated

11. Watercolor cartoon illustrating a conventionalized floral design for a plate painted by Helen F. Frazee. *CHS, gift of Mrs. Clifford Nolan, Sr.*

17

Atlan Ceramic Art Club, 1893–1921.

Following a suggestion from Florence Pratt Steward (Mrs. LeRoy T.), fifteen Chicago china painters organized the Atlan Ceramic Art Club in February 1893 with the goal of developing a style of ceramic decoration that would be "original" and "distinctively American." Other founding members included Eva E. Adams, Emma Kittredge, Lillie E. Cole, Mrs. Walter Greenleaf, Roxanna B. Preuszner, Mrs. D. B. Linstedt, Cornie H. Mann, Mrs. E. L. Humphrey, Louise Anderson, Mable C. Dibble, Grace H. Peck, Lettie McIntyre, Belle Foster, and Julia Wells.

Prior to 1917 other well-known Atlan members included Mrs. A. M. Barothy, Helen G. Cooper, Helen F. Frazee (Mrs. A. A.), May McCrystal (Mrs. J. B.), Matilda Middleton, Augusta Barton McGarn, Helga M. Peterson, Mrs. F. M. Sessions, Helen M. Topping, Mrs. J. V. D. Wright, and Mrs. J. E. Zeublin.

The Atlan Ceramic Art Club held a yearly exhibition of its members' work and participated in exhibits sponsored by the Chicago Arts and Crafts Society, the National Society of Mineral Painters, and The Art Institute of Chicago. The last reference to an Atlan Club exhibition appeared in 1921, although members may have continued to paint after that date.

Porcelain decorated by club members is often signed with the Atlan logo as well as with the name of the painter.

that not only the general public but also fellow china painters needed education in the comparative merits of conventional and naturalistic methods. "We were sometimes disappointed," wrote Atlan historian Florence Steward, "to find that some of the best designs, color schemes and almost perfect technique was given but a glance and turned away from in silence, to rave over a festoon of forget-me-nots, or a cupid balancing on the nose of a teapot."

In 1899 the Atlans began a second course of study with Mrs. Koehler, this time using nature as a source for their designs. Inspired by local fruits, flowers, and animal life, they learned to create designs and to adapt them to various porcelain forms. Their second exhibit of conventionally decorated china drew considerable praise from art critics writing for *House Beautiful* and *Brush and Pencil,* two Chicago magazines devoted to art, crafts, and "home culture." Moreover, they were invited to show their work at the Paris Exposition of 1900.

Following the lead of the Atlan Club, the Chicago Ceramic Association in February 1900 began a series of Saturday study courses at The Art Institute of Chicago under the direction of Louis J. Millet and professional china painter and manufacturer of ceramic colors, John W. Hasburg. Millet illustrated how conventionalized ornamental motifs could be derived from geometric and plant forms, while Hasburg demonstrated the practical application of conventionalized designs to ceramics. By the end of the course participants had caught the conventionalization fever. Seeing themselves as having joined the ranks of those who practiced the fine arts, they changed the name of their organization to the Chicago Ceramic Art Association.

Shortly after 1900 Atlan Ceramic Art Club members adopted conventional decoration as the only acceptable style for work shown in their annual exhibitions at the Art Institute. It soon became their trademark. "The Atlan Club has certainly established a new form of china decoration for the United States," wrote an eminent Eastern art authority in the preface of the club's exhibition catalog, "their work is far ahead of anything I have ever seen done here and compares favorably with the best of Europe." Another unnamed critic was quoted as saying that the Atlan Club "has certainly succeeded in presenting a new and beautiful form or ornament, and the public has *accepted* it; I see no reason why it should not become an established American style of decoration for china."

By 1915 conventional decoration had indeed become an established style of china decoration and membership in the exclusive Atlan Ceramic Art Club signified that one's work was among the finest in the nation. While the Atlans had originally limited their membership to twenty, they gradually expanded to thirty. To maintain their high standards, however, the Atlans instituted an associate membership to provide the benefits of a free winter class in design and color without the

12.   Ginger jar decorated with a
conventionalized floral design by
Atlan Ceramic Art Club member
Ellen Lovgren, 1915–17.   (h: 7½″).
Mr. and Mrs. Frank H. Whitehand

privilege of exhibiting with the club. As associates reached the appropriate level of achievement they were accorded full membership in the Atlan Club.

The Atlan Ceramic Art Club remained a vigorous and prestigious influence on Chicago ceramics for over twenty-five years—partly due to the adventurousness and orginality of its work and partly due to the energy and devotion of its founder, Florence Pratt Steward. A graduate of the Art Institute like most of the other Atlan members, Mrs. Steward had conceived the idea for the club and had initiated the winter study courses. After Mrs. Koehler's initial instruction, she had carried on the winter lessons, teaching members and associates and even adding French lessons as part of the course. A participant in every Atlan exhibition from 1893 through 1921, Mrs. Steward was the club's spokeswoman and one of its best china decorators.

In 1911 Mrs. Steward became nationally known for her *Conversational Set in Historic Ornament,* a dessert service composed of eight place settings. Each plate, cup, and saucer was beautifully executed in conventional designs representing various traditions in Oriental and Western ornament. Each piece featured a wide border of ornament encircling a proverb or saying drawn from the literature of the particular culture. By popular demand the set was displayed at numerous ceramic exhibitions, always drawing high praise from the critics.

Even the famous dessert service paled, however, next to Mrs. Steward's forty-eight piece *Meat Course Set* displayed in 1917. Consisting of twelve place settings, it was decorated with conventionalized ornament derived from twelve "epochs" in the history of art. Priced at $1,000 in that year's Art Institute exhibition, the set was accompanied by a dozen cups and saucers and bread and butter plates of similar design. These were sold separately at prices ranging from $8.00 to $10.00 each to those who wished to own an "epoch" but could not afford the entire set.

In addition to the Atlan study courses, Mrs. Steward taught classes at her home on East 60th Street and wrote instruction manuals such as *Ceramic Decoration* and *Flat Enamel Decoration on China,* two self-help guides which included suggestions for color schemes and conventional designs.

Another well-known member of the Atlan Club was Mabel C. Dibble, an energetic woman who had taught china painting in her hometown of Milwaukee before moving to Chicago in 1893. Sharing a studio in the Marshall Field Building with two other china decorators, Miss Dibble prepared watercolor studies and designs for the use of her many students and mixed and sold her own enamels, one of which was the popular Dibble Green. By 1906 she had been publicly acknowledged as one of the country's outstanding teachers of conventional enamel decoration, with *Keramic Studio* devoting its entire October issue to her work. Shortly thereafter Mabel Dibble became the first woman in the

13. Bowl with wheat-colored luster glaze and band of blue conventionalized spades by Mabel C. Dibble, 1912. (h: 1 13/16"). *Theodore N. Foss*

14. Japanese place setting from the *Conversational Set in Historic Ornament* decorated by Atlan Club founder Florence Steward, 1911. The plate is inscribed: *Smiles crown the welcome and make every dish a feast.* (d: 8⅝"). CHS

15

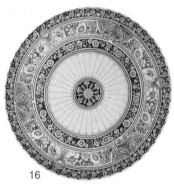

16

15. Plate with narrow bands of
pink, lavender, and yellow conventionalized flowers painted by
Helen F. Frazee, c. 1900.
(d: 10¼″). *CHS, gift of Mrs.
Clifford Nolan, Sr.*

16. Plate with predominantly
blue and lavender conventional-
ized design decorated by Helen
F. Frazee, c. 1900. (d: 10¼″).
*CHS, gift of Mrs. Clifford
Nolan, Sr.*

17. Satsuma vase decorated with
oblong black cartouches filled
with multicolored flowers, by Atlan
Club member Matilda Middleton,
c. 1915. (h: 14½″). *Gallerie
Areta, Miami, Florida*

17

18. Covered jar decorated with bright conventionalized flowers on a black background by Mrs. A. Berglund, 1914–21. (h: 14½"). *Thomas M. Tomc, Fly-By-Nite Gallery, Chicago*

19. Satsuma incense burner with conventionalized floral motifs painted by Mrs. A. Berglund, 1914–21. (w: 5"). *Thomas J. Neniskis*

20. Satsuma tray decorated with pink, yellow, blue, and green conventionalized flowers and pink triangles by Mrs. A. Berglund, 1914–21. (8⅞" x 12"). *Thomas M. Tomc, Fly-By-Nite Gallery, Chicago*

18

21

22

23

24

25

21. Box with five purple conventionalized pansies, handpainted
by Ellen Lovgren, 1915–17.
(d: 3⅞″). *Mr. and Mrs. Frank
H. Whitehand*

22. Potpourri jar with blue, green,
orange, and gold geometric design by Ellen Lovgren, 1915–17.
(h: 2⅜″). *Mr. and Mrs. Frank H.
Whitehand*

23. Porcelain box with blue,
orange, and gold conventionalized
floral design on the cover and
black and white stripes on the
sides, decorated by Ellen Lovgren,
1915–17. (h: 2 1/16″). *Mr. and
Mrs. Frank H. Whitehand*

24. Teapot handpainted with
conventionalized flowers in circular cartouches on a deep blue
ground by Helen F. Frazee,
c. 1915. (h: 4″). *CHS, gift of
Mrs. Clifford Nolan, Sr.*

25. Planter with pierced rim
decorated with colorful conventionalized flowers on a deep blue
ground by Ellen Lovgren, 1915–
17. (h: 5″). *Mr. and Mrs. Frank
H. Whitehand*

26

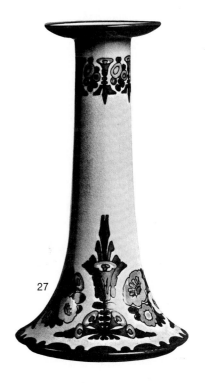

27

26. Lamp and shade of frosted glass painted with bands of conventionalized flowers by Ellen Lovgren, 1917. (h: 13¾"). *Mr. and Mrs. Frank H. Whitehand*

27. Candlestick with lavender, pink, and yellow conventionalized flowers by Helen F. Frazee, c. 1915. (h: 7¼"). *CHS, gift of Mrs. Clifford Nolan, Sr.*

Midwest to be honored as a Master Craftsman by the prestigious Boston Society of Arts and Crafts, and in 1909 she was invited to join London's Royal Society of Arts.   Eager to elevate the status of china painting, she frequently contributed designs and articles to art periodicals and in 1911 published a primer entitled *How to Use Enamels on China* for pupils in out-of-the-way places who had to work without the guidance of a teacher.

Ellen Lovgren was another talented Atlan Club member but, unlike Miss Dibble, she was shy and retiring and remained quietly at home caring for her younger sister.   Invited to become an exhibiting member of the Atlan Club in 1915, Miss Lovgren quickly became one of the club's most highly praised painters and over the next five years her work won numerous awards.   In 1917 the art critic for the *Chicago Sunday Tribune* singled out two of her pieces—a boudoir lamp and a desk set—for special mention in his review of the Atlan's annual exhibition.   The boudoir lamp, which featured wide bands of pastel conventionalized ornament, was notable not only for the quality of the design but for its application to glass, a material which had begun to capture the interest of china decorators.

Like her fellow Atlan members, Helen Frazee had been noted for figural and floral work before joining the Atlan Club in 1893.   After studying drawing at the Art Institute and participating in the Atlan and Chicago Ceramic Association's study courses, Mrs. Frazee began to produce colorful and imaginative conventional designs.   In her studio in the Auditorium tower, and later in the Fine Arts Building, she taught classes in enameling and executed conventional designs for customers.   Equally adept with mineral colors, enamels, raised paste, portraiture, or landscapes on porcelain, Helen Frazee became best known for the beautiful Oriental-inspired conventional designs she painted in low relief enamel on cream-colored Satsuma pottery imported from Japan.

According to an article by Agnes Gertrude Richards in *The Fine Arts* magazine of October 1915, the decoration of Satsuma originated in Chicago with Mrs. Frazee and the Atlan Club.   "Its members at first experienced much difficulty in procuring the undecorated ware and little encouragement of their efforts from the leading artists in the eastern states," wrote Agnes Richards, "The east indeed seemed inclined to regard the innovation rather doubtfully at first.   However, after viewing the exhibition of western enterprise along these lines they were led to follow in its wake so that decorating on Satsuma is now recognized throughout the country as a most important branch of ceramic art."

One of the city's best-known, non-Atlan china painters was Ione L. Wheeler, who applied conventionalized motifs to both porcelain and glass.   Her specialty, however, was luster ware, which she created by applying metallic glazes to glass or porcelain to create a shimmering, iridescent effect.   Rather than use the brown and dull tones favored by

28.   Helen F. Frazee (1858–1923) in her studio, c. 1910.   *CHS, gift of Mrs. Clifford Nolan, Sr.*

most ceramists, Mrs. Wheeler created greens, yellows, and other pastels. And instead of applying floral swags or bands, she usually covered the entire surface of the piece with the luster, omitting further decoration. Mrs. Wheeler, like most of the other decorators, gave instruction in china and glass decoration in her studio in the Fine Arts Building; later she served as an art instructor at Rockford College and at the Convent of the Sacred Heart in Lake Forest.

While Helen Frazee and Ione Wheeler had both studied painting at The Art Institute of Chicago and maintained studios in the Fine Arts Building, they otherwise represented two different types of women active in the Arts and Crafts Movement. Mrs. Frazee, who was the wife of a successful merchant and lived on fashionable Prairie Avenue, epitomized the Chicago woman of social rank for whom accomplishment in some form of self-expression—whether art, music, or needlework—was considered essential. The widowed Mrs. Wheeler, on the other hand, represented the growing number of ambitious, independent, and self-supporting women whose artistic talent provided their only means of livelihood.

Naturalistic versus Conventional Design

By 1905 the conventional approach was strictly adhered to by the Atlan Club, promoted by the Chicago Ceramic Art Association and the National League of Mineral Painters, illustrated in *Keramic Studio*, and taught by Bessie Bennett, Evelyn Beachey, Abbie Pope Walker, and other ceramics instructors at The Art Institute of Chicago. But although the movement quickly attracted many converts and much praise, many china painters continued to cover ceramic forms with the full-blown roses and dainty violets dictated by naturalistic design. "China painters have a decided lack of originality," lamented Teanna McLennan in her review of china decorating as an art industry in the June 1905 *Brush and Pencil*. If only more of the nation's 20,000 professional china painters would apply the principles of good design and strive for originality and the development of unique ideas like those put forward in Chicago by Mrs. Koehler, the Atlan Club, and other leading workers, she pleaded, "decorations that are at once well designed, well colored, and well executed" would be produced and would serve as landmarks in the advancement of American ceramics.

Even in Chicago, however, adoption of conventional decoration was far from universal. Nearly all admired the harmonious conventionalized patterns displayed in the Art-Crafts and ceramic club exhibitions, and many agreed that they were indeed original and the style of the future; but most continued to paint naturalistic motifs because their customers preferred them, and because they had to sell their work to

29. *Italian Garden* bonbon dish
decorated by Pickard artist Edward S. Challinor, 1912–19.
(6¼″ x 6⅞″). *Joel Cohen*

keep on painting. Some considered the conventional designs "too Cubistic" or "too Futuristic," taking more pleasure in the familiar pastel roses, succulent grapes, jolly monks, or sweet cupids which they depicted in mineral paints on porcelain. A clever few, such as Dominick Campana, combined artistic skill with business sense and mastered both styles, offering "figures, flowers, scenes, animals, conventional painted from life on china, etc." in his advertisements in *Keramic Studio*. The battle of naturalistic versus conventional continued as long as china painting remained popular, as shown by Burley & Company's decision to award equal numbers of prizes in the naturalistic and conventional categories in the annual exhibitions they sponsored through 1916.

In these competitions, prizes in the Naturalistic category were annually carried off by Edward Stafford Challinor, a talented artist who had joined the Pickard China Studio in 1902. Challinor would go on to achieve an international reputation for his work for Pickard during his fifty years there.

The Pickard China Studio

Early in 1889, while working as a salesman for a Chicago cut glass and china firm, Wilder Austin Pickard had admired a piece of Pauline art pottery displayed at Marshall Field & Company. Learning that it was made at Edgerton, Wisconsin, he contacted the firm and soon became the Pauline Pottery's first traveling agent. The association was successful, for in one season Pickard sold more goods than the pottery had sold in the previous five years of its existence.

The Pauline Pottery (see page 52) remained in operation until 1893, when the death of its chief financial backer, Oscar Jacobus (husband of the pottery's founder), forced its closing. To give employment to the young women artists who were thus thrown out of work, Pickard offered to buy white china blanks and art supplies for them and then to sell their products. The result was a new company, called The Edgerton Art Studio, with Pickard as salesman and Mae Johnson, one of the group's best painters, in charge of the day-to-day operation.

In 1894 Pickard moved the business part of the operation to the Chicago home of Minnie Verna Flood, whom he had recently married. The actual painting was carried on in the homes of the china decorators, whose numbers were swelled by additional young women, many of whom had also received instruction at the Art Institute. Mrs. Pickard, who did some painting (having taken up the art after she met her husband), devoted the major part of her energies to keeping the books for the business.

Gradually other members of the Flood family became involved in the operation, helping in their spare time to unpack the blank

The Edgerton Art Studio, Edgerton, Wisconsin and Chicago, 1893–1898.
The Pickard China Studio, 1898–1937.
Pickard, Inc., Chicago and Antioch, Illinois, 1938–1941; Antioch, Illinois, since 1941.

Founded by Wilder A. Pickard (1857–1939), the Pickard China Studio employed as many as fifty artists to create hundreds of different patterns and shapes including finely crafted vases, tablewares, and dresser sets handpainted with naturalistic and conventionalized designs. These designs were gradually replaced by decalcomania decorations, with very little handpainting being done after the death in 1952 of Edward S. Challinor, the firm's art director.

Gold-encrusted and gold-etched china, introduced in 1911, became the company's most popular line during the 1920s and is still produced today. In 1935 the firm developed a fine porcelain which, along with other Pickard products, was retailed at Marshall Field & Co. for the first time in 1938. Soon thereafter, the company expanded to a new plant in Antioch, Illinois.

Pickard pieces often bear three marks: the name or symbol of the manufacturer of the china blank, the Pickard logo, and the name of the painter, which can be found within the design.

Under the direction of Pickard's grandson, Henry Austin Pickard, Jr., several new shapes and patterns have been introduced, including a series of limited edition commemorative plates and bells first offered in 1970.

30. Pitcher with poppies, painted
at the Pickard China Studio
between 1898 and 1904.
Dorothy Pickard Platt

white china, deliver it to the decorators in their homes, collect it after it was decorated according to Pickard's specifications, fire it in the kiln located on the third floor, and pack and ship the finished product. French china blanks, primarily Haviland and Limoges, were used for decorating, with the finished pieces resembling Pauline art pottery in design and technique.

In 1898 the business moved out of the Flood-Pickard home into a carriage barn on Whiting (now Walton) Street and the name of the firm was changed to The Pickard China Studio. As the operation grew, Pickard rented other carriage houses on Oak Street and gradually replaced the student decorators and young women with full-time professional painters, for whom china decorating was a livelihood rather than a hobby or income supplement.

By advertising in ceramics journals and drawing from the large pool of talented artisans then arriving in Chicago from England, Germany, Italy, Russia, and the Austro-Hungarian Empire, Pickard soon assembled a staff of fifty or so highly skilled ceramic artists, mostly men trained in the great art centers of England and the Continent. Emil Aulich, Joseph Yeschek, Edward Challinor, Franz Vokernik, Dominick Campana, and Erhardt Seidel were among the outstanding decorators who joined Pickard early in the century.

Specializing in the "fancy china" then popular, the firm produced fruit bowls, pitchers, dresser sets, vases, and plates decorated with naturalistic fruits, flowers, nuts, and portraits. Orders were also taken for china painted with elaborate monograms in raised Roman Gold and beaded with turquoise and ruby enamels. After 1899 conventionalized designs were gradually introduced under the guidance of Pickard's sister, Anna Pickard Atkins, who served as the firm's art critic and sales advisor.

By 1904 the china-decorating enterprise had outgrown the carriage barns and Pickard began to search for a site where he could build a larger studio close to transportation, but far enough from the city to provide plenty of fresh air and sunlight. Selecting a site on East Ravenswood Park (later Ravenswood Avenue), on Chicago's North Side, he designed a Renaissance-style brick studio on a large tract surrounded by lawns, trees, and flowers. The building contained large, airy rooms outfitted for each stage of the operation from unpacking blanks to firing, as well as such innovations as a reading room and reference library. Just behind the studio was an apartment house where members of the staff could live if they chose and a play yard for the children.

Believing that the best work was done by men and women who enjoyed what they did and that pleasant surroundings and genial company were as important as proper tools and good equipment, Pickard attempted to create a social and intellectual environment in his Ravenswood studio not unlike that of the William Morris workshops in

31

32

31. Anna Pickard Atkins in the Pickard China Studio sample room, 1905. *Dorothy Pickard Platt*

32. Edward S. Challinor painting scenic plates in Pickard's Ravenswood studio, c. 1912. *Dorothy Pickard Platt*

31

33

34

35

32

36

38

37

33. Pickard bowl with pears in mellow tones of orange and yellow on a pale green ground, decorated by Dresden-trained painter Max Klipphahn, 1898–1904. (d: 10-9/16″). *Dorothy Pickard Platt*

34. Pickard cup and saucer with *Dutch Decoration*, painted by Adolph Richter, 1905–10. (h: 2¼″). *Dorothy Pickard Platt*

35. Pickard tankard with purple plums on pale yellow and green ground, decorated by Max Klipphahn, 1898–1904. (h: 6″). *Dorothy Pickard Platt*

36. Pickard claret jug featuring bright gold grapes on a deep matte green ground, painted by Tony Coufall, 1905–10. (h: 14-7/16″). *Dorothy Pickard Platt*

37. Pickard scenic vase with shadowy palm trees and moon on a matte gray ground, decorated by Curtis Marker, 1908–12. (h: 7⅛″). *Dorothy Pickard Platt*

38. *Easter Lily* plate, painted by Pickard artist Otto Schoner, c. 1901. (d: 8⅝″). *Dorothy Pickard Platt*

33

39. *Chinese Peacock* vase painted by Pickard artist Curtis Marker, 1925. An etched gold pattern covers the portion of the vase above the black band. (h: 12¾"). *Dorothy Pickard Platt*

40. Pickard gold-etched tea set, 1925–30. Its surface is etched with tiny flowers. (h: 6½"). *Elizabeth F. Cheney*

41. Pickard China Studio employee Frank Yeschek taking gold-etched china from a hydrofluoric acid bath. Areas where the glaze was to be preserved were covered with an acid-resistant paint called asphaltum. After the pieces were etched, they were covered with two coats of gold. *Dorothy Pickard Platt*

42. *Aura Argenta Linear,* one of Pickard's conventionalized designs, features silver flowers and a wide band of gold. Painted by Adolph Richter, c. 1910. (h: 7¾"). *Dorothy Pickard Platt*

43, 44. All of the employees who worked on the first plates made and decorated by Pickard in 1935 signed their names on the back in gold. The inscription reads: *MADE FOR AND PRESENTED TO/Mr. and Mrs. W. A. Pickard/ BY/THE PICKARD STUDIOS/ September Sixth/Nineteen Thirty Five.* (d: 10⅝"). *Dorothy Pickard Platt*

England several decades earlier. Relying on the honor system rather than supervision by a foreman, he put every man and woman to work to the best of his or her ability and also established a profit-sharing plan. Artists were encouraged to create original designs and submit them to the sales force, and each year some of these were added to the samples that the salesmen took into their territory.

By 1908 Pickard china was carried by more than a thousand of the most prestigious jewelry, department, and art stores around the country. There were more than a thousand different shapes and as many designs, done in both naturalistic and conventional styles, as well as figure work, with each piece signed by the artist who executed the design. Of the figural type, two patterns which remained popular for many years were the *Dutch Decoration* (featuring canals, windmills, tulips, and a Dutch maiden), and the *Praying Mohammedan* (a scene depicting an Arab on his prayer rug with two camels in the background). Typical conventional designs included *Cornflower Conventional,* with stylized flowers in blue, gold, and green; *Aura Argenta Linear,* a study in gold and silver; and *Pink Enamel Flowers,* clusters of pale pink blossoms set upon two parallel gold lines.

In 1911, inspired by hand-hammered gold metalware produced by the Tiffany Studios in New York, Pickard introduced gold-etched china. In addition to a line of all-over gold-encrusted china, several new designs featured heavy gold bands acid-etched with bas-relief designs in combination with colorful handpainted scenes or floral motifs. Patterns included *Bordure Antique,* in which the gold was relieved by a band of deep blue with conventionalized white birds; *Deserted Garden*, in which delicately tangled masses of foliage and grasses mingled with fallen fruit to portray an old abandoned garden; *Antique Chinese Enamels,* developed from designs on antique porcelains; *Encrusted Linear,* which combined bands of gold with olive green and lustrous purple blue; and *Italian Garden*, on which mountains and lakes contrasted with roses and vines trailing over marble columns.

Later, in 1913, Pickard introduced an all-over scenic design which he called *Wildwood,* featuring silvery birch trees and bushes on a pale gray background with delicate pink wild roses in the foreground— the whole treated with a vellum-like surface to produce a soft, dreamy effect. Scenic vases and plates showing local landscapes became very popular, with two English craftsmen, Curtis Marker and Edward S. Challinor, specializing in their production. Trained at the Royal Doulton Pottery, Challinor excelled at painting flowers, birds, fruit, and landscapes, eventually becoming Pickard's chief designer.

By the 1920s gold-encrusted and gold-etched pieces had become the company's trademark. Customers could select dinnerware with rich gold borders combined with a colorful handpainted design, or choose from all-over gold sets etched in four patterns: plain; trailing vine; silk moiré; or rose-and-daisy. Gold tracery—in which delicate snowflake-like motifs of fine gold lines were applied over a solid color, usually a brilliant luster of black, blue, or green—was available as an overall decoration or as a border. One particularly stunning design consisted of a wide border of gold tracery over deep blue, surrounding a center panel featuring an etched gold peacock.

In spite of their success the Pickards were dissatisfied with the imported blanks. Even before World War I Wilder Pickard had begun negotiations to purchase a factory in Limoges, France, so that he could make his own blanks. Although the outbreak of war in Europe ended that attempt, Pickard's dream was eventually realized by his younger son, Austin, who had joined the studio in 1925. Following the stock market crash of 1929, when production was again curtailed, Austin Pickard convinced his father to build and equip a laboratory at the plant where he and Adolph G. Simon, Jr., a young man with considerable skill, could begin experiments in china making.

Starting with a formula purchased from a Liverpool, Ohio, pottery that was going out of business, the two men worked for seven years to develop a formula that would meet the standards set by Wilder Pickard and his staff. The final product had to be vitreous (or as hard as glass), translucent, thin, light, and have a smooth, lustrous glaze that would not craze. In 1935 they succeeded and sent the senior Pickards the first dozen service plates made and decorated by the Pickard China Studios. On the back of plate No. 1 the name of each person who had worked on the set was signed in gold. The business established by Wilder Pickard continues to this day as Pickard, Inc., in Antioch, Illinois.

Small Studios

While the majority of Pickard's decorators remained at his Ravenswood studio for many years, a few stayed only a short time before establishing small studios of their own. Among the latter were Dominick Campana, Edward Donath, and Erhardt Seidel, all of whom learned about American marketing methods from Pickard but had distinctive artistic styles of their own.

Dominick M. Campana, a Venetian artist who joined the Pickard China Studio in 1900, left after two years to open his own studio in the Auditorium Building in the heart of the city's ''china painting district.'' Campana excelled in pictorial work and often painted his subjects from life. Executed in a technically flawless style, his work frequently incorporated poetic ideas. His vase, *The Vestals*, and his plaques *The Last Ray* and *Pyrus Flocks*—considered the most original pieces in the 1902 Chicago Ceramic Art Association exhibition—were examples of figural works which expressed romantic themes and reflected the ''charm not merely of uniqueness, but of personality.''

45. Plaque showing a tiger on a mountainside by Pickard artist Dominick Campana, c. 1900. (15⅞" x 12⅝"). *Dorothy Pickard Platt*

46. Vase with four large irises in
gold, lavender, rose, and green
on a pale yellow ground encircled
by black and gold bands.
Painted by Edward W. Donath,
c. 1910. (h: 13⅜"). *Richard J.
Donath*

One of Campana's best-known pieces was a plaque entitled *Sighs of the Pond,* which pictured "a woman's face thrust out of the water and kissing two butterflies." It was praised as far superior to the pieces usually exhibited and as a good example of Campana's personal style, which was "not imitative, but bold, free, with spirit and force." In addition to portraits Campana painted animals—particularly horses, lions, and tigers—noted for their strength and naturalness.

Around 1906 Campana began to diversify his activities by writing instruction booklets such as *The Teacher of China Painting,* and by mixing and selling his own line of Campana's Colors. By 1917 he had mastered the techniques of glass painting and written a series of articles on this topic for *Keramic Studio.* Moving to Wabash Avenue, he operated the D. M. Campana Art Co. for many years.

Edward W. Donath, a young German artist whose fruits and flowers reflected the lovely brown tones of the Minton school, left Pickard to open the E. W. Donath Studio in 1897. With the help of his sister and several other assistants, he produced handpainted china in his studio on North Clark Street and later North Avenue until 1926.

Another former Pickard decorator, Erhardt Seidel, had been apprenticed at the age of fourteen to a ceramics artist in his native Germany for four years before migrating to the United States early in the 1890s. After working for firms in New York and New Jersey, he came to Chicago in 1896 and joined the Pickard China Studio, where he stayed through 1907. Seidel's work was similar to Campana's in that it too was beautifully executed and used figures and animals, often in a storytelling or teaching context. Plaques or plates in this style, with titles such as *Musical Afternoon* or *Queen Louise Descending Stairway,* were usually sold framed to be hung as paintings.

Employing a technique popular around 1900, Seidel also transferred photographs to china, encircling the black or sepia portrait or scene with delicately painted floral borders. A master of dark-toned naturalistic fruits and flowers, Seidel produced work primarily in this line, for these designs were most appealing to the buyers for the large department and specialty stores which served as the major retail outlets for handpainted china. Seidel's wife Anna served as his sales agent, showing samples and taking orders for his work, which he executed in a home studio until 1909, when he moved his family to Seattle, Washington.

Yet another Chicago firm engaged in decorating china on a commercial basis was White's Art Company, "one of the largest decorators in the country" and the producer of White's Art China, distinguished by subdued matte colors and a liberal use of Roman Gold accents. A larger version of the individual studio, White's offered classes in etching and enamel work on china and sold custom-mixed Roman Gold and matte colors.

Other studios producing handpainted china included the Carlyle

47. Plate by Erhardt Seidel (1863–1916) with a sepia photograph of the artist's son, Walter Erhardt Seidel, surrounded by purple and orange pansies, c. 1902. (d: 9 11/16"). *Elsa B. Seidel and Walter E. Seidel*

48. Two birds hover over a nest perched on an apple blossom branch on this vase painted by Erhardt Seidel, 1908–16. (h: 8″). Its companion, a large pitcher, shows the mother bird caring for her fledglings. (h: 13⅝″). *Elsa B. Seidel and Walter E. Seidel*

China Art Company, the Carlsson & Rorabeck Company, the Gerard Company, Kenwood Studios, and the Schmidt Ceramic Company. Burley & Company rented studio space in its building on Wabash Avenue to a large number of china painters, who in turn supplied the firm with a line of exclusive designs for its customers.

Unlike most of the other products of the Arts and Crafts Movement, handpainted china was moderately priced, with most pieces within the range of those with moderate incomes. While punch sets and elaborate dinner services could be quite expensive, most items were sold individually and only the poorest family was without at least one handpainted cup and saucer or hatpin holder. Even the work of the renowned Atlan Club tended to be moderately priced, with Helen Frazee in 1915 offering a small vase for $3.00 and Frances Barothy pricing a three-piece tea set at $12.50 in the annual Art Institute exhibit and sale.

Methods of manufacture as well as the final product of studios such as Pickard's or White's differed considerably from those of the city's oldest commercial china-decorating establishment, the Chicago China Decorating Works. Established by 1880, the large Chicago China Decorating Works specialized in decorating the heavy utilitarian wares used by hotels and railroads, including all the china for Pullman dining cars. The processes involved were strictly mechanical rather than artistic and many young girls were employed to carry on the routine factory work. Their job was to press a paper pre-inked with the impression of letters or a logo onto a mug, plate, or whatever form was being decorated. When the paper was removed, the letters or designs remained stamped on the china. As in other china decorating factories, the kilns were loaded and fired by men.

Many of the young female decorators who worked for the small china decorating companies or opened studios of their own were graduates of the School of the Art Institute. Though instruction in most crafts had ceased by 1905, classes in pottery and ceramic painting were continued for many years because of their popularity and practical value. "No school in the country is doing better work in the department of ceramics than the Chicago Art Institute," declared *Arts and Decoration* in April 1911, "the work produced there, under the direction of Mrs. Evelyn B. Beachey, is strong in design and color, and shows continuous improvement." Design as well as the actual painting were taught in these classes. Pupils began with the simple problem of decorating tiles in straight lines and in tones of one color, then progressed to plate rims, cake plates in all-over patterns, and eventually to two-piece sets and more complicated vases, pitchers, and teapots.

The growing popularity of handpainted china encouraged the establishment of firms serving the needs of the hobbyist or amateur who lacked a steady hand for drawing or an aptitude for design. Such establishments also offered shortcuts for the harried professional decorator who needed to complete large dinner services or routine

49. Pitcher with gold conventionalized grapes outlined in black, decorated by White's Art Company, c. 1914. (h: 7¼"). CHS

pieces as quickly as possible. For those lacking the time or talent to draw or transfer designs on blank china, the Herrick Designs Co. offered an amazing and inexpensive variety of conventional patterns printed on a specially prepared paper that permitted tracing the design onto the china without the use of carbon or tracing paper. In 1911, for instance, their *Herrick Designs Book* illustrated 100 attractive conventional designs available at the bargain rate of fourteen for one dollar, accompanied by suggestions for colors to be used in decorating cups, saucers, plates, etc. The Coover Studio in the Auditorium Building—yet another firm dedicated to saving the "time, effort, eye and nerve strain" of the china painter—provided easily transferable designs in conventional, semi-conventional, and naturalistic styles for both enamel and flat-color work at prices beginning at twelve cents per dozen.

For those preferring to develop their own designs but lacking the time or patience to repeat them, the Time and Energy Co. on North Clark Street offered over 150 "dainty, practical and artistic" rubber stamps already molded with delicate flowers, scrolls, leaves, and border designs for use in decorating china. The company also provided trademark stamps and created unique designs for the exclusive use of a particular pottery or individual.

This type of mass production, which vulgarized the art of china painting, had two negative consequences. The proliferation of inexpensively produced china "gaudily decorated with cheap gold and stamped flowers" reduced the attractiveness of painted wares to the discriminating buyer. At the same time, the competition from the cheaply decorated china reduced the market for more artistically finished pieces.

The Impact of World War I

The china-decorating profession experienced a severe setback in 1914, when the outbreak of war in Europe slowed the importation of undecorated French china and stopped entirely the importation of German blanks. Suitable American porcelain was unavailable, as most potteries had turned to producing the less attractive but more profitable grades known as hotel china. Although limited quantities of Satsuma and Sedji porcelain continued to come from Japan, these wares were crudely made and marred by blemishes. Some of the shapes copied French and German porcelains, but most came in the same forms as the Japanese themselves decorated and sent over at very low prices, creating additional competition for the small-scale American china decorator.

As the war dragged on, many china painters abandoned their profession and turned to glass decoration and other types of craftwork. "I am tired and completely disgusted with the commercial work," one

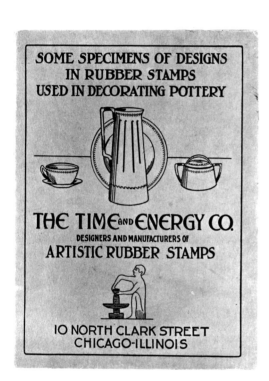

50. Cover of booklet illustrating rubber stamp designs available from the Time and Energy Co.
CHS

discouraged amateur decorator wrote to the editor of *Keramic Studio* in May 1917:

> *Just to give you an idea of the prices paid the worker: 10¢ a working for bread and butter plates, next size plates 12¢, next size 15¢ and so on. I know of this instance: a large French salad bowl, decorated in conventional basket motifs, all done in hard enamels with much gold, representing a good deal of work carefully done, sold for $4.50. Think of it, how can anyone make a living at such prices?*

In September of 1917, the Haegar Potteries of Dundee, northwest of Chicago, put on the market a new ornamental earthenware suitable for enamel decoration. Featuring a pale yellow glaze, the Haegar ware resembled Satsuma pottery, but was available in unlimited quantities and at much lower prices than Japanese ware. By then, however, the overall demand had shrunk and many decorators had given up their expensive downtown studios and were working at home because their former customers considered it unpatriotic to buy luxuries like painted china while the country was at war. The big ceramic supply houses suffered as well; by the end of the war Burley & Company, importer of fine ceramics and glasswares in Chicago since the city's founding in 1837, had gone out of business. The Pickard China Company managed to survive, in part because it developed a product for which there was a steady demand—Japanese blanks covered with layers of gold.

The demand for handpainted china resumed after the war but the trade became more and more concentrated in the hands of the few large firms still in business. Factories and large studios, such as the Pickard China Company, filled the demand for hand-decorated wares formerly met by individual painters and tiny studios. Large art supply stores met the needs for white china, brushes, and paints, often acting as retail outlets for the tubes and pots of gold and custom colors mixed by small operations such as those owned by Aulich, Hasburg, and Sleeper. Among the clubs and associations, china painting and other crafts encouraged by the Arts and Crafts Movement were adapted to serve as occupational therapy for soldiers recovering in hospitals or at home.

As shipments of china resumed, the leading china decorators became eager to reestablish their art as a paying proposition. Many realized, however, that fashions and markets had changed. Discussing the state of the art in an article in the March 1919 issue of *Keramic Studio*, assistant editor Henrietta Barclay Paist acknowledged that the exciting days of experimentation and emphasis on technique had passed, and that china decorators must take a fresh, hard look at current trends in interior design in order to anticipate the demand of the future. She predicted:

One of the strongest tendencies, which is not new, but has survived the war, and will, I am sure, grow, and influence the demand for art products, is the more orderly thought in home furnishings. The time has passed when intelligent people furnish their homes by collecting interesting things from every-where and huddling them into their living rooms regardless of harmonious relation. The thought to-day is more logical and orderly. Interior decorators and home makers now start with a definite idea and try to harmonize all the furnishings; woodwork, walls, draperies, furniture, decorative windows, all carry out some definite thought in color and design. This method of house-furnishing will more and more create a demand for special porcelains—for sets in special designs and color. It will be better for us to work more for the average home demand and less for the connoisseur; more for the table and not so much for the purely ornamental. The sun porch, the breakfast room, the nursery, the dining room, all call for their special service." [Henrietta Barclay Paist, "Keramic Art," Keramic Studio 20, no. 3 (March 1919): 172]

During the following decade, designs became more conventional-ized and geometric, with many featuring the stark geometric or distinc-tive floral motifs now popularly identified as Art Deco or Moderne by the end of the 1920s. Dinnerwares as well as other forms of house-hold ceramics assumed simpler forms and decoration was often re-duced to a few lines or a single motif. By 1933, *Keramic Studio,* once the bible of china painters, had been renamed *Design* and its pages featured art pottery and ceramic sculpture. At the dazzling A Century of Progress Exposition opening in Chicago that year, handpainted china was nowhere to be seen. Most of the small studios had already closed, their decorators deceased, retired, or pursuing other occupa-tions. F. B. Aulich, Erhardt Seidel, Helen Frazee, and Mabel Dibble were dead; Dominick Campana and John Hasburg had already become art suppliers. The Pickard China Studio had turned to sup-plying the gold-etched, gold-printed, gold-and-color stamped and decalcomania-decorated wares demanded by the public, limiting handpainting to a few floral designs.

As the country settled into the Great Depression, attics received mother's handpainted china to gather dust next to father's Mission rocker and grandmother's massive old Victorian dresser and bed-stead inset with floral tiles.

Max Klipphahn, famous for his flower designs, was trained in Dresden, Germany. An employee of the Pickard China Studio, he is shown here painting a vase in the *Seville* pattern, c. 1920. *Dorothy Pickard Platt*

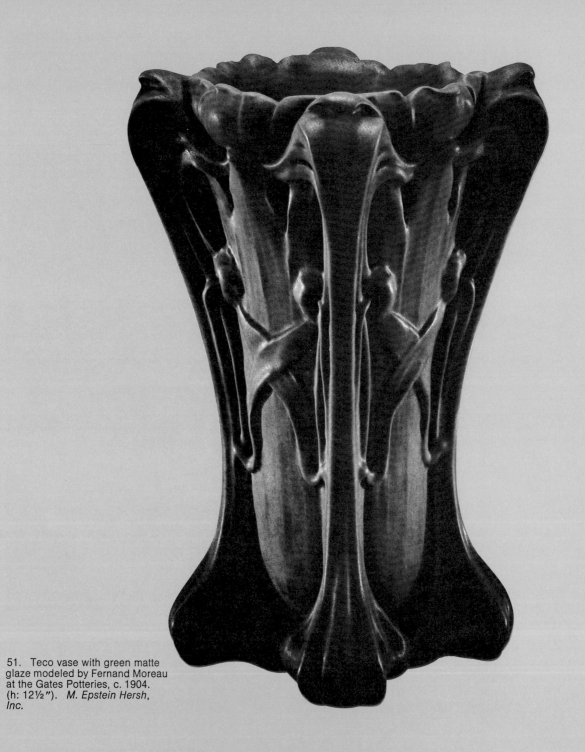

51. Teco vase with green matte
glaze modeled by Fernand Moreau
at the Gates Potteries, c. 1904.
(h: 12½″). *M. Epstein Hersh,
Inc.*

ART POTTERY

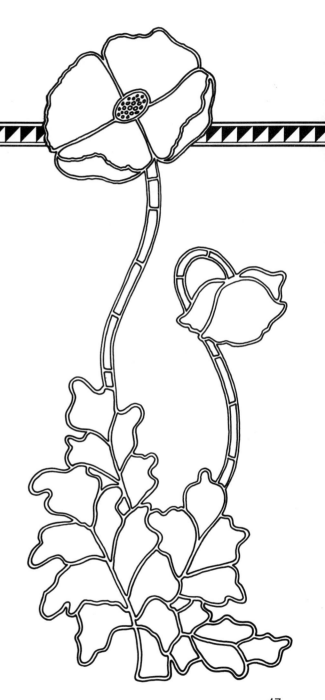

During the 1880s, many china painters expanded their scope to include the more complicated art of decorating handthrown earthenware blanks with mineral colors, slips, glazes, or sculpted ornaments to create one-of-a-kind pieces known as art pottery. The difference was one of technique: in china painting the decoration was applied over the glaze prior to a second firing; in the decoration of art pottery the ornamentation was applied before the piece was glazed and usually before it was fired. Earthenware could be decorated after it had already been fired once—in what is known as a bisque state—but ornamentation was more successful when applied on forms received directly from the hands of the potter. As a result, many china painters became artist-potters, going back to an earlier stage of production to make the earthenware forms themselves.

Chicago art potters imported most of their materials and techniques from the East Coast and Cincinnati, where experimentation in the decoration of earthenware pottery had been stimulated by Philadelphia's 1876 Centennial Exposition. But much of their inspiration and encouragement also came from within their city. Indeed, the Chicago Terra Cotta Works (see page 161) exhibited two redware vases and a teapot at the Centennial.

One important influence on Chicago art pottery was the Interstate Industrial Exposition, held annually from 1873 through 1891 in a huge pavilion located on Michigan Avenue at the foot of Adams Street, now the site of The Art Institute of Chicago. In 1877, following the example of the Centennial Exposition in Philadelphia, the sponsors of the Interstate Exposition decided to include "articles of Vertu or Bric-a-brac"— the contemporary collective terms for small ornaments valued for their rarity or artistic interest.

The Art Committee of the Exposition secured a large collection of European, Oriental, and American ceramics on loan, and installed the first large-scale exhibition of decorative ceramics shown in Chicago. For the education of visitors, the Art Committee published a *Hand Book to The Bric-a-brac Collection* which listed and described each of the objects in the exhibition. Included were enameled and painted

52. Unglazed redware vase made by the Chicago Terra Cotta Company, c. 1876. It was given to the Smithsonian Institution by the company's president, Sanford E. Loring . (h: 8⅞"). *National Museum of History and Technology of the Smithsonian Institution*

earthenwares from Faenza, Italy; porcelains from Dresden in Germany and Sèvres and Limoges in France, as well as from China and Japan; and examples of ancient ceramics from Europe and the Orient. Among the English artwares were decorated Minton tiles, the new Doulton ware, and Lambeth Faience. Reflecting the pervasive grip of English taste upon local household art, the handbook carefully noted that a particular Chinese preserve jar decorated "in old enamel colors" was "a facsimile of one figured and commended in Charles Eastlake's 'Hints on Household Taste.'"

The bric-a-brac collection had been arranged by the versatile Chicago artisan, Isaac E. Scott, who was also the maker of "the appropriate and tasteful" Gothic-style cases in which the ceramics were displayed. Scott, at the time a modeler at the Chicago Terra Cotta Works, was a native Philadelphian who had moved to Chicago a few years earlier.

On October 27, 1879, Mrs. John J. Glessner, one of Isaac Scott's best clients, noted in her journal that "Mr. Scott was making pottery for us in Boston." The reference was to four earthenware vases, still in Glessner House on Prairie Avenue, made at the Chelsea Keramic Art Works in Chelsea, Massachusetts, just north of Boston. All variants of the flat-sided pilgrim bottle, they featured crisply sculpted naturalistic ornament modeled by hand and applied to the molded body, a technique commonly used in the architectural terra cotta of the period (see pages 161–64). Like other "art pottery" of the day, the pieces were signed by the artist. Two of the vases featured a glossy, translucent, green glaze perfected in 1877 by Hugh C. Robertson, proprietor of the Chelsea Keramic Art Works; the remaining two were unglazed.

While Robertson's Chelsea Keramic Art Works produced pottery in classic and Oriental shapes, the Rookwood Pottery in Cincinnati made a variety of exotic molded shapes handpainted with flowers, landscapes, or Japanese-inspired motifs using a technique known as the Limoges method. This called for mixing mineral colors with slip (liquid clay) and applying them with a brush to the moist earthenware body. When the article was thoroughly dry, it was fired in a kiln. Afterwards, the piece was dipped in a transparent glaze and fired a second time.

This underglaze slip technique had been used on art pottery exhibited by Haviland & Co. of Limoges, France, at the 1876 Philadelphia Centennial Exposition, where it caught the attention of Mary Louise McLaughlin of Cincinnati. A devoted china painter, McLaughlin was dissatisfied with the blank forms supplied to her by others and began to experiment with decorating locally made earthenware. Inspired by French ceramics, she soon became the first American to master the Limoges method, which she described in detail in 1880 in her book *Pottery Decoration Under the Glaze*. The Rookwood Pottery, founded by Maria Longworth Nichols in Cincinnati that same year, soon adopted

53. Green glazed vase made by Issac E. Scott at the Chelsea Keramic Art Works in Chelsea, Massachusetts, for the John J. Glessner family of Chicago, 1879. (h: 8⅝"). *The Chicago Architecture Foundation*

McLaughlin's method of decorating pottery and before long so did other pottery manufacturers in that city.

In addition to decorating pottery under-the-glaze, the Cincinnati decorators used a variety of other techniques, including overglaze decoration, designs incised on the clay body, and carved-relief designs. Their efforts received national attention and had widespread appeal. When the Rookwood School for Pottery Decoration offered instruction in over- and underglaze painting, plus carved and modeled work in October 1880, it drew students from many regions of the country, including several from Chicago.

By 1881 white earthenware blanks were available from Rookwood and other Cincinnati potteries and many Chicago women had begun decorating them using McLaughlin's mineral paint and slip recipe. The paints, slip, and bisque blanks were easily obtained from Chicago art supply stores, but the city had no commercial kilns where amateurs could have their work fired. The only option was to send the decorated pieces to Cincinnati for firing. Being quite fragile, many were broken during shipping. This, combined with the apparent commercial success of the Cincinnati women, inspired several Chicagoans to find ways to have art pottery fired in Chicago.

Chicago's First Art Potteries

Among the first to envision making art pottery at home was Victorine B. Jenkins, a widow who had taken up china painting in the 1870s. According to the *Clay Record*, Mrs. Jenkins had, early in the 1880s,

become interested in painting on limoges and underglaze while visiting Cincinnati. After devoting some time to studying in the potteries she returned to Chicago and opened the first studio of the kind in the city and commenced teaching clay modeling. She experienced great difficulty in getting the work fired, having to send it to Cincinnati to be burned and glazed. At last a man who made flower pots took an interest in the work, but so much was returned broken that, after two years of persistent effort, the idea was abandoned. ["Ceramics Their Fad," Clay Record, (August 12, 1892): 84-5]

Although Mrs. Jenkins may have thrown or molded the pottery forms herself, it is likely that she modeled the articles in the rough with her hands, decorated them, and then gave them to the potter to glaze and fire.

Concurrent with Mrs. Jenkins's attempts to make art pottery in Chicago were those of Roxanna Beecher Preuszner, a widow who taught china painting and pottery in her studio at 66 Park Avenue on the city's West Side. Although it is not known whether she obtained

54. Terra cotta vase with glossy blue glaze decorated with a branch of white dogwood. This vase could have been made by a member of the Chicago Pottery Club. Incised *Morse/Chicago/1882*. (h: 12¾"). *Mr. and Mrs. Helmut Strauss*

her knowledge through publications, exhibitions, or friends, Mrs. Preuszner was aware of the work of Cincinnati women as well as of the over- and underglaze techniques employed by Charles Volkmar and John Bennett, well-known art potters working in New York. In November 1881 she purchased a kiln that would maintain the higher temperatures necessary for underglaze work and had a local china decorating firm fire it for her.

The highly successful results of Mrs. Preuszner's first firing were recorded in a November 13, 1881, *Chicago Daily Tribune* account headed "Decorative Pottery Can Now Be Done Wholly at Home." The article noted, "This should command the attention of the many lady amateurs of this city who have hitherto been under the necessity of sending their productions to Cincinnati for firing." The wares that came from Mrs. Preuszner's first kiln were of four types—"terra cotta, ivory white, Cincinnati ware, and Minton tile." Among the pieces were "two terra cotta plaques with decorations of Virginia creepers in autumn tints," three small vases "in the Volkmar style," featuring simple incised or built up designs, and "two large vases of Limoges faience, decorated with flowers and lizards in bold relief."

In 1881 blank Limoges ware and Minton tiles were available from the Western Decorating Works, A. H. Abbot & Co., or Burley & Company. The Cincinnati ware could have been obtained from one of several local crockery dealers; the terra cotta could have come from one of the small local potteries. Judging from the ware described, Mrs. Preuszner probably had not made the shapes herself, but had merely decorated them using the Limoges method or by applying hand-modeled relief motifs.

Mrs. Preuszner's work, continued the *Tribune,* was exhibited at Thayer & Chandler's art store, where ladies could "leave all orders and examine these productions with a view to encouraging the establishment here of permanent facilities for completing this fascinating work in an artistic and careful manner."

A few weeks later, in December 1881, the newspaper reported that Thayer & Chandler had "quite a large collection of decorated ware sent in by ladies to be fired on the 15th in the kiln for which this firm takes orders." By mid-January 1882, the art store announced the successful results "of the experiment in the production of art pottery made wholly in Chicago" and "ladies engaged in this plastic pastime" were encouraged to bring in more pieces.

While many women were content to decorate Cincinnati ware and Minton tiles, a few were determined to create art pottery from start to finish by designing the shapes, decorating, firing, and glazing the pieces themselves. Moreover, they proposed to do this as a commercial venture. One of these women was another former china painter, Pauline Bogart Jacobus. Inspired by an exhibition of painting and sculpture by the French actress, Sarah Bernhardt, held at O'Brien's Art

Pauline Pottery, 1882–1893.

Often credited with establishing the first art pottery in Chicago, Pauline Jacobus (1840–1930) taught china painting in her home before attending the Rookwood School for Pottery Decoration in Cincinnati, Ohio. Returning to Chicago, she opened a small studio on 36th Street, which operated between 1882 and 1888.

Early Pauline products resemble handpainted china of the period, with simple naturalistic decoration highlighted with silver or gold. Marks were incised or impressed on the bases of the pieces. Some of the early ones were also dated.

In 1888 the Pauline Pottery moved to Edgerton, Wisconsin, where a variety of products were made until the pottery failed in 1893. A year later the enterprise was reorganized as the Edgerton Pottery, which remained in operation until 1902. When this, too, went out of business, Mrs. Jacobus acquired one of the kilns and reassembled it behind her home in Edgerton. There she resumed her practice of making pottery during the summer and decorating it the following winter. In December 1909 the local paper announced Mrs. Jacobus's retirement.

Gallery in Chicago in January 1881, Mrs. Jacobus decided to try clay modeling herself. She persuaded her husband, Oscar I. Jacobus, then a wealthy member of the Chicago Board of Trade, to send her to the Rookwood.School for Pottery Decoration in Cincinnati.

In the midst of her studies Mrs. Jacobus received word from her husband that a group of women had organized the Chicago Pottery Club and were planning to open an art pottery in Chicago. Determined to be first, Mrs. Jacobus returned to Chicago, having hired Rookwood's kiln builder John Sargeant to build a kiln for her. With the help of Laura Fry, one of the instructors at the Rookwood School, she outfitted a small workshop on 36th Street. Hastily she made, fired, and exhibited, in 1882, the first decorated pottery created wholly in Chicago.

Using a heavy, dense clay imported from Ohio, Mrs. Jacobus, assisted by a presser (who shaped the clay using molds) and two student decorators, continued making earthenware vases, bowls, and other artware in her workshop. Pottery forms, some thrown, some molded, were decorated underglaze with blue, yellow, or dark green handpainted decorations or were covered entirely with glazes. Redware was decorated with incised and gilded designs. Her husband named the products Pauline pottery.

By 1884 Pauline pottery had achieved wide popularity and was sold at Marshall Field & Company's large department store as well as through a retail sales outlet on Wabash Avenue. Within a few years, however, the expense of importing large quantities of clay became prohibitive, and Mrs. Jacobus decided to find a source of supply closer at hand. After locating a fine clay bed near the small town of Edgerton, Wisconsin, she and her husband secured financial backing from several Edgerton businessmen to open a large operation which would include the production of porous battery cups for the Bell Telephone Company. In the spring of 1888 the Pauline Pottery moved to Wisconsin, where it continued to produce artwares until 1893.

Paralleling Mrs. Jacobus's efforts, about twenty ladies organized the Chicago Pottery Club in the fall of 1882, with Mrs. Philo King as president, Mrs. John B. Jeffrey as secretary, and the indefatigable Victorine B. Jenkins as treasurer and manager. Like Mrs. Jacobus, they hoped to take advantage of the growing demand for pottery and to turn their club into a business operation. By September 1883 the club had leased a cottage at 795 West Congress Street and completed arrangements for the erection of two kilns for firing and glazing art pottery. The prestigious English potter, Joseph Bailey, Sr.—who had assisted Mary Louise McLaughlin in Cincinnati and later joined the Rookwood Pottery—was hired to supervise the operation.

Moving into the cottage, Bailey created forms for the members to decorate while Mrs. Jenkins provided instruction in a studio located at the pottery. Despite the trouble and the expense of finding and shipping suitable clay from a distance, the club continued its work for

55. Redware vase with gold-painted poppies and butterflies made at the Pauline Pottery, 1883. Incised *Springer*. (h: 8⅜"). *State Historical Society of Wisconsin*

56. Teapot with gold flowers and black and gold bands, made at the Pauline Pottery, 1882–88. (h: 6½"). *D. Magner, American Arts and Crafts, Brooklyn, New York*

57. Planter decorated with gold and silver incised spiderwebs and flowers, made at the Pauline Pottery, 1883. (d: 8¾"). *State Historical Society of Wisconsin*

two years. Finally, in 1885, members realized that the pottery was not going to be a financial success and dissolved the club. Bailey returned to Cincinnati and Mrs. Jenkins moved to Baltimore, where she continued to teach pottery making. Returning to Chicago a few years later and unable to locate a kiln for firing her underglaze work, she opened a studio with Daniel F. and Folger A. Bigelow in the Athenaeum Building and resumed teaching china painting.

By 1890, when Mrs. Jenkins returned to Chicago, the Pauline Pottery had moved to Edgerton, Isaac Scott had moved to New York, and Mrs. Preuszner and several other amateur art potters had turned to philanthropic and educational activities. At this point ceramists once again turned their attention to china painting as they busied themselves preparing work for the 1893 Chicago World's Fair.

Although entries by Chicago ceramists in the 1893 Fair were confined to decorated china, it was not long before interest in art pottery revived. Stimulated in 1897 by the founding of the Arts and Crafts Society and the industrial arts program of the Central Art Association, tiny art potteries soon began to flourish alongside china decorating studios. But, repeating the pattern established a decade earlier, the small potteries tended to be short-lived, unprofitable ventures. Though operated by energetic, dedicated artisans, they revolved around the talent and perseverance of a few individuals and often failed to develop the sales force necessary to promote their product. When the local market or their friends failed to buy, when styles changed or the potter grew tired, the small pottery went out of business. Of at least a dozen potteries founded in Chicago between 1893 and 1933, only two remained in business longer than a decade. Only one, the Gates Potteries, operated for more than twenty years, and that because of the devotion of its owner rather than because of a ready market for its wares.

The Gates Potteries and Teco Ware

The Gates Potteries, which produced garden pottery as well as an art line called Teco ware, were an offshoot of the American Terra Cotta & Ceramic Company founded by William Day Gates in 1881 to produce drain tile, brick, and architectural terra cotta (see page 169). Since its founding, Gates and his staff had experimented with clays and glazes for architectural purposes, but, on the side, for the sheer love of it, had tried various clays and an infinite number of glazes in an effort to create some pottery that would approach their ideal in form, color, and texture.

Early in the 1880s, the branch of the firm known as the Gates Potteries had made and sold plain terra cotta vases for decoration by

58. The gold and white flowers applied to this early vase from the Gates Potteries may have been added by an amateur potter. Impressed *WM. D GATES*, 1880s. (h: 4½"). *George A. Berry III, TC Industries, Inc.*

54

amateur artists. By the end of the decade, however, Gates had decided to make and market a unique line of art pottery which would be distinguished by line and color. Pieces would be free of surface decoration and would depend for their beauty solely upon form. With his already prosperous terra cotta company providing financial backing, an extensive laboratory, and ample kilns, Gates was able to experiment for more than thirteen years until a superior product was achieved.

The first experiments were limited to subdued reds, buffs, and browns—the shades then popular in architectural terra cotta. By the mid-1890s, however, Gates had determined that the color and texture of the glaze were more important than the composition of the clay body and began to channel his efforts in that direction. With the help of two of his sons, Paul and Ellis, and his chief chemist, Elmer Groton— all three of whom had graduated from the department of ceramics at Ohio State University—Gates experimented first with glazes featuring marbled or mottled surface effects. Eventually he achieved a soft, waxy matte glaze in a cool, silvery green which became the hallmark of the pottery. Varying from a pale to a deep moss green, the color resembled the tones assumed by old bronze after long exposure to the weather. Although the glaze was suggestive of the green glaze of Boston-made Grueby pottery, Gates discounted any similarity as "a matter of accident and not of deliberate imitation."

Satisfied with the results, Gates named the new ware Teco (pronounced Tea-ko), derived from combining the first syllables of the two words terra and cotta. "We needed a distinctive name," Gates told an interviewer, "so I invented this." Though the name had been devised as early as 1895, Teco ware was not marketed until it had received the stamp of approval from Chicago's artistic community, which saw it for the first time in the Chicago Architectural Sketch Club's exhibition in 1900. It was first sold commercially the following year in a variety of shapes, some quite complicated, featuring the finely textured, matte green glaze.

About the same time a fluke in firing produced a vase with a shiny glaze reminiscent of the rich luster of metal. Both the green- and metallic-glazed wares were offered for sale in 1902 at prices ranging from one dollar for a small inkstand to fifty dollars for a lamp with a green Teco base and a leaded art glass shade. Compared to other art pottery of the day, Teco represented high quality at a modest price. "We are convinced," Gates told Walter Ellsworth Gray in a 1902 interview,

that there is a large element of the public cultured of taste and in love with the beautiful who cannot afford to indulge in the luxury of high-price articles of a decorative nature, and hence we feel that in putting the Teco ware upon the market in artistic

59. Green glazed terra cotta plaque from a gatepost at the entrance to the American Terra Cotta & Ceramic Company's factory at Terra Cotta, Illinois. (h:16⅞"). *George A. Berry III, TC Industries, Inc.*

60. Teco ware with metallic glazes, 1904–20. Left to right: vase (h: 8½″); vase (h: 12″); vase (h: 8⅝″); pitcher (h: 4⅛″); vase (h. 3½″). *Michael and Fern Abrahams, Brooklyn, N.Y.; Rosalie Berberian; George A. Berry III, TC Industries, Inc.; Joel Cohen; Thomas M. Tomc, Fly-By-Nite Gallery, Chicago*

The Gates Potteries, c. 1885–c. 1922.

Although terra cotta vases and garden ornaments were made at the American Terra Cotta & Ceramic Company's factory in Crystal Lake beginning in the mid-1880s, the name, Gates Potteries, did not appear until about 1890. Within the next five years, under the direction of owner William Day Gates (1852–1935), the pottery began to make Teco ware in many sizes, ranging from delicate vases to huge garden urns. Teco featured a variety of metallic, crystalline, and matte glazes, the most common of which was a velvety matte green resembling weathered bronze. The firm continued to produce vases, tablewares, tiles, landscape murals, and garden ornaments bearing the Teco trade name until the early 1920s, when the demand for architectural terra cotta allowed the workmen little time for creating art wares.

61. Teco vase no. 431 with green matte glaze, designed by William D. Gates, 1901–10. (h: 7⅜"). *Joel Cohen*

57

62. Teco waterlily vase no. 151
with dark green matte glaze,
designed by Chicago architect
W. J. Dodd, c. 1903. The 1905
catalog noted that the vase was
"expressly for cut flowers; the
lower part holds water while
flowers are carelessly arranged in
different openings, producing an
exceptionally pleasing and artistic
effect." (h: 11"). *Thomas M.
Tomc, Fly-By-Nite Gallery,
Chicago*

*designs, and with finishes comparable with those of more ex-
pensive ware, we will meet a public want. Our methods enable
us to do this."* [*Walter Ellsworth Gray, "Latter-Day Developments
in American Pottery,"* Brush and Pencil *9 (February 1902): 296*]

Another principle influencing the development of Teco ware was
the decision to make only those shapes which would serve some
useful purpose, whether household or horticultural. Following English
Arts and Crafts philosopher William Morris's advice to "have nothing
in your houses which you do not know to be useful, or believe to be
beautiful," Gates chose shapes that were clearly recognizable as
vases, urns, and bulb pots, and had strong bases which prevented
tipping or spilling. Forms were made to fit the hand, and protruding
and perpendicular parts—while not obtrusive enough to be called
handles—suggested the ease with which they could be lifted or moved.
Teco mugs and pitchers made fine flower holders, while nearly all the
vases could serve as attractive lamp bases. This was clearly demonstrated in 1902 when a dozen pieces of Teco ware which had been
converted into lamp bases were displayed at the first exhibition of Art-
Crafts held at the Art Institute.

The second annual Art-Crafts exhibition, in 1903, featured vases
designed by members of the Chicago Architectural Club. In the course
of doing business, Gates had become friends with most of the city's
best-known artists and architects, a number of whom offered designs
for Teco ware. Architect William LeBaron Jenney, "the father of the
skyscraper," was responsible for several vases with conventionalized
flower designs, while his partner W. B. Mundie designed at least three
jardinieres whose shapes had been derived by combining circular
forms with squares or rectangles. Another vase featured a slender
cylindrical body topped by gently flaring rectangular handles.

Many of the pieces were the work of younger Chicago architects
identified with the progressive Prairie School, whose particular concern
was residential design. Rejecting the historical revival styles that had
characterized American architecture during most of the nineteenth
century, members of the Prairie School had by 1903 begun developing
new forms which they considered more appropriate to the time. Calling attention to the beauty inherent in natural materials such as wood,
clay, and stone, they advocated the use of these materials in simple,
uncluttered forms. Ornament, when it appeared in their structures at
all, often consisted of a geometric composition or a single motif such
as a hollyhock, poppy, or thistle, which emerged gracefully from
within the material through carving or modeling.

When these same principles were applied to the design of Teco
pottery, distinctive shapes emerged. Simple and geometric, these
forms were distinguished by rectilinear handles, or thick vertical piers
which extended from base to rim. Ornament, when used, consisted

of conventionalized floral motifs or incised linear designs whose primary function was to emphasize shape.   William J. Dodd created a number of attractive vases, including one striking design whose modeled leaves were attached at the top and bottom only, allowing the form of the vase to show through.   Hugh M. G. Garden designed several jardinieres, including one which combined graceful contours with an openwork leaf design, and another whose simple barrel shape was enhanced by incised, parallel lines.   N. L. Clarke designed hanging vases or wall pockets to hold creeping vines or running flowers, while Max Dunning devised decorative vases "especially adapted for rooms with Mission furnishings, such as library, den, or office."

M. P. White, William K. Fellows, J. K. Cady, Howard Van Doren Shaw, George C. Nimmons, and Frank Lloyd Wright were among other Chicago architects who designed Teco pottery.   For Gates, Frank Lloyd Wright designed a thirty-two inch "triplicate vase" which sold for thirty dollars, making it one of the highest-priced pieces of Teco. For Wright, Gates's workers cast in terra cotta the lovely *Flower in a Crannied Wall* statuette and *The Moon Children* fountain, modeled by Chicago sculptor Richard Bock in 1902 for the entrance hall of the Susan Lawrence Dana house in Springfield, Illinois.

The product of a unique relationship between architect and pottery, Teco ware became the ceramic expression of the Prairie School.   This special relationship was acknowledged by Chicago architect Thomas Eddy Tallmadge.   Reviewing the work of the Prairie School architects in the *Architectural Review* for April 1908, he wrote: "In the realm of pottery Chicago architects have delved deep, and have encouraged by their demands and their designs the local development of the craft." This concept was reinforced by Gates's promotional material, which claimed that Teco was a new and distinctly American pottery.   It did not incorporate "the symbolisms of the ancient potters," rather, Teco embodied "modern ideas" in harmony with "the present creeds of modern home decoration."   Homemakers were being encouraged by architects and decorators to discard their Victorian clutter in favor of more austere furnishings and simple shapes.   Pottery pieces of subtle forms and finished with matte glazes were designed to harmonize with the new, fashionably plain furnishings and more informal style of living. Thus it was no coincidence that Teco ware was often shown atop fire-place mantles or in the center of tables in Mission-style or Prairie School rooms, whether in Frank Lloyd Wright's home and studio or in the most modest bungalow built from mail-order plans.

While not all Teco ware was designed by architects, each piece embodied the same philosophy of design.   Blanche Ostertag, a young Chicago illustrator active in the Arts and Crafts Movement, drew sketches for Gates.   So did Orlando Giannini—co-owner of the art

63.   Teco vase no. 252 with green matte glaze, designed by architect Hugh Garden, c. 1903.   Described as "very chaste in design" and "a great favorite" in the 1905 catalog, it cost $8.00. (h: 12½"). *CHS, given in honor of Theodore Tieken by his children*

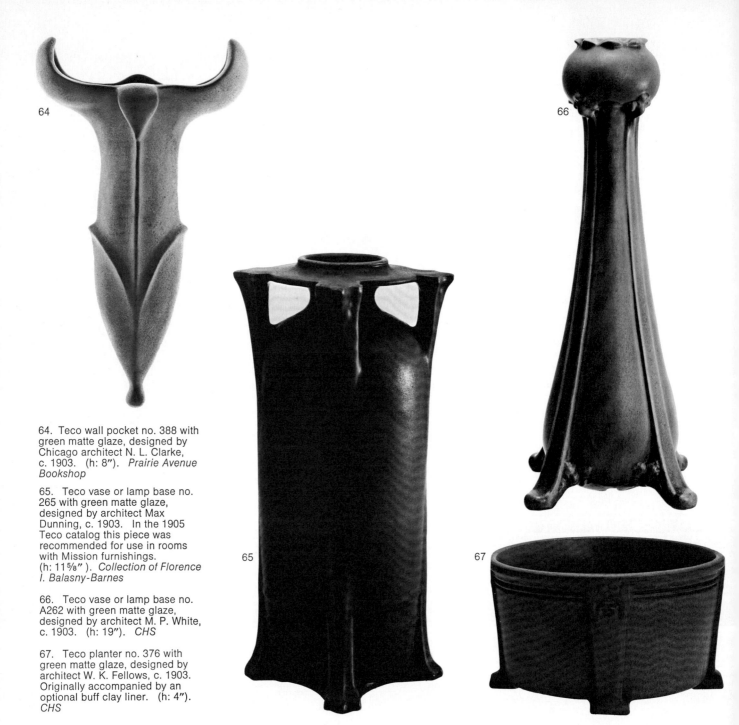

64. Teco wall pocket no. 388 with green matte glaze, designed by Chicago architect N. L. Clarke, c. 1903. (h: 8″). *Prairie Avenue Bookshop*

65. Teco vase or lamp base no. 265 with green matte glaze, designed by architect Max Dunning, c. 1903. In the 1905 Teco catalog this piece was recommended for use in rooms with Mission furnishings. (h: 11⅝″). *Collection of Florence I. Balasny-Barnes*

66. Teco vase or lamp base no. A262 with green matte glaze, designed by architect M. P. White, c. 1903. (h: 19″). *CHS*

67. Teco planter no. 376 with green matte glaze, designed by architect W. K. Fellows, c. 1903. Originally accompanied by an optional buff clay liner. (h: 4″). *CHS*

68. Lamp with green Teco base no. 271, designed by architect W. B. Mundie. The six-sided shade is composed of intersecting planes of green, white, and clear glass. Pictured in the 1904 catalog, the lamp was priced at $40.00. (h: 23"). Base: *CHS*; Shade: *Adrian Alexander*

glass firm of Giannini & Hilgart (see page 131)—who created a Teco lamp design incorporating a leaded glass shade with grape leaves in subdued tones of green and yellow. The 1904 Teco catalog also offered lamps with leaded art glass shades in geometric designs similar to those Giannini produced for Frank Lloyd Wright.

Some of the most unusual designs were created by the chief modelers of Gates's American Terra Cotta & Ceramic Company, Fritz Albert and Fernand Moreau. Both men had come to Chicago to work at the World's Columbian Exposition. Trained as a sculptor in Berlin, Fritz Albert had attracted Gates's attention by his work in the German Pavilion. Gates, impressed with Albert's ability, later hired him. At the American Terra Cotta & Ceramic Company, Albert divided his time between architectural commissions and the potteries.

Inspired by his love of nature, Albert designed Teco vases, low planters, and wall pockets in unusual forms incorporating naturalistic reeds or flowers modeled in low relief. One of his most unusual pieces featured long slender reeds spiraling upward from base to lip. Others were composed of overlapping leaves which resembled buds unfolding or half-opened water lilies, inspired no doubt by the rushes, reeds, lilies, and lotus growing in the little lake on the factory grounds. Teco vases and garden urns in classical Greek shapes were another of his specialties. In 1907, however, Albert left Gates to join the Northwestern Terra Cotta Company where his activities were confined to architectural modeling.

Teco pottery featuring the undulating curves and organic stalks associated with French Art Nouveau was the work of Fernand Moreau, a French sculptor. Moreau operated his own sculpture studio and taught evening clay modeling classes at the Art Institute before joining the staff of the American Terra Cotta & Ceramic Company in 1904. Of the vases modeled by him, at least four are decorated with naturalistic stalk-like motifs which appear to grow from the clay body of the pieces before unfurling gracefully or bursting into bloom. But Moreau also worked in a more linear style; one streamlined vase displays four sleek, stylized leaves supporting a bullet-shaped body. Like Albert, Moreau eventually became a modeler for the Northwestern Terra Cotta Company, although he continued to execute designs for Gates on a contract basis from time to time.

While many of the most exciting Teco shapes were contributed by friends or employees, at least half of those in production were the work of William Day Gates himself. His designs included interpretations of classic Greek or Oriental shapes, severely simple cylindrical vases, and a variety of sculptural vases, mugs, and candlesticks with coiled bodies or flat, angular handles. He also designed most of his firm's garden pottery, which consisted of enormous jars, giant garden vases, plinths, panels, sun dials, and window boxes. Gates's most striking pieces in this line were undoubtedly the four immense vases,

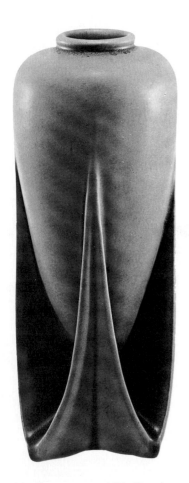

69. Teco vase no. 127 with pale green matte glaze, designed by Fernand Moreau, c. 1905. (h: 8⅝"). *Todd M. Volpe Collection*

70. Teco vase no. 310 with swirling leaves, designed by Fritz Albert, c. 1905. Green matte glaze. (h: 18⅛″). *Private Collection*

71. Teco vase no. 192 with twisted iris leaves attached at top and side, designed by Fritz Albert, c. 1905. This vase was described as being "beautiful for displaying large flowers or clusters of foliage." Green matte glaze. (h: 14″). *D. Magner, American Arts and Crafts, Brooklyn, New York*

70

71

each seven feet high, designed around 1909 for the Pompeiian Room of the Auditorium Annex (later the Congress Hotel) and executed in Teco green. In addition to the familiar green color, garden ware was also available in unglazed terra cotta or finished with stone-gray glaze.

The fact that many designers contributed to the creation of Teco ware gave the line such a variety of styles and glazes that no one piece of Teco pottery could be called representative of the company's output—an attribute that added to the interest of the ware. It also ensured that there was something to appeal to every taste. As a result, Teco became the only Chicago pottery to achieve and maintain artistry on a mass production basis.

The first Teco catalog, published in 1904, expounded the basic philosophy that had guided Gates in the creation of Teco ware. "In Teco Art Pottery," the booklet stated, "the constant aim has been to produce an art pottery having originality and true artistic merit, at a comparatively slight cost, and thus make it possible for every lover of art pottery to number among his treasures one or more pieces of this exquisite ware." The catalog illustrated sixty shapes available to the customer. One of the last catalogs, published around 1910, reiterated these basic democratic principles and added:

> Teco Pottery is not, rightly speaking, a commercial product. It is not the symbol of the money-hungry manufacturer, or merchant or exploiter. It is an ideal formulated and rendered tangible. Materially it is made of clay, but in reality it is the realization of the dreams, the patience, the industry, the research, the relationship and the love of art of William Day Gates. [Teco (Chicago: The Franklin Co.), c. 1910]

The advertisements Gates placed in *House Beautiful, The Ladies' Home Journal,* and other homemaker periodicals urged art lovers to send for the free booklet which explained the qualities that made Teco "beautiful, restful, artistic, and refined." Noting that "quiet, restful pottery" was one mark of a truly refined home, one 1905 advertisement advised homemakers that "one small Teco vase, costing perhaps a dollar, will do more to give that touch of elegance and artistic refinement to the home than any other one thing." A 1902 promotion directed at Christmas shoppers which had appeared in the November *Craftsman* described Teco pottery as "pleasing to the eye and soothing to the nerves." For the benefit of architects and contractors, Gates composed an eloquent ode "To a Teco Vase" for the company's house organ *Common Clay* and wrote short articles on the historic origins and artistic virtues of pottery.

While each Teco design could be attributed to a single artist-designer, the actual vase or garden urn was the product of a trio of craftsmen comprising a modeler, potter, and chemist. All Teco forms were cast, although the original model may have been thrown or

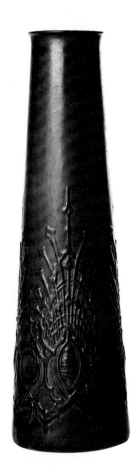

72. Teco vase or cane holder with delicate foliate design applied to standard form no. 73. Dark green matte glaze. (h: 25 ¼"). *CHS*

73

75

74

73. William D. Gates in his
living room in his home Trail's
End, c. 1908. A Teco humidor
no. A270, designed by architect
W. B. Mundie, sits on the small
table near his chair. The fireplace is faced with Teco tiles in
blue, lavender, and beige surrounding a landscape tile painted
by Hardesty G. Maratta. On the
hearth stands a Teco umbrella
stand with three satyr heads, while
sconces designed by Orlando
Giannini hang on the wall. Sample tiles showing the glazes available at the American Terra Cotta
& Ceramic Company cover the
entire floor. *Family of William
Day Gates*

74. Unmolding and finishing
Teco ware at the Gates Potteries,
c. 1905. *Family of William Day
Gates*

75. Gates in his garden at Trail's
End, c. 1908. While the graceful
seven-foot tall vases were made
as early as 1897, the best-known
examples later stood in the
Pompeiian Room of the Congress
Hotel. *Family of William Day
Gates*

modeled by hand. After the model was made, discussed, and adopted, it was turned over to a mold-maker, who made an exact cast of it in plaster of Paris. Teco ware was known by number rather than by pattern names and although all pieces received the impressed Teco mark, none was signed by the individual designer or makers. However, designers were identified by name in many of the company's catalogs.

By adapting mass-manufacturing techniques such as casting and assembly-line processing to the production of art pottery, Gates was able to produce far greater quantities of wares at a lesser cost than would have been possible by using hand building or throwing. At the Gates and similar large potteries, one workman filled the mold and later removed the dried vase; another potter cleaned away all traces of mold seams with modeling tools and, if necessary, added to the piece handles or feet which had been cast in separate molds. A kiln-setter placed the vase in clay receptacles called saggers and then in the great circular oven in preparation for firing. After the firing, another potter sprayed the pieces with liquid glaze using pneumatic pressure; others returned them to the kiln for the final firing. While not handmade by a single craftsman from start to finish, Teco ware was still the end product of a time-consuming, expensive process requiring much handwork and skilled labor. The conditions under which Teco ware was produced and the spirit which predominated in the pottery were characteristic of the Arts and Crafts Movement.

Gates's enthusiasm for his work must have communicated itself to his workers. Visitors to the works at Terra Cotta rarely failed to comment on the natural beauty of the site and the dedication of the workmen. In the first of a series of articles devoted to American potteries, the well-known potter, Susan Stuart Frackelton, wrote:

> *The potteries are beautifully situated in a picturesque valley, amid delightful surroundings of wood, field, and lake. Mr. Gates firmly believes that beautiful surroundings tend to inspire beautiful thoughts. One must have enthusiasm for his work to give it individuality and charm, hence the beautiful lily-ponds built and stocked with rare aquatic plants near the clear, little lake, and the profusion of flowers cultivated round about. The potteries stand in the heart of this lovely country, with no other buildings near save the home of the "Master Potter." There is none of the usual factory squalor; nothing dejected and hideous to look upon, no children at work; no half-paid pinched-faced women; none but men who have the air of being fitted to accomplish what lies before them during the day and of doing the day's work with poise and sincerity.* [Susan Stuart Frackelton, *"Our American Potteries: Teco Ware,"* The Sketch Book 5, no. 1 (September 1905): 14]

Teco joined Grueby of Boston, the Rookwood Pottery of Cincinnati,

76. The American Terra Cotta & Ceramic Co. factory as seen from across the lily pond, c. 1897. The October 1897 *Clay Worker* noted that "the modeler's room at Terra Cotta overlooks on one side a lovely little lake, whose placid waters are framed in willows and rushes and covered with lily pads. On the other a wooded park-like slope, covered from spring till fall with the flowers of the season, stretches away to the West." *Family of William Day Gates*

and the Van Briggle Pottery of Colorado as one of ''the big four'' in American ceramics when it received highest honors at the 1904 World's Fair in St. Louis. The Gates Potteries exhibit in the Palace of Varied Industries consisted of three lines of Teco ware displayed in a stunning pavilion of leaded glass: the early ware which used soft green glazes on well-designed vases and lamp bodies; richly colored vases whose high glaze embodied tiny metallic flakes; and a new Teco crystal ware, whose surface was covered with tiny crystals similar to the frost which appears on windowpanes in winter. In the Mining Building were exhibited huge garden vases and large landscape murals executed on terra cotta panels. The color in the murals was achieved by applying slip to damp terra cotta. Executed at the factory by the Chicago artist, Hardesty Gilmore Maratta, these murals won a gold medal for Gates, while his display of Teco ware was awarded the Grand Prize.

Although Gates was the first to introduce an Americanized version of a crystalline glaze—one of the novelties of the 1893 World's Fair—he did not capitalize on his discovery. With a generosity rare in such a competitive industry, Gates presented the formula for the beautiful glaze to the American Ceramic Society when he became its president in 1905.

In 1910, when polychrome (multi-colored) glazes were becoming a popular choice for architectural terra cotta, the distinctive, soft Teco green glaze was supplemented by new autumn-inspired colors such as mellow golds, rich browns and buffs, stone grays, and tones of rose. A few pieces, turned out in much smaller quantities, featured metallic blues and purples and even a bright canary yellow. Although considerably less subdued than the earlier greens, these new colors immediately found favor among tastemakers. In the August 1911 *Fine Arts Journal*, for example, Evelyn Marie Stuart praised the cheery new colors and declared that ''as a background for flowers and greenery no other fabric could be more appropriate and satisfying than these various shades of Teco.'' While the range of colors was expanded, most of the shapes remained the same. The new colors were merely applied to the most popular shapes, selected from an inventory now numbering over 500 designs. ''Teco Tones are colors to *live with*,'' declared a 1910 advertisement, adding, ''Teco *forms* inspire something like affection.''

The scope of Teco was further widened around 1910 by the addition of Teco art and faience tiles. Entire fireplace mantels were constructed using Teco art tiles in pleasant shades of green, brown, dull orange, blue, lavender, and gray, interspersed with landscape tiles painted with clumps of trees, gently undulating hills, or clouded skies in soft, muted tones of gray, green, blue, or brown.

The faience tiles were more ornate, featuring relief carving, such as delicate conventionalized foliage or fruits and flowers glazed in bright

77. Teco tea set with gray matte glaze, c. 1910. (h: 6"). *Robert A. Furhoff*

78. Collection of matte glazed
Teco ware, 1901–20. (Left to right,
back row): green vase no. 256
by Max Dunning (h: 11⅝″); green
vase no. 182 by William D. Gates
(h: 16⅛″); dark green vase no.
151 by W. J. Dodd (h: 11″); blue
vase no. 420 by Fernand Moreau
(h: 12¾″); gray vase no. 72 by
William D. Gates (h: 18¼″).
(Middle row): yellow vase no. 427
by William D. Gates (h: 5″); apple
green vase no. B60 by William D.
Gates (h: 8½″); brown vase no.
283 by Fritz Albert (h: 9¼″);
black bookend (h: 6⅞″); rose
vase no. 444 (h: 10½″); salmon
vase no. 335 by Fritz Albert
(h: 11¾″); mauve vase no. 336
by Fritz Albert (h: 7⅞″). (Front
row): green/tan mug (h: 3⅜″);
cream and glossy green bookend
(h: 6⅞″); tan pitcher no. 58 by
William D. Gates (h: 4″); gray
sugar bowl (h: 2¼″); blue vase
no. 60 by William D. Gates
(h: 6⅝″); pink vase no A402
(h: 6⅝″). *(Lenders, in alphabe-
tical order): Collection of Florence
I. Balasny-Barnes; George A.
Berry III, TC Industries, Inc; Joel
Cohen; Robert A. Furhoff; Thomas
J. Neniskis; Thomas M. Tomc,
Fly-By-Nite Gallery, Chicago.*

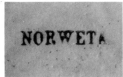

Norweta Pottery, c. 1907–c. 1920.
Chicago Crucible Company, c. 1920–c. 1932.

An art pottery line produced briefly by the Northwestern Terra Cotta Company at 2525 Clybourn Avenue, Norweta ware included delicate vases with blue, lavender, or green crystalline glazes as well as sturdy vases suitable for use as lamp bases or umbrella stands.

These products were discontinued around 1920 when Northwestern acquired the Chicago Crucible Company and introduced pottery vases, lamp bases, and ashtrays with mottled glazes in shades of green or blue. Other products included wall plaques featuring relief portraits and whimsical open-mouthed frogs.

Northwestern also produced terra cotta garden ornaments, urns, and benches from 1877 through the 1940s.

colors. A few pictured low-relief sailing ships framed in pale blue and white. Others displayed strictly geometrical arrangements of various contrasting colors. Plain green Teco tiles with simple incised or low-relief designs were recommended for use in masonry or tile walls. While attractive Teco tiles were created for the factory office and Gates's own fireplace, the most spectacular use of Teco faience tiles appeared in 1912 in the large landscape mural created by Chicago artist Charles Francis Brown for the "Teco Inn" of the Radisson Hotel in Minneapolis, Minnesota, when the company opened a branch office in that city.

Also new in the Teco line were tea services and chocolate sets available in pearly pink, greenish brown, or pinkish tan earthenware. Noting its rather heavy weight, which she considered an asset, Evelyn Marie Stuart, in the same 1911 *Fine Arts Journal* article, praised the new tea ware, adding that it called up "alluring visions of its beauty in combination with mission arts and crafts, bamboo trays, wicker or rustic tea tables, and the curious handwrought effects in silver and linen which one sees offered for sale in the studios and art shops of the handicraft workers." This, no doubt, pleased Gates, for it showed that his new wares had not strayed from his original aim of combining the artistic and the practical.

The new faience tiles and tea wares were exhibited in Chicago at the first Clay Products Show sponsored by the ceramic industry in 1912. After that no further innovations were made in the line. Although the ware remained in production for another decade, only the simpler forms requiring little hand finishing were produced. Large and frequent orders for architectural terra cotta left workers with little time to devote to pottery making, and Gates and his sons, Major Earl and Neil, were kept busy supervising the Chicago office, the factory, and branch offices in Minneapolis and Indianapolis.

Norweta Ware and Other Art Pottery

Like the Teco ware of William Gates, much of the other art pottery produced in Chicago before World War I was the inspiration of men connected with the architectural terra cotta industry. By 1907 the Northwestern Terra Cotta Company (see page 168) had introduced a line of art pottery called Norweta. (Like Teco ware, it took its name from that of the parent company.) During what must have been a short-lived experiment, two lines of pottery were produced. One featured delicate porcelain vases covered with a crystalline glaze. The other, a line of terra cotta vases also suitable for use as lamp bases, consisted of twisted treetrunk forms or tapering cylinders with stylized leaves and flowers modeled in low relief, usually finished in a cucumber green or a dark blue monochrome glaze. Some were highlighted

80

81

79. Norweta vase with dark green crackled matte glaze made by the Northwestern Terra Cotta Company, 1907–20. (h: 14″). *CHS*

80. Vase or lamp base with turquoise and avocado green mottled glaze marked Chicago Crucible Co., c. 1920. (h: 7″). *CHS*

81. Norweta vases with pale blue crystalline glaze made by the Northwestern Terra Cotta Company, 1907–20. (h: 4¾″). *Collection of Sonia and Walter Bob; Robert A. Furhoff*

79

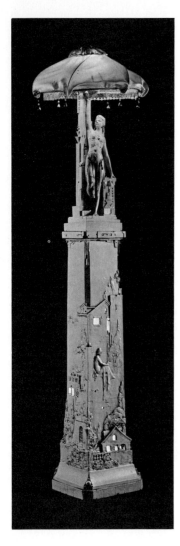

82. Lamp and pedestal base with cream semi-matte glaze made by the Northwestern Terra Cotta Company, c. 1920. The sylph, modeled by Fritz Albert, wears a gown highlighted with gold, pink, and green glazed jewels. The pedestal, designed by Fernand Moreau, features a village scene with towers and cottages, young women, and animals. (h: 76"). *M. Epstein Hersh, Inc.*

with touches of a contrasting color in the manner made popular by the Grueby Pottery of Boston.

In 1911 the Northwestern Terra Cotta Company entered four examples of Norweta ware (three green terra cotta vases and one crystal vase) plus a terra cotta lamp standard in the Art-Crafts exhibit at The Art Institute of Chicago. The company produced a variety of lamp standards, but the most spectacular were those bearing whimsical landscapes modeled in low relief by Fernand Moreau or Fritz Albert. Houses, trees, young women with Gibson-girl hairdos, owls and pussycats modeled by Moreau, or a complex composition of triangles by Albert, encircled the square white-glazed pedestals, which supported jewel-arrayed sylphs who held aloft three electric light bulbs. Simpler, columnar standards were also available in several architectural styles.

Around 1920 the Northwestern Terra Cotta Company expanded its facilities by acquiring the Chicago Crucible Company. About this time Northwestern discontinued its Norweta line and began to produce a new line, marked Chicago Crucible Company, instead. This ware included small, somewhat bulbous vases and lamp bases with speckled blue or yellow-green glazes. Made sporadically between architectural terra cotta orders, the Chicago Crucible Company pottery was phased out a few years later when it proved unprofitable.

Pottery in simple shapes featuring matte and metallic glazes similar to those used on Teco ware was produced between 1913 and 1915 by Duane F. Albery, a former employee of the American Terra Cotta & Ceramic Company. After graduating from Ohio State University with a degree in ceramic engineering, Albery worked in Gates's ceramic laboratory for four years before leaving in 1913 to open a pottery in Evanston, just north of Chicago. His wife, Frances Huxtable Albery, recalled: "We built a pottery factory in our back yard, and had a flourishing business. We taught some of the Northwestern [University] students the art."

In their small works, called the Albery Novelty Pottery, the young couple produced vases and wall pockets, advertising novelties, and pottery featuring monograms "not painted over the glaze but worked into the body of the pottery itself." They also made small terra cotta castings and fired decorated china for other ceramists. Albery was especially proud of two terra cotta casts of *The Bust of a Child* made for the Chicago sculptor Emil Zettler in 1914. That same year Albery succeeded in creating a genuine black pottery "free from the usual tints such as dark blue or gray." Within a year, however, the high cost of materials forced the Alberys to give up their pottery and move to Perth Amboy, New Jersey, where Albery had accepted a job in a ceramic laboratory.

As early as 1898, Sven Linderoth, a Swedish architect who had dedicated many years to experiments with enameled tiles, produced art pottery along with filter tubes and flower pots at his small works, the

Albery Novelty Pottery, 1913–1915.

In 1913 Duane F. Albery gave up his job as a ceramic engineer at the American Terra Cotta & Ceramic Company and moved to Evanston, where he and his wife, Frances Huxtable (a former Evanstonian), built a pottery in the backyard of their home at 431 Sherman Avenue. There they produced art pottery and clay novelties featuring matte and glossy glazes, some of which resembled those used by Albery's former employer in the production of Teco ware.

When the pottery closed in 1915, Albery accepted a position with a terra cotta firm in New Jersey, but by 1922 he had returned to Evanston and was working for the Northwestern Terra Cotta Company.

83. Two vases made by the Albery Novelty Pottery, 1913–15. The tall vase has a green matte glaze, while the smaller one features a glossy brown glaze. (h: 7⅛″, 2¾″). *Private Collection; Thomas J. Neniskis*

Linderoth Ceramic Co., on South Elizabeth Street. Around 1906 he began producing pottery shapes for decoration by members of the National League of Mineral Painters and, a year later, agreed to share his facilities with members of the Atlan Ceramic Art Club who wished to try their hand at pottery work. About the same time, probably inspired by the glowing mosaic tile interior of the Alhambra palace in Granada, Spain, he renamed his pottery the Alhambra Ceramic Works and began to offer a line of art pottery.

Modeled by a Swedish sculptor named LeVeau, the vases and pitchers produced by the Alhambra works had intricately carved surfaces, C- and S-scroll handles, and elaborate applied ornamentation reminiscent of what had been so roundly condemned in England by taste-setters Charles L. Eastlake and William Morris. "Mr. LeVeau's taste in decoration," politely reported *Keramic Studio* in an article featuring the works,

> *seems to lean a little toward classic, rococo and old fashioned styles which do not appeal very much to modern ideas, but his handling of the modeling tools and especially his modeling of figures are remarkably good. We have seen a couple of statuettes in clay, one of them a lifelike bust of Ericson which showed better than anything else his talent as a modeler.* ["The Alhambra Ceramic Works," Keramic Studio 8, no. 12 (April 1907): 272-3]

Small potteries were also established by several women known for their work as china decorators. Nellie Agnes Cross, assisted by her sons Richard Watson Cross, Jr., and Charles William Cross, operated the Crossware Pottery at their home on Farwell Avenue in Rogers Park on the city's North Side. Mrs. Cross, who served several terms as president of the National League of Mineral Painters, had specialized in glass and china decorating before beginning to help her sons make art pottery around 1905. In the 1908 Chicago Ceramic Association exhibition she displayed "several pieces of Crossware consisting of some pleasing little pottery tiles, vases, bowls and a most refined green pottery fern dish," according to a review in the August 1908 *Keramic Studio*. Although Mrs. Cross exhibited the ware under her own name, Lillian Gray Jarvie, who operated the Jarvie Shop in the Fine Arts Building, went so far as to say that Crossware was actually made by one of the Cross boys (Richard), who was "barely out of his teens." She indicated that he also made nearly all of his own machinery and mixed all of his glazes, rather than purchasing them ready-made from a commercial firm, as was the practice of most amateur potters.

A similar venture, the Barnet Pottery, was conducted at 6228 Wabash Avenue by Belle Barnet Vesey, another china decorator who succeeded Mrs. Cross as president of the National League of Mineral Painters. Tiles and bases decorated with floral and geometric designs and vases with black outlines and open-work borders were designed by Mrs. Vesey and executed by Charles Barnet Wirick and Jean Paul Wirick, and displayed in the annual Art-Crafts exhibition at the Art Institute in 1910. Shortly after this the pottery seems to have gone out of business. In the same 1910 exhibition appeared the work of another short-lived pottery, the Beggs Shop, operated briefly at 1744 North Humboldt Street by Helen W. and Stephen J. Beggs.

It is possible that Mrs. Cross and Mrs. Vesey had been encouraged in their art pottery efforts by Susan Stuart Frackelton, the founder of the National League of Mineral Painters and an accomplished art potter who had moved to Chicago from Milwaukee in 1902. In Milwaukee, Mrs. Frackelton had developed a portable gas kiln for china decorators and experimented extensively with making salt-glazed stoneware and other types of pottery from local Wisconsin clay. Originally made to show what an earnest craft worker with a high artistic ideal could do with common material, the stoneware met with so cordial a reception that Mrs. Frackelton continued to produce it in limited quantities. The grayish white pieces were made in a variety of forms, but the decorations were always in shades of blue. In Chicago, Susan Frackelton continued her ceramic work for another eight years, teaching pottery classes in her studio in the Fine Arts Building and writing and lecturing on ceramics and other handicrafts.

Two other potters who were well known in Chicago but whose major work had been done elsewhere were former Art Institute students Elizabeth and Edward Dahlquist, who, with Gertrude Singleton Mathews had founded the Shawsheen Pottery in Billerica, Massachusetts, in 1906. Moving to Mason City, Iowa, a year later, the Dahlquists became known for their black and dark green glazed handcoiled pottery made in the Indian fashion with strips of clay pressed one upon the other. Later, much of their work was thrown on a potter's wheel. Their output included vases, bowls, jardinieres, and tea sets, much of it the work of students.

The Dahlquists moved to Chicago in 1911. Elizabeth taught classes in art and pottery in her Hyde Park studio and Edward periodically taught pottery at the Art Institute. After 1915, when Elizabeth opened the Ho Ho Shop on the North Side to sell Chinese porcelains and objets d'art, the Dahlquists stopped making ceramics.

In addition to these professionals and semi-professionals, a small army of amateur potters worked in basements, in sheds, even in bedrooms of small city apartments, producing art pottery for their own pleasure or to sell through the Jarvie Shop, the Swastica Shop, or similar outlets which specialized in the handcrafted furniture, metalwork, weavings, and pottery identified with the Arts and Crafts Movement.

84. Candlestick with blue anthemion and peacock feathers by Susan S. Frackelton, 1909. One of the last known pieces of signed and dated Frackelton ware. (h: 7"). *State Historical Society of Wisconsin*

Frackelton Pottery, 1902–c. 1910.

Before moving to Chicago in 1902, Susan S. G. Frackelton (1848–1932) had acquired an enviable reputation as a china painter and art potter. During the 1880s, while head of the Frackelton China Decorating Works in Milwaukee, Wisconsin, she had developed Frackelton Dry Water Colors, invented a portable gas-fired kiln, and published *Tried by Fire* (1885) to aid fellow china painters. By 1892 she had organized the National League of Mineral Painters.

In the early 1890s, Mrs. Frackelton began to use Milwaukee's creamy clay to create artistic salt-glazed stoneware with cobalt-blue incised and applied decoration. Later she added a line of blue-decorated underglazed art pottery which resembled the Delft ware produced in Holland.

After Mrs. Frackelton moved to Chicago to live with her daughter, she continued to make her Blue and Gray pottery for at least another eight years. In an interview published in the September 1903 issue of *The Sketch Book*, she related: "Each piece is thrown upon the wheel and no duplicates are made, so the output of my work is small. I have never made a piece from a mold. One of the tests of handmade pottery is that the base is always smooth, whereas the base of those which are made from molds have rims or hollows." Frackelton pottery carries an incised signature and, occasionally, a date.

After 1910, Mrs. Frackelton turned to book illumination and oil painting, often exhibiting her work in the annual Art-Crafts exhibitions at the Art Institute.

85. Pitcher with blue jack-in-the-pulpit decoration by Susan S. Frackelton, 1906. (h: 9½″). *State Historical Society of Wisconsin*

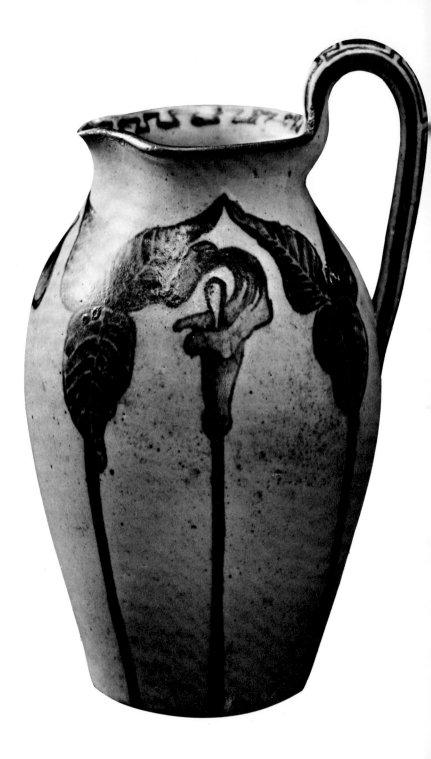

A Return to Traditional Styles

In the years after World War I, Chicago's art pottery, like its architecture, reflected a return to traditional, historically inspired styles. In architecture this expressed itself in a revival of Gothic, American Colonial, Tudor, and Spanish styles; in pottery it manifested itself in lavish and exuberant forms or imitations of simple peasant wares. Large pottery classes continued to be taught at The Art Institute of Chicago, the Lewis Institute (a technical school), the Chicago Normal College, and the University of Chicago, as well as in various high schools throughout the city. Now, however, the focus was on the practical and artistic uses of clay and on the manual dexterity fostered by clayworking rather than on the moral uplift to be derived from this activity or on the contributions it was expected to make to American art.

At the Art Institute, Myrtle Merritt French taught designing, glazing, and firing to classes numbering about sixty students a year. In addition to imparting the basic skills, she gave special attention to experiments with glazes and clays, with particular emphasis on clays found in the United States. Instead of opening their own studios, most Art Institute graduates now became teachers or found their way into the pottery industries of Ohio or New Jersey.

In the late 1890s Jane Addams had established a pottery at Hull-House where immigrants could learn the marketable skills associated with pottery production. Located at the settlement house complex on Halsted Street, classes were conducted by resident social worker William Bulger and other members of the Chicago Arts and Crafts Society. Describing the Hull-House pottery workshop in 1904, Marion Foster Washburne wrote in *The Craftsman*:

> *. . . here in the alcove of the wood and metal working rooms is a big vat of clay, a couple of potter's wheels, and a case of admirably modeled, glazed, and decorated pottery. Standing at the table is a clean old German kneading clay, his squat, bowed legs far apart, his body leaning forward, his long and powerful arms beating upon the clay like piston rods. He rolls it into a long cylinder and breaks it off with exactitude into a half dozen little lumps. As he carries it across the room, walking with a side-wise straddle, one sees that he is bent and twisted by his trade, conformed to his wheel. Upon this he slaps his clay, and thrusting out a short leg, sets it whirling. Above the rough lump he folds his hands, and, in a minute, from that prayerful seclusion, the clay emerges rounded, smoothed, and slightly hollowed. His hands open, his thumbs work in; one almost sees him think through his skillful thumbs and forefingers: the other fingers lie close together and he moves the four as one. Like some mystery of organic nature, the clay rises, bends, and becomes a*

86

87

86. Vase with yellow matte glaze made by W. C. Strauss in a pottery class at The Art Institute of Chicago, 1917. (h: 3½") *Thomas M. Tomc, Fly-By-Nite Gallery, Chicago*

87. A pottery class at the School of the Art Institute of Chicago, c. 1923. *Chicago Commerce. CHS*

88. Green glazed planter with
applied decoration supported by
four donkeys, made by Miguel
Juarez at the Hull-House pottery,
c. 1930. (h: 15"). *Jane Addams
Memorial Collection, University of
Illinois at Chicago Circle*

Hull-House Shops, c. 1898–c. 1940.
Hull-House Kilns, 1927–c. 1940.

The social settlement founded by Jane Addams and Ellen Gates Starr at 800 S. Halsted sponsored at least three pottery operations: the Labor Museum, in which neighborhood immigrants practiced old-country crafts with traditional implements and where all types of handicrafts were exhibited and sold; the Hull-House Shops, where evening classes were conducted by social workers who belonged to the Chicago Arts and Crafts Society; and the Hull-House Kilns, an outgrowth of the pottery department of the Labor Museum which was formally organized in 1927 by Myrtle M. French, instructor of ceramics at The Art Institute of Chicago.

As early as 1898 *Brush and Pencil* described vases, jars, and bowls in the Chicago Arts and Crafts Society exhibition which had been made by Hull-House social worker William Bulger and decorated with incised lines by resident Frank Hazenplug. Made from red Illinois clay mixed with buff-colored clay from Minnesota, the pieces were all under six inches in height so that they could be fired in Bulger's small kiln. Like all Hull-House pottery, they were simple in shape and strictly utilitarian in design.

Products of the Hull-House Kilns tended to be restricted to bowls, tea sets, pitchers, plates, and other tablewares, although whimsical animals and figures were occasionally created by children. Made from dense, heavy clay, the pieces were often heavily glazed in shades of bright red, yellow, orange, green, or blue. Some were decorated with incised or handpainted designs. Hull-House pottery was sometimes signed with the name of the maker; at other times pieces were marked on the base with a rubber stamp that read *Hull-House Kilns*.

In the late 1930s emphasis shifted to other programs, but craft classes still continue today in neighborhood centers affiliated with the Hull-House Association.

89. A young potter finishing a bowl at the Hull-House Kilns, c.1930. *Jane Addams Memorial Collection, University of Illinois at Chicago Circle*

79

vase. "Look at that thing grow!" an excited boy exclaims, forgetting the crowd of onlookers. "See it, see it!" The old potter rises, lifts the vase in his mitten-like hands and, bending, straddling sideways, his face unmoved, carries it tenderly to its place." [*Marion Forbes Washburne, "A Labor Museum,"* The Craftsman *6, no. 6 (September 1904): 573-4*]

In 1927 the pottery classes at Hull-House were reorganized into a commercial operation known as the Hull-House Kilns by Myrtle French, instructor of ceramics at the Art Institute. The pottery was staffed by students from the Hull-House Art School who showed an aptitude for claywork and who wished to earn their livelihood as potters. Handmade plates, teapots, bowls, and other tableware were duplicated from a line of samples and sold, along with one-of-a-kind pieces, at Hull-House and through the Hull-House Shop on North Michigan Avenue. Hull-House furnished the materials and the students did most of the work. Hull-House shared the proceeds with the potters.

While the potters secured a modest income, the primary value of this activity lay in the stimulation it provided for the workers and in the fact that it brought together people of different nationalities to share ideas and techniques. As a result, the output of the Hull-House potteries often reflected ethnic traditions and tastes. Mexicans, for example, employed a special method in building figures of animals and often decorated their plates and bowls with colored slip in a manner reminiscent of Indian designs. Others preferred to decorate their work with designs incised into the damp clay, by modeling designs above the surface, by using different colors of an unfired glaze to create majolica, or by painting designs using various colored slips. Amateurs spent their leisure hours in the pottery, and the same room and equipment were used by children after school and by adults in the evening.

Only three other potteries operated in Chicago between 1920 and 1933: the Faenza Pottery, the Kay Bee China Works, and the newly-added pottery of the Pickard China Studios, which had previously confined itself to china decorating. Of these, the Faenza Pottery specialized in producing imitation antiques while the other two directed their efforts toward creating hard porcelain suitable for use as fine dinnerware or vases.

In 1920 Charles Barnet Wirick and Jean Paul Wirick, the two brothers who had executed pottery for the Barnet Pottery, took over the aged Sven Linderoth's Alhambra Ceramic Works at 5844 South Elizabeth Street, where Charles had been apprenticed eighteen years earlier. Changing the name to the Faenza Pottery, the Wiricks modeled candlesticks, decorated tiles, and made other wares out of shale clay, obtained from the Indiana coal mining region, mixed with small quantities of kaolin. All their wares, according to the August 1923 *Chicago Commerce*, were replicas of antique Spanish and Italian

HULL-HOUSE SHOP, ITALIAN COURT,
619 NORTH MICHIGAN AVE., CHICAGO

FIRST BIRTHDAY EXHIBITION AND
SALE IN THEIR NEW QUARTERS
MARCH 19, 1932 TO APRIL 19, 1932

POTTERY, CHILDREN'S PAINTINGS,
WEAVING, WOOD, METAL, PRINTS,
ETCHINGS, FURNITURE RECONDITI-
ONED, BATIK, LESSONS IN WEAVING.

90. Advertisement for the Hull-House Shop on North Michigan Avenue, 1932. *Jane Addams Memorial Collection, University of Illinois at Chicago Circle*

peasant pottery and were marketed by three Michigan Avenue shops.

In 1923, after five years of experimentation, a group of Chicagoans succeeded in producing a true porcelain and for a short time their pottery was the only one in the country making a genuine hard paste china. Known as the Kay Bee China Works, Inc., the firm was described as follows in *Chicago Commerce:*

> *For years Fred B. Kammermayer, of 5688 New Hampshire Avenue, and Julius H. Brauer, an artist, of 2338 Larrabee Street, spent all their spare time and savings experimenting with various American clays in an effort to produce hard china. An almost white clay from North Carolina finally yielded the desired effect. Vases and other articles equal to the finest Dresden were molded in the basement of Mr. Kammermayer's home and fired in a small kiln erected in his back yard.*
>
> *Although success had crowned their efforts, the two struggling experimentors faced failure through lack of business ability until H. Heine, of Highland Park, president of the Heine Chimney Company, 123 West Madison street, and Oscar Leistnner, importer and manufacturer of artificial flowers at 323 West Randolph street, became associated with the enterprise. They formed a corporation with Mr. Kammermayer as president, Mr. Brauer as secretary and Mr. Heine as treasurer. The Norwood Park avenue plant was established, with one double-deck kiln and approximately 15,000 square feet of floor space, producing about $40,000 worth of porcelain a year. Plans have already been drawn for the erection of three more kilns which will give the plant a production capacity of about $250,000 in plain white china, which, when decorated will be worth $750,000. ["Chicagoans Solve Secret of Porcelain," Chicago Commerce 19, pt. 1 (August 18, 1923):7]*

Vases comprised the principal output of the Kay Bee China Works and thirty different shapes and sizes were produced at its plant at 5210 Norwood Park Avenue. Originally the vases, upon removal from the molds, were decorated under-the-glaze using enamels and gold-etch at the Brauer Art Studio on Milwaukee Avenue, but later their manufacture and decoration were consolidated under one roof. Plates, cups, and other tablewares were thrown on a motor-driven potter's wheel, while elaborately hand-sculpted figures of men and animals were applied to the vases or fired separately as ornaments.

Together, the Pickard China Studios and the Kay Bee China Works had brought to fruition a long cherished dream. In just over fifty years emphasis had shifted from handpainted china, to art pottery, and back again to handpainted china. But the efforts of Pickard and Kay Bee meant that this time Chicago decorators practiced their art on blanks manufactured in their own city.

91. *Sunburst Globe* pattern
carafe and tumblers, cut in the
factory of Pitkin & Brooks,
c. 1900. (h: 7¾"). *Mr. and Mrs.
Charles O. Zollar*

CUT &
ENGRAVED GLASS

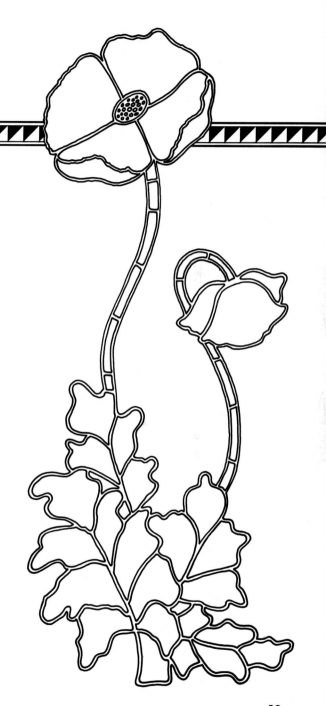

In Chicago the glass cutting and engraving industry which developed at the end of the nineteenth century shared a number of characteristics with china painting and the production of art pottery. Like china painters, glass cutters were concerned with the decoration rather than the manufacture of the object itself, and practiced their art on blank glass forms manufactured in Indiana, Ohio, Massachusetts, and New York. Unlike china painters and art potters, however, many glass cutters did not sign their work. Because innovation in glass cutting was limited by the fragile nature of the medium, glass cutters tended to follow prescribed patterns. Thus originality of design was less important than the quality of the execution, that is, the depth and precision of the cut.

American cut glass was widely admired for its brilliance, which was a consequence of the materials used in the manufacture of the glass blanks. American sand was especially fine and when mixed with oxide of lead in combination with potash, allowed manufacturers to make glass of exceptional clarity. Although all glass could be cut, the peculiar attributes of lead glass—its softness and high index of refraction—made it particularly appropriate for cutting because there was less chance of breakage than with harder, more brittle glass. To create a prismatic sparkle, American cutters combined a variety of geometric fans, stars, diamonds, flutes, and mitres, covering most of the surface with deep and intricate incisions. The high index of refraction inherent in lead glass gave the American cut glass the brilliance of diamonds.

Not only were local glass blanks superior to European, but American advances in glass technology also contributed to an exceptionally fine product. Steam-, gas-, and later electric-powered machines allowed the craftsman to turn out work of a uniform standard; the invention of new steel cutting wheels allowed a smoother and deeper cut; and better brushes gave a finer polish to the glass. The flow of European immigrants brought both experienced entrepreneurs and skilled craftsmen to put American technology and assembly-line techniques to good use.

Glass cutting was a difficult and laborious occupation requiring steady hands, good eyesight, and intense concentration. To create a cut glass article, the cutter marked the main outlines of the geometrical pattern on the plain, smooth surface of the glass blank with a reddish pigment, then roughed in the design with iron wheels or discs which were kept moist under a constant dripping of sand and water. The deepest cuts were always made first, since they were the most difficult. With the principal cuts completed, the piece was passed on from one workman to another, each one cutting a different part of the design using the appropriately sized wheel and materials until the piece was completed. Thus, rather than one man doing the entire piece, each man executed a part of the design.

When the article came from the cutting room, the cuttings were gray (matte) and had to be polished on wooden wheels fed with a mixture of water and pumice, or rottenstone. Next, brush wheels were used and a final polish given with a felt wheel or a cork wheel moistened with putty powder. A cheaper and quicker polishing process—in which the cut glass was dipped into an acid bath—came into use in the mid-1890s and increased the output of a typical glass manufactory by 25 percent. However, despite the fact that acid-polishing was less harmful to the health of the workmen, many old-timers preferred to continue hand polishing, because they thought it gave the surface a higher brilliance and left sharper cuts. But hand polishing was a luxury few manufacturers could afford in the highly competitive cut-glass business, in which nine-tenths of the cost of the article represented the wages of highly skilled workers.

The American "rich cut glass" fashionable at the turn of the century had been introduced to the public by American manufacturers as early as the 1876 Centennial. But consumers were slow to buy it, considering imported glass superior. To sell the native product, many wholesale and retail dealers misrepresented it as imported from England or the Continent. Indeed, some even shipped American glass abroad and "imported" it back to get a higher price.

All this changed in 1893 when American cut glass manufacturers, who had begun an extensive advertising campaign to make the public aware of American "rich cut glass," achieved international recognition at the World's Columbian Exposition in Chicago. While all the major manufacturers contributed to a magnificent display, the Libbey Glass Company of Toledo, Ohio, erected a large, fully equipped factory on the Midway Plaisance where crystal blanks were made, cut, and polished in full view of admiring spectators. One of the main attractions was Libbey's Crystal Art Room, where rich cut glass glittered and gleamed in a setting resplendent with huge plate glass mirrors and draperies of lustrous spun glass. Visitors to the Fair bought thousands of tons of American rich cut glass, from knife rests and napkin rings to enormous punch bowls and table lamps. This was the turning point as

92. A cutting room at F. X. Parsche & Son, c. 1903. The founder's son, Frank Parsche (standing), supervises apprentices cutting bowls. *Parsche Studios*

American cut glass manufacturers embarked on their most successful years.

Contributing to the dazzle at the World's Columbian Exposition were Chicago's two cut-glass manufacturers, Pitkin & Brooks and F. X. Parsche & Son. The firm of Pitkin & Brooks had been manufacturing "high grade, rich cut glassware" since the mid-1880s in its large establishment on the corner of Lake and State streets. By contrast, F. X. Parsche & Son was a small, family-run concern which had been cutting glass for just about a year. Both firms, however, cut their patterns on thick, blown-glass blanks obtained from glass factories located outside of Chicago, since the city's immediate surroundings lacked the fine-grained sand required to manufacture glass.

Pitkin & Brooks

At the showrooms of Pitkin & Brooks, one of the largest glass and china wholesalers in the country, Chicagoans could select from a staggering number of patterns and shapes. In the catalogs sent to retail jewelers and department stores, Pitkin & Brooks illustrated more than 300 different vases and serving pieces in 17 different patterns and in three grades or price ranges. Their finest line, the P & B grade, featured a profusion of deep cuttings on heavy pure crystal shapes; their Standard grade was alleged to be "equal to the cut glass sold generally throughout the United States"; and their least expensive grade, a line known as Imported glass, was cut abroad according to their own design. Except for the imported grade, all of Pitkin & Brooks's glass was cut in two factories located in Chicago or in a third factory that the firm operated in Chicago Heights. Glass blanks were obtained from the firm's own subsidiary, the Chicago Flint & Lime Glass Company of Chesterton, Indiana.

Some of Pitkin & Brooks's patterns were offered in more than one grade, but those cut in the more intricate patterns were available only in the expensive P & B grade. In the 1906 catalog, for example, bonbon dishes were offered in fourteen patterns, ranging in price from $2.13 for a Standard grade *Erminie* pattern cut with rather simple stars and fans, to $6.88 for an elaborate scallop-rimmed P & B grade *Pinto* bonbon dish with deep-cut fans and diamonds. An exquisite P & B grade *Plymouth Pattern* punch bowl supported on a graceful pedestal base cost $175.00, or nearly four months' wages when figured at the average 1906 manufacturing scale of 17½¢ per hour. At such prices only the very wealthy, the White House, or the heads of foreign governments could afford to buy complete dinner services or decorate their homes extensively with rich cut glass. Cut glass made an impressive wedding, anniversary, or birthday gift and elaborate services were often commissioned for special presenta-

Pitkin & Brooks, 1871–c. 1923.
Founded by Edward Hand Pitkin and Jonathan William Brooks, this firm quickly became one of the largest wholesale and retail dealers of china and glassware in the Midwest. The firm manufactured its own cut and engraved glassware beginning in the 1880s; by 1906 much of its cut glass was produced in two Chicago factories and in a branch factory in Chicago Heights. *American Cut and Engraved Glass* by Albert Christian Revi (1973) and *American Brilliant Cut Glass* by Bill and Louise Boggess (1977) illustrate and list a number of patterns patented by Pitkin & Brooks. Only top quality P & B grade pieces were signed.
The firm is not listed in the Chicago city directory after 1923.

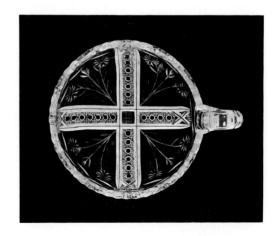

93. Nappy cut with cross of hobnails separating engraved flowers by Pitkin & Brooks, 1910–23. (d: 6"). *CHS*

94

95

94. Cylindrical vase with two wide bands of engraved gooseberries and pears separated by narrow bands of cut diamonds, executed by Pitkin & Brooks, c.1910. (h: 14″). *CHS*

95. Vase with geometric patterns including buzzstars, diamonds, flutes, crosshatching, and steps, cut by Pitkin & Brooks, c.1900. (h: 24½″). *Mr. and Mrs. Charles O. Zollar*

tions. But by choosing the less expensive grades, homemakers in even the most modest circumstances could secure a cut glass vase, bowl, or perfume bottle to bring a bit of sparkle to their boudoir or dining table.

F. X. Parsche & Son

Franz X. Parsche, founder of F. X. Parsche & Son, began as a glass engraver rather than glass cutter. A Bohemian by birth, he migrated to New York in 1873. A year later, seeing a newspaper advertisement placed by Burley & Tyrrell, he moved to Chicago to work in that firm's large crockery and glass establishment. In 1876 he opened his own shop. Parsche specialized in fine engraved glass until 1892, when, most likely in preparation for the upcoming World's Fair, he and his sixteen-year-old son Frank C. Parsche began producing heavy cut glassware.

F. X. Parsche & Son occasionally filled orders for Pitkin & Brooks and other wholesalers, but the majority of the firm's cut glass was retailed through the prestigious Chicago department store of Marshall Field & Company. For many years the Parsches cut the elegant *Owasco* and *Cayuga* patterns featured in the store's downtown showrooms, offered through its mail-order catalogs, and sold to jewelers and other dealers through its wholesale store.

Marshall Field & Company was known for the high quality of its merchandise and accepted only the finest cut glass. The store's inspectors routinely visited the Parsche cutting rooms to measure the depth of the cuts in the glass. If the glass did not measure up to Field's standards, it was rejected. Since the rejected glass was cut in Field's own patented patterns, such pieces were unsaleable and represented a substantial financial loss. Understandably, F. X. Parsche & Son aimed for high standards of workmanship and hired only the finest cutters.

By 1903, when the popularity of cut glass was at its peak, F. X. Parsche & Son employed fifty cutters. Many were young boys aged twelve or thirteen who worked as apprentices, executing the simpler cuts and learning the trade from the older, skilled workmen. Apprentice cutters earned $3 for six 10-hour days; the most highly paid foreman and cutters made $20 a week. Cutters were always men, although women were employed to wash the cut glass, to remove the polishing powders, and to wrap and pack the finished items for shipping.

F. X. Parsche, 1876–1898.
Koch & Parsche, 1899–1901.
F. X. Parsche & Son Company, 1902–c. 1920.
Parsche Studios, since c. 1920.

Franz X. Parsche (1842–1929) had been apprenticed to a glass engraver in his native Bohemia and had worked in a glass factory in Scotland before emigrating to New York City in 1873. Moving to Chicago a year later he worked for Burley & Tyrrell until 1876, when he opened his own glass engraving shop. In 1892, with the help of his son Frank, he began to manufacture rich cut glass.

After a brief partnership with Edward J. Koch, the Parsche glass-cutting enterprise grew very rapidly. At its peak in 1905, the firm employed 50 cutters. In 1902, Frank C. Parsche patented his *Pinwheel* pattern featuring a large rosette enclosed in a wreath of crossed sheaves or feathers; his *Heart* pattern, patented in 1907, consisted of a brilliantly cut heart-shaped motif surrounded by a wreath, rosettes, and buttons. Generally pieces were not signed.

After 1918, when the cut glass business began to decline, the Parsches added a line of hand-painted china decorated by Fran Haenisch. They also produced cut glass bar bottles, etched special designs for liquor distillers such as Chapin & Gore and Sunnybrook, and fired company names and logos on inkwells and other novelties. In addition they engraved mirrors and stemware.

The last stemware was cut around 1952. Since then, Parsche Studios, operated by grandson Donald C. Parsche at 4606 N. Western Avenue, has specialized in grinding chipped stemware and creating custom lamps.

96

97

96. Page from the 1898 Marshall Field & Company catalog showing rich cut glass. *Marshall Field & Company*

97. *Cayuga* pattern pitcher, cut by F. X. Parsche & Son for Marshall Field & Company, c. 1896. (h: 11¼"). *James Mattucci*

88

Other Chicago Companies

The brisk demand for cut glass and the relatively small amount of equipment needed to start a shop encouraged ambitious workmen to leave large companies such as the Libbey Glass Company or Pitkin & Brooks to set up their own glass-cutting businesses. Before 1893 Chicago had only two cut-glass manufacturers; by 1906 it had at least a dozen. Shops were opened in small storefronts, in walkup lofts in manufacturing districts, and even in homes, sheds, or barns. Patterns were usually variations of those in the public domain, but unique and fashionable ones developed by master cutters and covered by patents were occasionally "broken" by varying a cut or two when the design was copied. The finished product was commonly sent to one of Chicago's large jewelry or dry goods wholesalers or sold through the Cut Glass Products Company, H. H. Buckley, or the Empire Cut Glass Company, all of which specialized in distributing cut glass.

The first large cutting shop to open after the 1893 Fair, the American Cut Glass Company was organized by William C. Anderson, a former supervisor of the cutting department at the Libbey Glass factory. By 1897 Anderson had gathered a number of employees from the local firm of Pitkin & Brooks, set up a shop at 300 West Jackson, and received patents for four new patterns.

In 1901 a number of employees left the American Cut Glass Company to go to work for a new firm, the Monarch Cut Glass Company, established by Richard, Emil, and Otto Heinz, and Herman E. and Frank Kotwitz. Within four years their factory had outgrown its quarters on the corner of Union Street and Carroll Avenue and Heinz Brothers (as the operation was then called) moved west to a new location in St. Charles, Illinois. Here the firm employed an average of 80 to 100 cutters, making it one of the largest cut-glass manufacturers in the Midwest.

Two more cut-glass firms had been established by immigrant Swedish glassworkers by 1906. The Central Cut Glass Company, founded by Herman T. Roseen and Andrew Swanson, at first employed only 5 cutters. Ten years later it had 200. The firm made only heavy cut glass, most of it acid polished. Indeed, in 1915 Roseen patented a dipping device for polishing several pieces of cut glass in an acid solution in one operation. The other firm, the Johnson-Carlson Cut Glass Company, also experienced rapid growth, for by 1911 its Chicago headquarters was supervising cutting shops in Minneapolis, Minnesota, and Warsaw, Indiana.

Edward J. Koch, founder of the successful Koch Cut Glass Company, had first gained experience working for Burley & Tyrrell, then for the Massachusetts-based Mt. Washington Glass Company, and finally with F. X. Parsche, before establishing his own company in 1901. Like several other Chicago manufacturers, Koch created heavy rich cut

Koch & Parsche, 1899–1901.
Edward J. Koch & Company, 1901–1911.
Koch Cut Glass Company, 1912–1915 (factory in Elgin, 1912–1914).
Midland Cut Glass Company, 1916–1927.

A designer and salesman rather than a glass cutter, Edward John Koch had worked for Burley & Tyrrell for fourteen years before joining Franz X. Parsche in 1899 in manufacturing cut glass. When this partnership ended, Koch formed his own company to produce rich cut and engraved glass. Among other custom designed patterns, Koch offered *Hobstar and Wreath* and *Rose Window*, two designs patented by his firm in 1902 and 1910 respectively. Glass cut or engraved by the company was unmarked.

After the firm (renamed the Midland Cut Glass Company in 1916) went out of business, Koch became a sales representative for the Hunt Glass Company.

glass vases, punch bowls, water sets, baskets, and decanters, as well as elaborately engraved mirrors, many of which were cut to order.

The Koch Cut Glass Company maintained a large display of blank crystal samples from which customers could choose the shapes they desired. Edward Koch would then assist them in selecting an appropriate and distinctive pattern. Because of his years of experience as a glass salesman, Koch was very familiar with the most fashionable cut glass patterns and could easily recommend a standard cutting or create a custom design. Once the pattern was determined, the drawing and the blanks were passed on to the glass-cutting staff headed by the proprietor's nephew, Robert Koch. Needless to say, custom-designed and custom-cut glasswares were exceedingly expensive.

Rich cut glass in a variety of shapes and patterns was also produced by the United States Cut Glass Company, a firm organized in 1902 by Herman E. Kotwitz (a former partner in the Monarch Cut Glass Company) and Albert L. White. Heavy glass blanks were intricately cut until 1914, when the firm was reorganized as the Western Cut Glass Company and a line of lightly cut and engraved glass was introduced.

By 1914 the labor involved in cutting an all-over brilliant pattern or engraving an elaborate design had become so costly that most factories began turning out simpler designs and less expensive pieces. To create new styles and decrease cost, Chicago cut glass manufacturers introduced copper wheel and stone engraving. Like adherents of the Arts and Crafts Movement in other media, they turned to nature for their inspiration for new designs. Birds, insects, flowers, and plants all appeared in conjunction with lightly cut geometric patterns. Flowers dominated to such a degree, however, that these years are often referred to by collectors as the "flower period" of cut glass. Eventually figured blanks—which had been blown or pressed into molds containing part of the pattern—began to be substituted for undecorated blanks. This meant that the craftsman cut only the flowers and not the leaves, substantially reducing the cost of cutting.

The difference between cutting and engraving glass was one of technique. A cutter used large wheels, usually of stone, to make deep cuts, holding the object to be cut between himself and the wheel. His artistry and skill were determined by how well he manipulated the glass and followed the pattern marked on the blank. An engraver, by contrast, used stone or copper wheels of small diameter, mounted on a lathe. He could see where the wheel was abrading the surface and often worked freehand. Most engraving was shallower than cutting, but not always. Stone engraving lacked the fine detail of copper wheel engraving, but lent itself especially well to creating fruits and flowers on the glass surface. Stone engraving was also left unpolished, so that the grayish matte surface of the design contrasted with the clarity of the background.

During the years just prior to World War I, most of the Western Cut

98. Bowl with swirling flowering vine, cut and engraved by the Koch Cut Glass Company, c. 1915. (d: 9″). *Collection of Mr. and Mrs. Theodore W. Koch*

Glass Company's output of cut and engraved glass was consigned to Marshall Field & Company for sale through its store or mail-order catalog. Two of the most popular designs in the lighter, primarily engraved, wares were a sunburst pattern, in which the sunbursts were repeated three times, and a pattern featuring matte gray grapes and bright cut leaves and tendrils. Designed by Herman Kotwitz, these patterns, like others with wide popular appeal, were quickly copied by competitors. The rampant copying of designs and the breaking of patents among glass manufacturers makes it difficult, if not impossible, to assign unmarked cut glass to a particular company or glass cutter.

As the popularity of heavily cut wares declined and cut glass manufacturers competed to capture a shrinking market, even the Koch Cut Glass Company supplemented its elegant heavily cut wares with a line of lighter, partially pressed cut glass. Called "Koch-Kut," its name implied a resemblance to the inexpensive "Prescut" imitation cut glasswares produced in large quantities by the McKee Glass Company of Pennsylvania.

Decline of the Cut Glass Industry

With America's entry into World War I in 1917, the production of glass slowed down considerably because the government needed lead—the essential ingredient of prismatic glass—for the war effort. Unable to get the necessary materials, many glass manufacturers, and subsequently many glass-cutting firms, were forced out of business. By the early 1920s the American Cut Glass Company, the Western Cut Glass Company, and even the long-established firm of Pitkin & Brooks had all closed.

During the 1920s the remaining Chicago companies turned their attention to producing less costly glass. The use of figured blanks, shallower cuts, and lightweight glass decreased the cost of production and put the product within the reach of the average consumer, but diminished its appeal for those who had been its chief buyers. When "a few manufacturers decided to make cut glass on a ton basis, by using pressed figured blanks," lamented Frederick Carder in the 1923 *Journal of the American Ceramic Society,* they removed it "from the pedestal it formerly occupied in the public estimation." "Cheapness," he warned, "will ruin the industry." But by 1923 fashions had also changed and lighter weight stemware with shallow, polished engraving and colored or color-trimmed glassware were both now in demand.

After 1925 the Central Cut Glass Company, which had become Roseen & Collins, abandoned heavy cut wares in favor of lightly cut and fine rock crystal glassware. Cut crystal stemware also became F. X. Parsche & Son's biggest seller, and was often purchased in combination with the hand-painted china which the company had added to

99. Bowl with three hobstars separated by strawberry diamonds, cut by the Koch Cut Glass Company, c. 1913. (d: 8⅛"). *Collection of Mr. and Mrs. Theodore W. Koch*

92

its inventory.   But during the years of the Great Depression, even this business fell off and, as Donald C. Parsche, grandson of the founder, recalled, they all "darned near starved."   One by one Roseen & Collins, the Koch Cut Glass Company, Johnson-Carlson, and Heinz Brothers closed.   By 1932 only the Parsches remained to struggle through the Depression.   This venerable firm, renamed Parsche Studios, remains in business today primarily as a glass repair establishment.

100.   Bowl engraved with flowers in cartouches connected by strawberry diamonds by the Koch Cut Glass Company, c. 1915. (d: 7 15/16"). *Collection of Mr. and Mrs. Theodore W. Koch*

ARCHI·
TECTVR
AL·ARTS

INTRODUCTION TO ARCHITECTURAL ARTS

Both the stained glass and architectural terra cotta industries already had a foothold in Chicago before 1871, but on a relatively small scale. It was the massive rebuilding of the city in the decade after the Great Fire which created a heavy demand for these products and encouraged the development of new designs and materials. Fueled by the needs of Chicago's constantly expanding population, the building boom continued through the end of the century, providing work for the thousands of highly skilled European craftsmen who were drawn to the city.

While stained glass and terra cotta are distinctly different materials, their manufacture shared several common characteristics. To begin with, both were strongly affected by changes in building technology and architectural styles. When techniques or styles changed, stained glass and terra cotta products also had to change or their manufacturers soon went out of business. Second, both were labor-intensive, primarily handcraft industries, dependent upon the skills of artisans who could interpret architectural drawings and upon procedures which could not be mechanized. And finally, realizing that their work was "half art, half business," both stained glass and terra cotta manufacturers attempted to ease growing conflict within their industries by forming national associations to regulate competition and maintain high standards.

However, the stained glass and terra cotta industries differed considerably in scale of production. The making of stained glass windows or lampshades required few tools and little equipment and could be carried on in a small workshop or even a basement or attic. This was hardly the case with terra cotta. The manufacture of architectural terra cotta required tremendous quantities of clay and fuel, carefully prepared glazes, and huge kilns, not to mention the services of architects and large numbers of skilled and semiskilled workers. This difference in the production process had an important consequence. Even after the Depression reduced the demand for stained glass, artisans were able to continue some production of stained and ornamental glass in small workshops. But once the terra cotta plants closed down, there was no way that their workmen could continue to practice their craft.

Many of Chicago's finest stained glass windows and terra cotta buildings can still be found and appreciated in all parts of the city. It is to be hoped that future generations will not be denied the opportunity to enjoy these reminders of a rich past.

101. Tools used by Fernand Moreau (1853–1920) to model architectural terra cotta. *M. Epstein Hersh, Inc.*

(overleaf)
102. Detail of a leaded glass window with red opalescent poppy motif, c. 1910. *The Art Institute of Chicago, gift of Mrs. Eugene A. Davidson*

STAINED & ORNAMENTAL GLASS

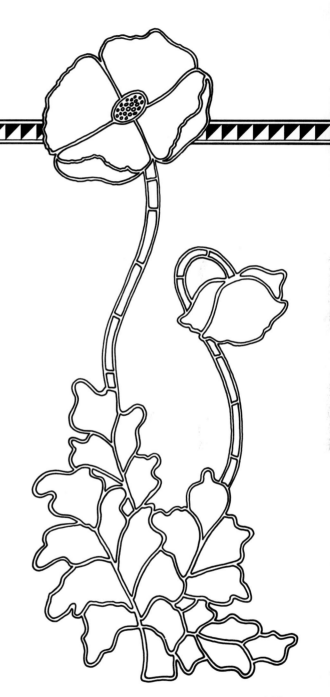

Two stained glass manufactories, W. S. Carse & Co. and Otto Jevne & Co., were in business in Chicago as early as the 1850s, producing ornamental windows for churches. But it was in the period of feverish reconstruction after the Great Fire of 1871 that the local stained glass industry experienced a period of rapid expansion, which carried it beyond the production of church windows to the creation of stained glass for a variety of decorative uses.

As an article in *The Inland Architect and Builder* a decade after the Fire indicated:

> *The use of stained glass, for so many centuries confined to the decoration of churches and palaces has become so universal, that scarcely a house of any architectural pretentions can be found that has not stained glass in door or window, and even to firescreens its use is applied, and here, as everywhere that the effect of light is available, its beauty is enhanced. . . .* [The Inland Architect and Builder *I, no. 4 (May 1882): 52*]

Going on to discuss the ambitious subjects and wonderful color effects achieved by local artists, the writer of the article predicted that ''the West has in her Chicago stained-glass artists one of the factors that will in the near future give to her homes much beauty, and win for her well-deserved renown.''

The sheer volume of post-Fire construction in Chicago had encouraged experimentation with new decorating schemes for churches, public buildings, and residences. City dwellers in particular found colored glass appealing, for it captured the sun's rays and carried them indoors, blotting out the narrow, crowded streets and smoke-filled skies. Concurrent technological advances, such as the use of natural gas and steam-driven machinery, made the production of glass in America economically feasible and led to the development of new types of glass, such as opalescent and cathedral glass.

Otto Jevne—who with Peter Almini had produced *Chicago Illustrated*, an impressive set of tinted engravings depicting Chicago before the Fire—advertised fresco painting as well as stained glass, and often

101

combined both to create distinctive church interiors. In 1873 the firm of Otto Jevne & Co. displayed an intricate and colorful stained glass window, *Adoration of the Angels*, in the city's first Interstate Industrial Exposition. The window was 4½ feet wide and 11 feet high, and showed fine gradations of color in the flesh tints and drapery folds. Particularly interesting was the method of its production. "The process of manufacturing," the exposition catalog stated, "is to paint the glass with mineral colors, and then introduce it several times into a kiln until it is vitrified, and then, by 'leading up,' to fit the portions into a complete window."

While the term stained glass covers "colored, enameled, or painted glass," Chicago's pioneer "glass stainers," as the above quote indicates, were primarily glass *painters* who used dark brown vitreous oxide and silver stain to paint designs on pieces of colored and/or opaque white glass. After the firing the pieces were assembled like fragments of a puzzle and connected to each other with strips of malleable lead—called cames—which were fitted and soldered around each piece to create the full window.

This same procedure for creating stained glass windows was also followed in Germany, England, and France, where the art of glass staining had been revived earlier in the century. Windows were occasionally imported from abroad, although local craftsmen were capable of making nearly identical ones because many had been trained in European methods. This was the case with some of the most prominent founders and workmen of Chicago's stained glass firms. John McCully of McCully & Miles, for example, had been a stained glass worker in England; George and Adolph Misch of George A. Misch & Bro., and Max Suess of the Chicago Stained Glass Works, had learned their trade in Germany.

George A. Misch & Bro., in business since 1864, made dozens of windows illustrating Christian doctrine and biblical scenes. By 1886 the firm had installed windows in numerous local houses of worship, including the First and Union Park Congregational churches, the Temple of the Sinai Congregation, and the Cathedral of the Holy Name. In addition, this firm, along with comparable manufacturers such as the Chicago Stained Glass Works and W. H. Wells & Bro., furnished hundreds of panes of simple stained glass for the high, narrow windows typically found in the simpler Victorian Gothic churches scattered throughout the Midwest.

When the use of steam-driven machinery became common and large sheets of clear plate glass became available, Misch added a line of what he called ornamental glass to the stained glass he was already producing. By 1873 his factory employed thirty men and was equipped with a 15-horsepower steam engine, which greatly simplified cutting at angles (beveling) the edges of glass sections used to create prismatic diamond-like transoms and door lights.

GEORGE A. MISCH

MANUFACTURERS
·OF·
ART AND STAINED GLASS

103. Advertisement for George A. Misch's stained glass manufactory from John M. Van Osdel's *A Quarter Century of Chicago Architecture*, 1895. *CHS*

Using similar machinery, another firm, James Berry & Co., supplied transparent "ground, cut, and embossed" glass in tremendous quantities for the imposing Grand Pacific, Tremont, and Palmer House hotels then under construction. In the 1873 Interstate Industrial Exposition Berry's works exhibited a magnificent example of cut glass in the form of a sheet of clear glass incised with the United States seal surrounded by the names of the presidents from Washington to Lincoln. According to the *Inter-state Exposition Souvenir:*

> *it was a splendid piece of workmanship, and done with a precision and nicety that seems almost impossible when aware that all this ornamental "cutting" is done by a revolving stone wheel worked by steam power. All the delicate characters to be cut are first traced in pencil, and then manipulated by the workman upon a flying wheel, and the result is, such specimens are daily produced as the one exhibited.* [Inter-state Exposition Souvenir *(Chicago: Van Arsdale & Massie, 1873): 72]*

By the end of the 1870s narrow panels of diamond-like clear glass or vibrant colored glass were commonly used as transoms or as border panels for windows and doors. Usually geometric or floral in composition, the panels were inset with faceted cut or pressed glass "jewels" or painted with flowers, birds, bamboo, or insects. Pictorial representation, earlier associated only with religion, began to appear in secular settings, with every topic from moonlit lakes to popular poems considered suitable for public buildings, libraries, and staircase landings.

Among the first pictorial windows to attract attention in Chicago were those made in 1883 by McCully & Miles, illustrating scenes from Sir Walter Scott's romantic poem *The Lady of the Lake.* Both blown and machine-made glass were used. Executed for the library of an elegant Milwaukee residence, the windows featured the legendary figures painted on sheets of antique glass framed in a border of jewels and opalescent glass. A recent American invention, opalescent glass was a machine-rolled multicolored glass with a milky-textured, iridescent appearance. By itself, opalescent glass was somewhat porcelain-like in appearance, but, against the light, and at certain angles, it had much of the fire and changing hue of opal. Opalescent glass and, eventually, drapery glass—an uneven textured glass used to simulate the folds of garments or other special effects—were imported to Chicago from Indiana, New York, Pennsylvania, and other major glass-producing states. Hand blown glass—known as antique glass—was made in both America and Europe, but the European variety was often preferred because of its more brilliant color and translucence. Bubbles, streaks, ripples, and varying thicknesses made it more appealing to the glassworker than the monotones of machine-rolled colored glass.

Colorful windows with serious themes were considered essential

104. Stained glass window with red, green, blue, and yellow glass painted with geometric and floral designs made for All Saints Church, Chicago, c. 1880. (h: 29"). *The Art Institute of Chicago, gift of Charles Hayes*

103

for important public buildings, as shown by the designs submitted in the contest conducted in 1884 to select stained glass windows for the new Chicago Board of Trade. Of the twenty competitors, five were from Chicago. McCully & Miles's designs, for example, featured circular pictorial medallions representing agriculture and industry, set in a rich mosaic border. The new firm of Healy & Millet proposed lunettes depicting heroic sculptors, blacksmiths, woodworkers, and goddesses. George A. Misch chose a contemporary theme, submitting watercolors showing such steam-powered farm machines as reapers, mowers, and corn-shellers against a background of wheat and corn fields. Although the designs of John LaFarge of New York were the final choice, the Chicago stained glass artists made a very creditable showing.

Healy & Millet and Other Decorators

As stained glass became esssential for the stylish interior, three local decorating firms—Healy & Millet, Mitchel & Halbach, and Spierling & Linden—met the demand by creating windows that were unique in design and beautifully executed.

When George L. Healy and Louis J. Millet, two young graduates of L'Ecole des Beaux Arts in Paris, founded their decorating firm in Chicago in 1880, they offered the usual range of wallpapers, stained glass, ornamental tiles, and artistic frescoes, but it soon became clear that their forte was stained glass. In 1884, when they opened their new building on Wabash Avenue for public inspection, all attention focused on the unusual motifs and novel effects presented in their brilliant display of stained glass. "Some of the designs shown were a pleasing surprise, their originality and freedom of design carrying the thoughts beyond the present to the future," recounted an admiring *Inland Architect* reporter who had been among the visitors to this "veritable artist's den."

Healy and Millet came by their talent naturally: Millet was the nephew of the French sculptor Aimé Millet, while George Healy was the son of Chicago's renowned portrait painter G. P. A. Healy. Though little is known about Healy, Louis Millet was highly visible in artistic circles and developed an enviable reputation as instructor of architecture and design at the School of the Art Institute of Chicago between 1886 and 1918.

In his classes at the Art Institute and in his own work, Millet advocated the use of conventional designs rather than naturalistic motifs. Following the theory of "organic ornament," Millet created designs based on plants and flowers conventionalized or reduced to their basic structures and maintained that ornamentation should be a part of, rather than applied to, an object or structure. Whether for stenciling, frescoing, mosaic tile, or stained glass, Millet's ornament harmonized

105. Healy & Millet's shop and studio, 223–25 S. Wabash Avenue, c. 1885. *Ryerson and Burnham Libraries, The Art Institute of Chicago*

with its surroundings yet retained a distinctive character of its own.

In every medium Millet sought to create new effects unhampered by historicism or tradition. He felt that all decorative work should be original or "a new effort," as he explained in an 1883 article on interior decoration:

> Decoration of our day is not, and cannot be on account of the complicated lives we lead, an art of perfect quiet and harmony, such as the ancients practiced. But it may become an art of strong effects, and although it is still slightly barbaric in its modes of execution and wild in its tendencies toward unlimited originality, it has the great redeeming feature of being a new effort, with no guide beyond the artist's taste and reason; with the widest of scopes as compared with the groove into which it had run, and without a tradition back of it. [Louis J. Millet, "Interior Decoration: Its Development in America," The Inland Architect and Builder I (February 1883): 3]

In addition to embracing non-traditional concepts in design, Healy & Millet employed new techniques, especially in the way they assembled their stained glass windows. Rather than using paint for lines and shadows, they employed a mosaic principle, whereby tiny fragments of colored and textured opalescent glass were used to create the contrast and detail as well as the main design. When two windows in this new "mosaic" style were exhibited at the Paris Exposition in 1889, they created quite a sensation. One reviewer noted:

> MM Healy et Millet, de Chicago, ont exposé une collection font remarquable de petits panneaux qui nous revelent une partie des applications auxquelles le verre nouveau donne lieu dans leur pays.* ["Le Vitail Depuis Cent Ans et L'exposition de 1889," Revue des Arts Décoratifs X (1889–90): 148, 152]

The French Government was so impressed that it purchased Healy & Millet's entire exhibition of "American glass" for installation in the national Musée des Arts Décoratifs in Paris. According to Herwin Schaefer, it was actually Healy & Millet and John LaFarge, rather than Louis C. Tiffany, who introduced this new way of making stained glass windows to Europe.

In Chicago, much of Healy & Millet's best work was done in conjunction with the architectural firm of Adler & Sullivan. Louis H. Sullivan, one of the partners, had known both Healy and Millet in Paris, and in Chicago the three continued their close friendship. Acknowledging

---

*Messieurs Healy and Millet, of Chicago, have exhibited a remarkable collection of small panels which reveal to us some of the uses to which the new glass is being put in their country.

Healy & Millet, 1880–1899.
Louis J. Millet, 1900–1923.

George Louis Healy (1856–?), son of G. P. A. Healy, the prominent Chicago portrait painter, and Louis J. Millet (1856–1923), a native of New York City, met while attending L'Ecole des Beaux Arts in Paris. Completing their courses in architecture and decoration in 1879, they moved to Chicago and opened a decorating establishment a year later. An immediate success, the firm provided frescoes, stained glass, glass mosaics, and other decorations for some of the city's most notable buildings, including the Auditorium (1889); McVicker's Theatre (1891); the Schiller Theater (1892); the Chicago Stock Exchange (1894); the Chicago Public Library (1897); and Fullerton Memorial Hall at the Art Institute (1897). Among their employees were Charles Holloway, designer of the "I Will" figure (1892) symbolizing the spirit of Chicago, and Christia M. Reade, an Art Institute graduate active in the local Arts and Crafts Movement.

From 1886 until 1918 Millet was associated with The Art Institute of Chicago, founding its Department of Decorative Design and serving as head, with W. F. Shattuck and W. K. Fellows, of the Chicago School of Architecture. After ending his long partnership with Healy in 1899, he went on to design the skylight of the Art Institute's Ryerson Library (1901) and the decoration of the James A. Patten house (1901) designed by George W. Maher. During 1903–04 he served as chief of mural and decorative painting for the St. Louis World's Fair. Later he assisted Louis H. Sullivan in the interior decoration of banks in Owatonna, Minnesota (1908) and Sidney, Ohio (1918).

Although most of Healy & Millet's memorial windows remain unidentified, one attributed to the firm may be seen in the Second Presbyterian Church at 1936 S. Michigan Avenue. Entitled "Cast Thy Garment About Thee and Follow Me," the window was commissioned by Mrs. George M. Pullman in memory of her mother, Mrs. Mary McKibben Sanger.

106
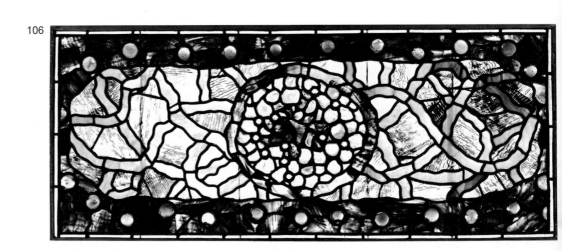

107

106. Stained glass panel designed by Louis H. Sullivan and executed by Healy & Millet for the Morris Selz residence, 1883. A blue ribbon motif surrounds a central cartouche of irregularly shaped multicolored glass fragments. (45¼″ x 18¾″). *David Norris*

107. Stained glass panel from the skylight of the Auditorium Theatre, Healy & Millet, 1889. A deep amber knot design surrounds a pale blue conventionalized flower on a light gold ground. (56¼″ x 33⅜″). *Roosevelt University*

106

108

109

110

109.   Lamp fixture with intertwined dolphins in gold iridescent glass made for the lobby of the Fisher Building, 343 S. Dearborn Street, c. 1896.   (26⅜″ x 16″ x 7¾″). *The Art Institute of Chicago, gift of Mr. and Mrs. Gustave Spiesel*

108.   Skylight designed by Louis J. Millet for the Ryerson Library, The Art Institute of Chicago, 1909. *The Art Institute of Chicago*

110.   Panel of pale green and rose glass from an Auditorium Building skylight, designed by Adler & Sullivan and executed by Healy & Millet, 1889.   *Private Collection*

that they shared a similar philosophy of ornament, Sullivan collaborated with Healy and Millet to produce the leaded glass, frescoing, stenciling, and other two-dimensional details for his commissions.

In 1889 Healy & Millet, using Sullivan's sketches, executed the glass for the Auditorium Hotel and Theatre, one of Adler & Sullivan's most spectacular productions. Describing the ornamentation of the Auditorium in 1891, Sullivan wrote:

> A single idea or principle is taken as a basis of the color scheme, that is to say, use is made of but one color in each instance, and that color is associated with gold. . . . The stained glass, of which a moderate use is made, is carefully harmonized with the prevailing tone of color in the decoration. [Industrial Chicago: The Building Interests 2 (Chicago: The Goodspeed Publishing Co., 1891): 490]

In the hotel lobby, stained glass was limited to large lunettes of pale gold glass featuring scrolls of amber glass highlighted with jewels. From the rich but somber lobby guests went up the grand staircase to be met by streams of light in golden hues from the skylight and windows on the mezzanine landing of the second story. On the south side of the lobby, a smaller staircase, subtly lit by simple geometric patterned windows, led upward to the tenth-floor dining room. At the top, a glass window-wall of large conventionalized daisy-like flowers of pale gold, yellow-green, and lavender burst into bloom.

At the entrance to the Auditorium Theatre on Congress Street, heads of theatrical figures emerged from lavender-hued flowers on the large lunettes in the vestibule. In the main auditorium, the color scheme was simple and grand, consisting of gold and old ivory in graded tones. Above, flowers of opaque cream-colored glass encircled by deep amber Celtic knots floated on a sea of pale amber cathedral glass.

During their eighteen-year partnership, Healy and Millet executed stained glass and glass mosaics for numerous Chicago office buildings, clubs, churches, and residences. In 1895 The Inland Architect noted that the firm had been commissioned to do a vaulted ceiling of glass mosaic for the lobby of the Fisher Building, a new office building under construction on South Dearborn Street. In a whimsical play on the name of the owner, Lucius G. Fisher, large ornamental fish were etched on the clear glass vestibule doors, while iridescent fish frolicked on the handsome leaded glass light fixtures which hung nearby. It is probable that these, like the glass mosaic ceiling, were the work of Healy & Millet.

Following the demands of fashion, several other Chicago decorating firms added glassworkers to their staffs to accommodate the wishes of their clients. One such firm was Mitchel & Halbach, which specialized in ornamenting the interiors of palatial theaters and mansions.

The partnership of Otto William Mitchel and J. Frederick Halbach dated from 1885, when the two secured the contract to decorate the interior of Chicago's new City Hall. Their work—both stylish and executed at one-third the price of the highest bid—attracted so much attention that they immediately received commissions to decorate several major Chicago theaters, including Hooley's Theatre, the Columbia, Havlin's, the Chicago Opera House, and the Lyceum, as well as several large theaters in Boston and New York. Later commissions included large hotels, churches, and residences for Chicago brewer Conrad Seipp, industrialist Richard T. Crane, and meat packer Philip D. Armour, among others. By 1886, when they remodeled the interior of Marshall Field's imposing Prairie Avenue residence, the partners were renowned for magnificent stained glass, executed by a staff of artisans working under their supervision.

Stained glass was also the specialty of the Linden Glass Company, an offshoot of the decorating firm organized in 1882 by Frank L. Linden and Ernest J. Spierling. Like Healy & Millet, Frank Linden excelled at fresco painting as well as stained glass, and many of the city's most elegant residences featured ceilings delicately watercolored with roses, Linden's favorite subject. Although best remembered for work later executed for Chicago architect Frank Lloyd Wright, the Linden Glass Company was known during the 1880s and 1890s for the fine stained glass it executed for some of Chicago's most celebrated clubs, residences, and public buildings.

In 1890, for example, the firm supplied the stained glass for the new Grand Central Station at the corner of Harrison and Wells streets. Designed by Solon S. Beman, the waiting room featured nine immense windows topped by lunettes of stained glass. Of American-made cathedral glass in tones of blue and amber, the windows had a textured surface resembling translucent onyx. Commenting that textured cathedral glass was chosen because it gave "good effects from both sides," a promotional booklet praised Linden's work while reminding readers that "the finest specimens of modern stained glass are invariably in private residences, and to see the best work of the Linden Glass Company one must go upon Prairie and Calumet avenues, and along the Lake drive."

Chicagoans also imported stained glass windows, known as Munich windows, directly from that German city. Destined for churches, these windows were primarily pictorial, depicting saints and heroic figures and incorporating elaborately painted detail. Today they are found in churches in Chicago's old ethnic communities, for they were favored by the German, Polish, and East European immigrants who gathered together in these neighborhoods.

In the mid-1880s, several German companies actually opened branch offices in Chicago. At least one firm, the Pyrographic Glass Company, found it advantageous to ship its entire plant and employees to America rather than pay the high tariff of 45 percent which American manufacturers succeeded in having imposed in 1883 on imported stained and painted windows. In May 1885 *The Inland Architect* noted that the Pyrographic Glass Company had ''just imported from Munich, Bavaria, a large plant of machinery and hands, and have located at 216 & 218 E. Monroe St., for the manufacture of every class of ornamental glass, and also embossing on glass in different colors and shades by an entirely new process'' which involved burning designs on glass using a heated tool. A few months later, the periodical recorded that ''the original plant and all the original designs and appliances brought to this country from Munich'' had been installed and that ''probably no better collection of beautiful designs of ornamental glass for churches'' could be found in the country than those owned by this ''wide awake and reliable'' company.

Artistic Glass for Everyone

As demand escalated, more than a dozen firms specializing in stained glass appeared in the city's directories in the decades between 1880 and 1900. While some were founded by glassworkers newly arrived from the Eastern states or overseas, most were organized by former employees of long-established Chicago glass firms.

The case of Joseph E. Flanagan was typical. From being foreman of the art glass department of McCully & Miles, Flanagan went on to join William C. Biedenweg, a skilled German glassworker, in founding the Flanagan & Biedenweg Co. in 1878. That same year, John D. Kinsella, another local glass craftsman, opened modest quarters to manufacture ''modern stained glass designs for churches, residences, and public halls.'' Max Seuss, once manager of the Chicago Stained Glass Works, opened the Seuss Ornamental Glass Company in 1886, while George H. Bradshaw, a former employee of W. H. Wells & Bro., established the Chicago Art Glass Company in 1887. Bradshaw sold this firm two years later when he was offered the opportunity to develop an art glass department for the H. M. Hooker Company, then Chicago's largest paint and glass dealer.

The new arrivals came from countries with long traditions of glass making. John Scott, an English glassworker, migrated to Chicago in 1885 to join local workers D. X. Dahinten and John Feulner in establishing Dahinten, Feulner, & Scott, a firm specializing in memorial and chancel windows for churches. Similarly, Hugo Eberhardt & Co. was founded in 1891 by a German glass cutter who had come to Chicago nine years earlier. George E. Androvette founded an art glass firm in 1890, while Abrahm J. Schuler and Max A. Mueller opened the Schuler & Mueller Co. to manufacture stained and ornamental glass in 1891. Orlando Giannini, a talented Italian designer, and Fritz Hilgart, a

111. Sample design for a sandblasted doorlight from a broadside advertising the Seuss Ornamental Glass Co., 1893. *CHS*

110

German glassworker, formed the firm of Giannini & Hilgart in 1899. Other stained glass artisans worked out of their homes or in small shops scattered around Chicago.

As the output and availability of artistic glass increased, numerous articles appeared to guide consumers "not blessed with taste of their own" in selecting stained glass windows for their home. In the July 1884 *Inland Architect and Builder,* Chicago architect Francis Le Baron published a list of suggestions for architects, builders, and home-owners, including such helpful hints as "figures larger than life should be avoided as injurious to the proportion of a building" and "the best windows for imitation are those of the twelfth century." Believing that stained glass was being misused, Le Baron recommended that it be placed in hallways and stairways and wherever desirable to shut out unpleasant views such as vacant lots, stables, backyards, or alleys. He considered stained glass windows "wholly unsuitable" for rooms occupied by the family, especially those in which work or reading was to be done. Even in dining rooms, warned Le Baron, stained glass should be used sparingly:

> An artistic panel over a sideboard is very ornamental but our guests and friends are not improved in appearance by being seen with purple hair, or green noses, or yellow lips, or variegated foreheads. The vulgar combinations of cheap stained glass that are stuck into every window of every "flat" are simply abominable. They corrupt the taste, for by constantly looking at them we grow to like them. [Francis Le Baron, "Stained Glass," The Inland Architect and Builder *III, no. 6 (July 1884): 77*]

Despite such admonitions against the overuse of stained glass, a tremendous building boom between 1880 and 1900 created an un-precedented demand for stained and ornamental glass. As the *Clay Record* pointed out:

> The use of decorative glass in modern buildings is becoming more and more widespread every day. Stained glass is used not only in transoms and door lights, but the ordinary clear glass used in windows, doors, and partitions is either embossed by an acid process or etched by a sand blast, creating a new world of decorations. . . . The decoration consists of scroll, diamond, square and circular repeats, decorated borders, monograms, and numbering and lettering of all kinds for commercial purposes. A panel of chipped glass that seems to be sliced from the irregular face of a crystal rock is a brilliant accompaniment to its decorative surroundings. [Clay Record *I, no. 7 (October 13, 1892): 253*]

Much of the "chipped glass" referred to above was made by Rawson & Evans, a local company which had patented the process.

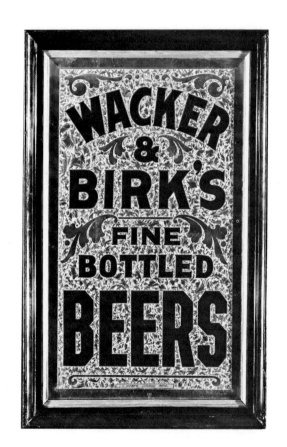

112. Chipped glass advertising sign with black letters on a gold foil ground, made by J. H. Weber Sign Co., Chicago, 1894–95. (28¼" x 17¼"). *CHS, gift of J. H. Weber*

111

Western Sand Blast Mfg. Co., 1876–c. 1920
Western Sandblast Mfg. Co., since c. 1920

From 1876 on this firm has specialized in the production and repair of sandblasted, chipped, etched, and beveled ornamental glass; chipped glass and enameled advertising signs; and colorful glass dials for slot machines and other mechanical devices. Until the 1920s the company also made leaded art glass windows for churches and residences as well as advertising novelties such as art glass pharmacy mortars and barber poles. Later it executed glass designed by Edgar Miller as well as for various Chicago architects.

Now owned by R. J. Pyne, who inherited the business from his father, the firm continues in business at 2015 W. Race Street.

113. Zinc stencil used by the Western Sand Blast Mfg. Co., c. 1890. *R. J. Pyne, Western Sandblast Mfg. Co.*

According to the firm's catalog, chipped glass was produced by "actually fracturing the surface of ordinary glass, producing a surface of broken crystal, interspersed with a running tracery of delicate and graceful lines" and was recommended for use in doors or for advertising signs.

Brilliant, enduring, and easy to read, chipped glass signs looked complicated and impressive. Actually, they were made by a rather simple, if time-consuming process, which involved applying a layer of hide glue to the back of a sheet of glass. As the glue dried, the glass chipped. The resulting crystalline surface was backed with thin metallic foil, or designs were created in combination with paint. For emphasis, colored letters, usually of black, dark green, blue, or maroon, were used on a background of chipped silver or gold. Occasionally the color scheme was reversed, with chipped silver or gold letters appearing on a colored background. Used to advertise everything from cigars to corsets, chipped glass signs appear so frequently in photographs of business districts taken at the time that one is tempted to believe Rawson & Evans's claim that their signs were "Better than Any Other Signs on Earth."

Colored advertising signs and mirrors were also a specialty of the Western Sand Blast Mfg. Co., one of the city's largest producers of ornamental glass. Employing approximately fifty men, the firm produced chipped and painted glass signs as well as etched, embossed, and sandblasted glass for use in vestibule doors, transoms, and the counter partitions of banks, office buildings, factories, saloons, shops, and railroad stations. As its name implied, the company's workmen used a blast of air or steam carrying sand to etch designs upon the glass. An article in *The Inland Architect* described the process as follows:

> a plate of glass is covered with a thin layer of foil; on this the design is traced and then deftly cut and lifted out, leaving the remainder of the foil intact. In this condition the plate is given a coating of melted wax, and before this is too much hardened the rest of the foil is stripped off, which leaves the design clear cut in wax on the glass. The plate is then put into a huge box filled with machinery, where sand blast acts upon the glass, cutting all the surface not protected by the wax, and bringing out the design perfectly. [The Inland Architect and News Record *XI (June 1888): 79*]

While office doors and advertising signs were necessarily custom designed, many of the other items were chosen from a large assortment of stock designs ranging from simple linear borders to ornate geometric or scenic compositions which covered nearly every inch of the glass. In 1887, for example, one Western Sand Blast Co. advertisement pictured thirty-two different patterns for vestibule doors. Three displayed simple swags or borders; the remainder featured birds on

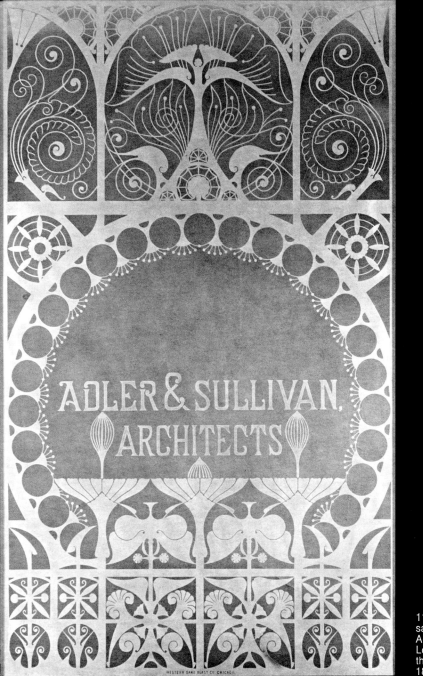

ADLER & SULLIVAN,
ARCHITECTS

WESTERN SAND BLAST CO. CHICAGO.

114. Doorlight of clear and
sandblasted glass for the office of
Adler & Sullivan, designed by
Louis H. Sullivan and executed by
the Western Sand Blast Mfg. Co.,
1883. (46 11/16″ x 28¾″). *CHS*

branches, bamboo and fans, or spindly-legged cranes standing in marshes of cattails—demonstrating that the craze for Japanese themes extended beyond the home and into the commercial sector.

Only cut and beveled products were produced by Schreiber & Annas, whose ornamental glass factory on South Canal Street devoted itself solely to "artistic glass cutting in its highest perfection, in all its branches." According to *Industrial Chicago*:

> *this concentration of their abilities made it possible for them to furnish perfect work of the most difficult descriptions, such as making jewels of any size to pattern or drawing, glass engraving, hammered, beaded, mitred, scored and fancy beveled glass. They introduced many new and effective ideas in this line and established an extensive business, being both ambitious and determined that no eastern concern should lead Chicago in turning out artistic work* [Industrial Chicago: The Building Interests 2 (Chicago: The Goodspeed Publishing Co., 1891): 797]

Schuler & Mueller, however, manufactured all types of ornamental glass, including leaded, beveled, leaded beveled, leaded clear, and leaded stained glass, appropriate for residences, public buildings, or churches. The company's *Book of Designs*, published at the turn of the century, showed compositions suitable for execution in either clear or colored glass. To secure a particularly artistic composition, the catalog suggested that the background of these designs "be worked out in one style of glass of some smooth effect and the ornamentation carried out in a rough glass, with a rippled or granite surface" in order to produce a sparkling and pleasing effect without obstructing the passage of light.

Ornament and utility were uniquely combined in the small squares of prismatic glass developed in the 1890s by the American Luxfer Prism Company. Installed above display or basement windows, Luxfer prisms effectively diffused light into the interior of stores and offices. Utilizing the principle of light refraction, the prisms comprised two small plates bonded together electrolytically. While most of the plates featured simple geometric designs, some bore highly conventionalized floral patterns patented by up-and-coming local architect Frank Lloyd Wright.

Stained glass was not restricted to churches, residences, and public buildings. Symbolizing art and luxury, especially on the raw frontier, stained glass rode the rails in opulent Pullman palace cars. Throughout the 1880s and 1890s, transoms and domes of colorful stained glass and door lights of etched and beveled glass were among the luxurious appointments which made the dining, sleeping, smoking, and parlor cars outfitted by the Pullman Palace Car Company of Chicago a legend throughout the world. With soft plush seats, gilt chandeliers, delicate marquetry, and colorful stained glass, Pullman's fleet of traveling cars ennobled the humblest passenger. Even the renowned author Nathaniel Hawthorne was moved to assert, "They spiritualize travel."

All of the art glass, along with the woodwork and furnishings, were the products of workshops owned and operated by the Pullman Palace Car Company on the city's South Side. Expert artisans, many of them from Germany or Italy, manned the glassworking shop and created transoms, lighting fixtures, and door lights in hundreds of special designs, for no two diners or parlor cars were exactly alike.

Influence of the World's Columbian Exposition

By the time of Chicago's 1893 Fair, colored glass was being used so extensively and in such startling color combinations that some concerned glassworkers expressed the fear that the widespread "abuse of color" would degrade the entire art glass industry. "This kind of work has been used with the most indiscriminate profusion, often regardless of cost or propriety," complained glassmaker George E. Androvette in the January 1893 issue of *The Inland Architect & News Record*, noting that "the demand for this doubtful sort of decoration has caused what should be an art industry simply to become a mechanical pursuit." Androvette, like many other local glassworkers, was afraid that the prevalence of cheap colored glass and jewels "arranged to catch the fancy of the uneducated eye" would lessen the desirability of stained glass, causing architects and builders to abandon the use of colored glass in favor of the new varieties of crystal or leaded glass.

This fear proved unfounded when the exquisite stained glass windows and glass mosaics displayed at the World's Columbian Exposition by American glass firms established the supremacy of American glass and stabilized the Chicago art glass market for a decade to come. Of the eleven American stained glass firms displaying their work, seven were from Chicago. George E. Androvette & Co., Flanagan & Biedenweg, Healy & Millet, McCully & Miles, and the Wells Glass Company exhibited stained glass for domestic and ecclesiastical purposes. Rawson & Evans and the Seuss Ornamental Glass Company showed ground, chipped, cut, embossed, beveled, and enameled glass.

Evoking the most comment and winning fifty-four medals was the work of the Tiffany Glass & Decorating Company of New York, which displayed a complete chapel shimmering with glass mosaics and stained glass, in addition to a stunning collection of lighting fixtures and lamps. Tiffany's stained glass windows featured brilliantly colored scenes and highly realistic figures in clear, jewel-like tones. As a result of Tiffany's display, church interiors were soon revolutionized by the addition of landscape scenes among the biblical figures, while a

Flanagan & Biedenweg Company, 1885–1953.
Joseph E. Flanagan (1858–1928), a former employee of George A. Misch & Co. and McCully & Miles, and William E. Biedenweg (1853–1914) began manufacturing "stained, enameled, embossed, beveled, cut and ground glass" in 1885. By 1900, their firm had become the largest of the Chicago producers of art glass for residential and ecclesiastical uses.

The Flanagan & Biedenweg Co. was noted for the superior quality of its work and its fine glass artists. Joseph A. Luxheim, one of the country's best-known designers of memorial windows, worked for the firm from 1904 until 1922; three sons of the co-owner, James R., Thomas C., and William C. Flanagan, had also been trained as artists. In 1904 the company had the distinction of winning the Grand Prize for American Glass at the St. Louis World's Fair.

Although the firm's domestic work was usually unsigned, memorial windows bearing the name of Flanagan & Biedenweg appear throughout the United States, particularly in the Midwest. In the Chicago area, examples can be found in St. Vincent's Church, 1010 W. Webster; St. Ita's Church, 5500 N. Broadway; and St. Andrew's Episcopal Church, 1125 Franklin, Downers Grove.

Joseph Flanagan was instrumental in organizing the National Ornamental Glass Manufacturers' Association in 1903 and was its first president. For twenty years he served as editor of the association's *Ornamental Glass Bulletin* (later renamed *Stained Glass*).

The Flanagan & Biedenweg Co. was located on W. Illinois Street from 1894 until 1942 when, under different ownership, it moved to 3754 N. Wilton where it was last listed in the telephone directory in 1953.

scenic window became a necessity for the staircase landing or library of every Chicago millionaire's mansion. The great diversity in surface and thickness of American glass compared to European glass, drew a great deal of attention, just as Healy & Millet's stained glass had at the 1889 exposition in Paris. An article describing the stained glass at the Columbian Exposition pointed out the ways in which it differed from traditional European and earlier American stained glass:

> *Our painted glass is not painted in the sense foreign glass is; Germany paints her figures, her draperies, her background, with the most brilliant and often inharmonious colors. France and England treat glass in much the same way, while we simply paint in clear brilliant coloring the flesh-tints and hair, having stained glass to fulfill the mission of background and drapery.* [American Architect and Building News *42 (November 11, 1893):74*]

In the American glass displayed at the 1893 Fair, effects of light and shade were obtained by using glass of unequal thickness or by superimposing one layer of glass upon another. When the color of a piece was too strong, it was backed with another less strongly colored piece so that when light was transmitted through the end product, the color was weakened and softened. If a color was too weak, it was backed with glass of stronger tone. On one side, the window became a mass of protuberances and depressions, varying in thickness from a quarter of an inch to four inches, with the elevated portions securely leaded down to the first sheet of glass.

Another American novelty to be seen at the Fair was stained glass designed and made by women. Over the north entrance to the Woman's Building were stained glass transoms by Elizabeth J. Abel of Philadelphia, who also gave demonstrations of stained glassmaking inside the building. In the Manufacturers' Building a stained glass window, *The Queen of the Elves*, made by Chicagoan Marie Herndl, hung among the exhibits of the major manufacturers. By 1893 women were employed as designers by many of the large firms, although few were involved in the actual execution of windows or light fixtures.

One exception was Chicago designer Christia M. Reade, a versatile artisan whose talents ranged from metalsmithing to china decorating. After graduating from The Art Institute of Chicago, Miss Reade turned her attention to "the industrial side of art, making the everyday useful things of life beautiful." Working for the firm of Healy & Millet, she "had much practice in the designing and making of stained glass windows, often selecting the glass for the workmen as well as making the detail drawing." In 1897, after becoming familiar with all aspects of window making from initial sketch to installation, she opened The Krayle Workshop in the Marshall Field Building. Here she designed and made stained glass windows, jewelry, and bookplates. Although better known for metalwork than stained glass, she completed several

115. Detail from a window made by the Flanagan & Biedenweg Co. showing the layers of glass used to create variations in color. *DePaul University*

windows, among them a memorial window, *The Worship of the Wise Men*, for the Episcopal Church in Wheaton, Illinois.

The World's Columbian Exposition kindled a burst of pride in the past which was expressed in stained glass and glass mosaic. In the new Church of St. Catherine of Genoa on West 118th Street, the landing of Christopher Columbus and Father Marquette's first visit to Chicago were memorialized in the sanctuary windows installed in 1893 by the innovative firm of McCully & Miles. That same year, Columbus's discovery of America and his triumphant return to the court of Isabella escorting American Indians were depicted in stunning glass mosaic murals installed in the lobby of the Columbus Memorial Building. Two years later glass mosaic panels by J. A. Holzer, depicting Father Marquette's exploration of the Illinois country in 1763, were installed in the Marquette Building, a new office structure nearing completion in Chicago's central business district.

Famous canvas paintings supplemented legends and historical events as subjects for stained glass. For churches, such popular artworks as Holman Hunt's *Light of the World*, Jean François Millet's *The Sower*, and Bernhard Plonkhurst's *Christ Blessing Little Children*, were reproduced over and over by local glass firms. For a domestic interior, Flanagan & Biedenweg's rendition of *The Three Arts* by F. Lafon won high praise from *Arts for America* in 1896.

The influence of Art Nouveau posters was also evident in the stained glass of the late 1890s. The dramatic posters of Alphonse Mucha, who taught at the Art Institute for a time, and of other popular illustrators provided appealing subjects for art glass workers, who found swirling, sensuous curves and bold lines ideal for translation into translucent windows. "In stained glass the whole idea is to obtain an effect," *Arts for America* explained in 1898, "and it has been demonstrated that poster designs lend themselves admirably to these effects when the ensemble is a euphony of color and drawing."

At the time, poster art windows were admired for their comparative simplicity, for they required fewer pieces of opalescent glass and fewer lead lines. Sinuous mermaids, maidens with vermicelli tresses, unfurling lilies, and similar motifs appeared in the advertisements and catalogs of Flanagan & Biedenweg, Chicago's largest producer of "poster art glass." In lieu of stock designs, customers were encouraged to give their homes a personal touch with poster art glass recalling "delightful associations and pleasant memories." "A view of one's native place," "the happy face of a dearly loved child," or "the stately poster girl of one's own family" were suggested as particularly appropriate for a bedroom, dining room, or entrance hall.

Windows featuring water lilies or roses on thin, curvaceous stems or heart-shaped blossoms in tangled boughs in the style of French or Belgian Art Nouveau were produced by nearly all of Chicago's art glass firms. Rarely signed by the maker, the windows were character-

116. Advertisement from *House Beautiful*, February 1904, for a Flanagan & Biedenweg Co. window inspired by poster art. *University of Chicago Library*

117

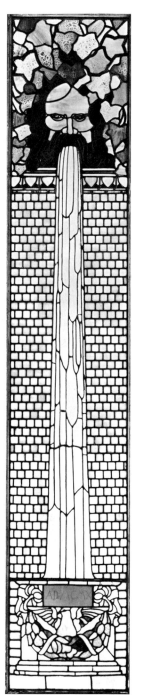

117. Art glass panel with red poppies and green leaves made by the Flanagan & Biedenweg Co. for the Joseph E. Flanagan residence, c. 1900. (17½″ x 33½″). *Marianne Flanagan Zeman*

118. Art glass panel featuring a conventionalized pomegranate of clear rippled glass with a green opalescent border, designed by architect Howard Van Doren Shaw for the Second Presbyterian Church, 1936 S. Michigan Avenue, 1900–1901. (18″ x 23⅜″). *Second Presbyterian Church of Chicago*

119. One of the glass door panels executed by Giannini & Hilgart for Peacock Alley in the Congress Hotel, 1910. Wearing a crown of gold-veined leaves, the mythological figure spews segments of blue/white glass into a multicolored urn set against a ground of tiny gold squares. (78½″ x 14¾″). *CHS*

118

119

zed by the use of opalescent glass, occasionally in combination with antique glass. Colors were bold and fruity. Golds, oranges, pinks, reds, and yellow-greens predominated, with dark blues and purples used sparingly, often only for contrast, as in a bunch of grapes or for a narrow border. Fruits and flowers provided the major themes for "stock" windows, which could be ordered from most manufacturers' catalogs for about $2.50 per square foot. Landscapes of opalescent glass sold for approximately $5.00 per square foot.

In the 1890s stiff cames of grooved copper or zinc had begun to replace the soft lead cames used to bind the segments of art glass together. Because they reduced the likelihood of buckling and thus eliminated the need for bracing, the new cames expanded the range of uses for art glass. Architects employed them for windows and doors, while cabinetmakers used them for furniture. Easily cut and preassembled with a minimum of hand fitting, these new cames made it possible to mass produce art glass for a variety of purposes. More-over, the stiff cames proved highly adaptable for use in the geometric designs which became popular and pervasive after 1900 and obtain-able in all price ranges.

Chicagoans were immensely proud of their achievements in the field of stained glass, as shown by the following:

> The old notion about the incapacity of Chicago artists engaged in the production of art glass is rapidly dying out, and the wealthy and refined of our city are now honoring the artistic creations of local artists by placing them in their residences, and employing glass decorations profusely to embellish their homes. Stained glass is extensively used by architects, who take pride in their achievements, not only for decorative, but architectural purposes, combining as it does utility and orna-ment, beauty and design, and by its judicious use they are enabled to relieve the tiresome monotony of plain windows. It may be undeniably asserted that the American artist far excels the European in this particular sphere of art. Because of the greater number of fine residences annually constructed here, he has a wider range for the development of ideas and putting his imaginative fancies into actualities. [Arts for America 5 (March 1896): 67]

Several Chicago architects as well as stained glass artists were putting their "imaginative fancies into actualities" by designing art glass. Their work would shortly revolutionize window design and lead to the development of a unique Midwestern style.

119

Giannini & Hilgart, since 1899.

Orlando Giannini (1861–1928) and Fritz Hilgart (1869–1942) specialized in residential art glass, glass mosaics, and lampshades during the early years of their partnership. Hilgart had been trained as a glass stainer, while Giannini had studied sculpture in Cincinnati. When Giannini, who executed murals and art glass for architect Frank Lloyd Wright, moved to California around 1907, he was replaced by his nephew Joseph R. Giannini, who had attended the Cincinnati Art School before moving to Chicago. By 1920 Joseph had also acquired part interest in the James Corday Co. which manufactured electrical elements used in light fixtures.

By the early 1930s Giannini & Hilgart had begun to specialize in ecclesiastical stained glass windows, some of which still remain in their former showroom at 2134 Lewis (now N. Magnolia). Under the direction of Lubomyr Wandzura, who took over operation of the firm upon the retirement of Fritz Hilgart's son, Fred, the firm remains in business at 1359 N. Noble Street.

120. View of the dining room in the Warren McArthur house showing the art glass designed by Frank Lloyd Wright and executed by Giannini & Hilgart, 1902. In each panel the elongated diamond of opaque white glass represents a blossom while the leading represents a stem. The rows of lead balls appear to be seeds. *Photo by William R. Boles*

A New Midwestern Style

While scenic and poster art windows reigned supreme, the young Chicago architect Frank Lloyd Wright was incorporating a revolutionary new style of art glass into his low, terrain-hugging "Prairie houses." In startling contrast to the whiplash curves and undulating forms of Art Nouveau, Wright's windows featured severe geometric shapes and highly conventionalized plant forms.

In his earliest designs for art glass Wright used abstractions based on flowers and plants. Erect, stylized flowers appeared as early as 1897 in the bands of casement windows designed for the Isidore Heller home on South Woodlawn Avenue, providing a pleasing vertical contrast to the general horizontality of the structure. In 1900 windows featuring fuchsia were installed in the B. Harley Bradley house in Kankakee, Illinois.

Two years later Wright updated the dining room of the Warren McArthur house (1892), one of his first commissions, by installing new lighting fixtures, French doors, and a built-in buffet incorporating striking art glass in a conventionalized floral pattern executed by the Chicago firm of Giannini & Hilgart.

Luminous orange and yellow glass dominated the complex windows and light fixtures executed in 1903 for the Susan Lawrence Dana house in Springfield, Illinois. The motif was the sumac plant, conventionalized and reduced to its basic geometric components. Bold, golden wing-like leaves rose sharply from straight, leaded stems composed of tiny parallelograms. This motif was repeated in windows, lighting fixtures, and in arched bands of glass which formed a dramatic entryway. In the dining room, four hanging lamps resembled suspended geometric butterflies. Composed of numerous planes and angles, the lamps presented an intricate interplay of orange, yellow, red, and green hues created by the use of sandblasted, clear, colored, and iridescent glass.

All the Dana residence glass—more abundant and more intricate in design than that used in any other Wright house—was executed by the Linden Glass Company of Chicago. Frank L. Linden, Jr., son of the company's owner, recalled Wright selecting the glass from large bins in the firm's workroom on Michigan Avenue, which used only European glass and employed only European-trained craftsmen.

Variations of flower forms appeared as standard ornamentation in the art glass of other Wright houses when cost permitted. Some windows, like those in the McArthur house, were self-contained units; others, like those in the 1912 F. W. Little house living room (currently being reconstructed in the Metropolitan Museum of Art in New York) were part of a single geometric design which continued across a line of casement windows. All brought an element of nature indoors. The view through the window was enhanced, yet not obstructed. Of these

Linden Glass Company, c. 1888–1909.
The Linden Company, 1910–1934.

Operated by Frank Louis Linden (1859–1934), a partner in the decorating firm of Spierling & Linden, this firm specialized in the production of stained glass windows, glass mosaics, and lighting fixtures. Some of its first commissions included stained glass for the George M. Pullman residence in Alexandria Bay, New York, as well as for the Chicago mansions of Edwin Partridge, W. S. Jones, and G. M. Moulton. Later, the firm executed art glass for several residences designed by Frank Lloyd Wright, including those of Susan L. Dana, Springfield, Illinois; Darwin D. Martin, Buffalo, New York; Avery Coonley, Riverside; and Frederick G. Robie, Chicago. Frank L. Linden, Jr., the founder's son, recalls that his father's firm also provided art glass for the Midway Gardens designed by Wright and for the Ernest Magerstadt house designed by George W. Maher.

Located at 1216 S. Michigan Avenue, the company closed soon after Linden's death in 1934.

early windows Wright commented that "this use of natural foliage and flowers for decoration is carried to quite an extent in all the designs, and although the buildings are complete without this 'efflorescence,' they may be said to blossom with the season."

But the exuberance of the stained glass in the Dana house was not maintained in Wright's later work. As early as 1902 he had begun to experiment with asymmetrical geometric shapes in the swinging doors to the kitchen, the skylight, and the windows designed for the Ward Willits house and executed by the Linden Glass Company. Before long Wright's designs for art glass gave less and less indication of the flower or plant which had provided the initial inspiration.

The rectangle, triangle, and diamond provided the basis for Wright's later glass designs, for these shapes were easily executed and one of Wright's design principles decreed that ornament "should be . . . designed with a thorough knowledge of what today's machinery can do most efficiently and well." When machinery was used, straight lines were more easily and more accurately cut than curved lines because glass breaks in straight lines, not curves. These principles were acknowledged by Wright when he developed his basic formula for designing art glass windows. As he explained:

> *The windows usually are provided with characteristic straight line patterns absolutely in the flat and usually severe. The nature of the glass is taken into account in these designs as is also the metal bar used in their construction, and most of them are treated as metal "grilles" with glass inserted, forming a simple, rhythmic arrangement of straight lines and squares as cunning as possible as long as the result is quiet. The aim is that the designs shall make the best of the technical contrivances that produced them.* [Frank Lloyd Wright, "In the Cause of Architecture," The Architectural Record 23 (March 1908):161]

Wright maintained that doors and windows should be "integral features of the structure, and if possible act as its natural ornamentation." Disliking fabric draperies, he substituted what he regarded as curtains of glass. These art glass windows let in the light while screening the interior from the gaze of passersby.

In structures intended for amusement, such as the playhouse designed for the Avery Coonley family in 1912, Wright added a touch of whimsy. Bright red, green, and blue circles representing balloons float in a sky of multicolored glass squares which represent confetti. In some, an American flag appears in the corner, recalling the parade theme which inspired the design of the windows. For the Midway Gardens—an entertainment center on Chicago's South Side modeled after the outdoor garden restaurants of Germany—Wright in 1913 designed windows composed of fanciful geometric shapes that repeated the decorative motifs used throughout the interior and exterior of the complex and represented toy blocks.

Whether inspired by plant or geometric forms, Wright's art glass windows and fixtures were imbued with a subtle radiance and originality that could not be overlooked. They did not dominate the decorating scheme, but were visual expressions of his conviction that "the ornamental forms of one's environment should be designed to wear well. This means that they must have absolute repose and make no especial claim upon the attention; to be as far from realistic tendencies as a sense of realities can take them."

While Frank Lloyd Wright may have conceived of his designs as having "no especial claim upon the attention," they immediately caught the eye of other architects and local glass companies, creating a new style of art glass whose appeal would prove nationwide.

Minutely leaded geometric and highly conventionalized floral designs became standard fare in Prairie-style houses and in the pages of the catalogs issued by Chicago art glass manufacturers. By 1908 they were so common that architect Thomas Eddy Tallmadge, describing "The Chicago School" in the April *Architectural Review,* wrote: "Mr. Wright's creations in leaded glass have been adopted, as their own, by most of the local glass concerns." In this article Tallmadge went on to discuss the work of Frank Lloyd Wright, Howard Van Doren Shaw, George W. Maher, and others associated with the Prairie School. Stressing these architects' interest in residential design, he noted their preference for straight lines and strong horizontal planes, which he termed "an absolute result of the inspiration of the prairie."

The conventionalized or natural vegetable forms appearing in glass designed by these Prairie School architects often were inspired by the local setting. Frank Lloyd Wright, for example, frequently used flowers or plants growing on or near the construction site for inspiration. As mentioned earlier, prairie sumac provided the theme for the Susan Lawrence Dana house; the motif for the art glass in the Oscar Steffens house (1909)—located on a hill overlooking Lake Michigan—was the sun abstracted into a gold square over a lake symbolized by aqua and white stripes. Hollyhocks, which covered the hilltop chosen in 1917 by Aline Barnsdale, oil heiress and manager of the Little Theatre in Chicago, provided the theme for the glass in her Los Angeles house.

Similarly, George W. Maher often chose a single floral motif to integrate glass with furniture, fabrics, metalwork and wall decoration, and to unify visually the interior and the exterior. In the Evanston mansion he designed in 1901 for Chicago grain speculator James A. Patten, Maher used the thistle, which grew wild on the suburban site. In 1902 a hollyhock provided the dominant motif for the Harry Rubens house in the northern suburb of Glencoe; poppies served as the central theme for the Ernest Magerstadt house (1908) in Hyde Park. The hollyhock lent itself so well to conventionalization that Maher used it in the

121. View of the dining room of the Ernest J. Magerstadt residence showing the poppy motif art glass windows designed by George W. Maher, 1908. *HABS, Library of Congress*

123

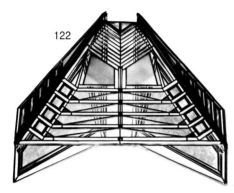

122

123

124

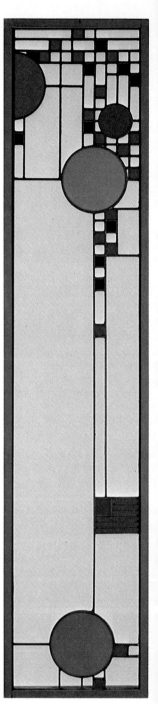

125

122. Hanging lamp designed by Frank Lloyd Wright and executed by the Linden Glass Company for the Susan Lawrence Dana residence, Springfield, Illinois, 1903. (19″ x 23½″ x 23½″). *The Richard W. Bock Sculpture Collection, Greenville College, Illinois*

123. Dining room window with red, yellow, and opaque white geometric motif made for a six-flat apartment building at 425 Greenwood Street, Evanston, designed by Thomas McCall, 1912. (16⅛″ x 28⅛″). *Mr. and Mrs. Helmut Strauss*

124. Sumac motif window designed by Frank Lloyd Wright and executed by the Linden Glass Company for the Susan Lawrence Dana residence, Springfield, Illinois, 1903. (46¼″ x 31½″). *The Richard W. Bock Sculpture Collection, Greenville College, Illinois*

125. Window for the Avery Coonley playhouse, Riverside, Illinois, designed by Frank Lloyd Wright, 1912. (61 13/16″ x 13½″). *Walter and Dawn Clark Netsch*

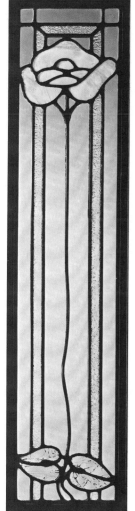

126

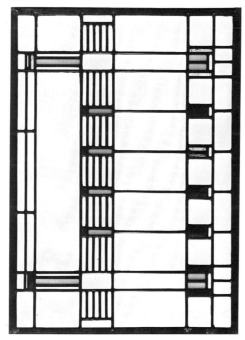

127

128

126. Window with blue/white opalescent poppy designed by George W. Maher for the Foler P. Stone residence in Wausau, Wisconsin, c. 1903. (23⅞″ x 5¾″). *Robert and Kathy Coleman*

127. Window of clear and opaque white glass, designed by Frank Lloyd Wright and executed by Giannini & Hilgart for the Ward Willits house, Highland Park, 1902. (20¾″ x 15¼″). *Mr. and Mrs. Alan Dobry*

128. Window with blue, green, white, and amber geometric motif similar to those designed by Prairie School architect George Grant Elmslie. (33¼″ x 35″). *Robert A. Furhoff*

129. Pair of doorlights with white, amber, and green conventionalized flowers and gold squares made by Drehobl Bros. Art Glass Company, c. 1925. (72 1/16″ x 9 13/16″). *Drehobl Bros. Art Glass Company Inc.*

stylish two-flats on Ellis Avenue commissioned by Chicago lawyer E. Schoenfeld and physician Joseph B. DeLee in 1909. Spiky holly-hocks in brilliant hues of blue and green still grace the entrance doors of Dr. DeLee's building, although the art glass windows, French doors, and glass mosaic fireplace—all executed by the local firm of Giannini & Hilgart—were removed long ago. Next door, in the apartment building designed for the Schoenfelds, a simpler version of the holly-hocks still graces the windows of the staircase landing.

Among young Chicago architects glass was considered an excel-lent medium for calling attention to innovative designs. "Its ease of manipulation gives it the advantage of being seized upon by a mind seeking a means of expression, while color and brilliancy attract attention to its possibilities as a medium of original thought," wrote George R. Dean in an article called "A New Movement in American Architecture." In pointing to new architectural trends in London, Munich, and Chicago, Dean observed that the greatest expression of the new modern style was found in its glass. Commenting on the glass designs of his fellow Chicago architects he wrote:

> They show a great variety of treatment, from almost natural forms to conventionalization so severe that the original form is lost and only the character remains. In some cases no especial form produced the motive, but only a type of form, or perhaps a feeling of growth without the semblance of natural forms. Glass lends itself charmingly to this last thought; the extremely brittle, crystal character of the material cries out against naturalism and leads one to sharp and severe outline. One of the characteristics of the school is the desire to produce a decorative effect without the aid of light passing through the window. In our mode of life much of our time is spent at home in the evening when the ordi-nary stained-glass window looks dead and uninteresting. Very decorative effects are obtained by means of gold and opaque glass in black and white. These are used in small pieces in such a manner that as dark spots they enhance rather than destroy the value of the window by day. In some a rich effect is obtained by burning gold on the surface of clear glass. By night this has the appearance of solid gold, while by day the gold, being deposited in minute particles, lets the light through, giving a soft, purple-gray tone. By burning on colored glass any desired tone may be obtained. [George R. Dean, "*A New Movement in American Architecture,*" Brush and Pencil 2 *(April 1900): 33–34*]

By 1905 Flanagan & Biedenweg, Schuler & Mueller, Giannini & Hilgart, and the other art glass manufacturers were supplying builders with inexpensive geometric or stylized floral patterned windows in prices ranging from 70¢ per square foot for "Clear Double Strength Glass, with spots of White or Color," to $2.25 a square foot for "Double

Strength Background [Crystal]; ornament Opalescent effect.'' The windows featured colored squares, triangles, and rectangles arranged in linear patterns obviously inspired by the original designs of Wright and other architects of the Prairie School. A few designs incorporated opaque white glass triangles or conventionalized blossoms.

Leaded art glass in similar patterns was also available from millwork supply firms such as E. L. Roberts and the Morgan Company. These served as outlets for various manufacturers, supplying everything in wood or glass required by the builder. E. L. Roberts and several other millwork suppliers carried the work of Flanagan & Biedenweg and other local glass producers, but the Chicago Millwork Supply Company actually produced all of the designs offered in its catalog. The 1910 catalog stated:

> We have our own art glass factory under the personal supervision of one of the most skillful artists in this line and are equipped for the production of strictly first-class work of any description. We can make up any design wanted in art glass—whether shown in this catalog or the catalogs of other houses.

Prices were competitive, with simple colored geometric designs selling for 70¢ per square foot and floral Art Nouveau compositions beginning at $1.50 per foot. While not cheap, they were well within the range of many homeowners.

Interior decorators such as Evelyn Marie Stuart, writing in 1912, urged homemakers to take full advantage of artistic windows in creating an impressive decorating scheme. "To accomplish this," Miss Stuart stated, "a window must be leaded in many small sections, so arranged as to express something." Clear glass aroused no emotion, and was therefore unacceptable.

> A simple many-paned window with wide fancy leadings, adds distinction to a building, especially to a home. These leadings may be in copper, zinc, or other of the harder materials, and in finishes to match the doorknobs or other structural hardware, which has a distinct harmonious advantage. Windows are thus leaded to match bookcase doors in the library in many of the newer buildings. Leaded glass French doors are also often used between connecting rooms, where it is desirable to shut them off from each other without obscuring the light.
> Tiny squares of crystal, gray, or amber are introduced in these fancy leaded windows of plain glass, often adding greatly to the interest of the composition. Little mosaic fruit or flower motifs also enliven such conceptions agreeably, fruit being especially appropriate in the dining room. Designs relying for their beauty upon color and line only, and upon straight lines at that, prove to be unexpectedly charming. [Evelyn Marie Stuart, "The Artistic

130. Bookcase doors with amber and green branch crossing a linear design of opaque and iridescent glass made for a Chicago bungalow, c. 1920. (50¼" x 35¾"). *Frank Milligan, Milligan Antique Galleries*

127

Development of American Ornamental Glass," Fine Arts Journal
26 (June 1912): 386–99]

Leaded windows in geometric patterns were turned out by the thousands for the new, one-story bungalows that dominated the medium-priced housing market. Spots of gold and iridescent glass glittered in the band of casement windows which faced the street, adding a touch of elegance to rows of otherwise identical houses. Similar art glass compositions appeared in the doors of the built-in bookcases or in the dining room buffet. Built by architects, contractors, and real estate speculators, clusters of bungalows remain in all sections of the city, their simple art glass windows recalling the day when Chicago was the art glass center of the Midwest.

Conflict and Competition

After 1900 the competition among Chicago firms for church and secular commissions increased as more glass shops opened in the city. By 1920 at least fifty manufacturers were at work. Of these, no fewer than three were the offspring of Flanagan & Biedenweg, the city's largest stained glass manufacturer. In 1903 Joseph J. Vogel, foreman of the firm, had become treasurer of the new Temple Art Glass Company, while employee Dennis Shanahan joined Max Guler in organizing The Munich Studio to specialize in ecclesiastical work. Frank Drehobl, a glazier who had worked his way up to foreman at Flanagan & Biedenweg, formed a partnership with his brother Joseph in 1919 and established Drehobl Bros. Art Glass Company in a storefront on Lincoln Avenue. Other firms founded between 1893 and 1912 included The Clinton Glass Co., Willy H. Lau & Co., the Colonial Art Glass Co., Walter A. Schuler & Co., Ford Bros., and the Lutwyche Glass Co.

The demand for church and residential stained glass remained strong, yet local craft practices worked against the best interests of the studios. Employment was very unstable, with journeymen moving from shop to shop, locating temporarily where work was plentiful. In turn, proprietors hired on a short-term basis, paying high wages to get a job done and then laying off workers until another large job came along. As a result many workers joined the Amalgamated Glass Workers International Association (A.G.W.I.A.) to gain some security. Organized in August 1900, the union lobbied for an eight-hour workday, higher wages, and the regulation of child labor.

Brief strikes occurred in 1905, followed by a crippling strike that lasted from December 1905 until May 1907. Six hundred union men, members of Chicago Local No. 1, stopped work because of wage reductions and their desire to limit the number of apprentices employed in each shop, since these were doing much of the work at very low

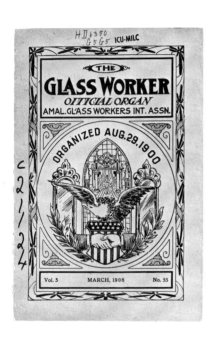

131. Cover of *The Glass Worker,* official organ of the Amalgamated Glass Workers International Association, August 1906. *The Center for Research Libraries*

128

wages.   The seventeen-month strike was reported in great detail in *The Glass Worker*, the official organ of the A.G.W.I.A., published in Chicago between 1906 and 1911.   Although not conceding defeat, union members eventually gave up in 1907 after their numbers had been reduced to fewer than 100, for most of their fellow glassworkers had been forced to leave town or enter other professions in order to support their families.

Competition, both from abroad and among the local companies, promoted uneven quality and pricing.   By 1907 the high tariff on foreign windows had been eliminated, allowing painted and stained glass windows to come in duty free as works of art.   American glass manufacturers, whose labor costs were four times those of foreign producers, suffered as churches placed orders for windows with German, Austrian, and Hungarian factories.

To capture large contracts, local manufacturers often reduced prices.   This encouraged architects and church committees to sponsor competitions or to shop around rather than place their order with long-established, prestigious firms.   As manufacturers attempted to squeeze some profit from an unrealistically low bid, inferior glass was often used and workmanship became shoddy.   Salesmen took to carrying sample windows as a way of influencing customers since they proved far more persuasive than the traditional watercolor sketches.   Firms which produced high quality, and therefore expensive, work deplored this peddler's approach, as revealed by a letter from George H. Bradshaw to the editor of the *Ornamental Glass Bulletin* in 1912. Bradshaw, who was head of the church glass department of H. M. Hooker Co., a major supplier of religious windows, condemned this "foolish habit of carrying great boxes full of sample windows when going into a competition, and I am sorry to say Chicago has recently gone into the same unbusinesslike, expensive and useless practice." "Why," he asked, "is it necessary to carry our studios around with us?"

Producers of church and memorial windows also had to protect their work from degradation by the glassworkers who specialized in mass-producing inexpensive painted biblical figures.   These would be used as the centerpiece of the window and borders of plain or opalescent glass would then be added on to fill in the window space, whatever its size or shape.   The Chicago Art Glass Studio and the American Ecclesiastical Studio, among other such "artists to the trade," turned out untold quantities of "painted figures of The Good Shepherd, Christ Knocking, and Gethsemane in three sizes" for sale to suppliers of low-budget windows.

Confronted with labor unrest and cut-throat competition, manufacturers throughout America came to realize that a serious effort had to be made to organize the studios if the stained glass industry was to survive and develop in proper directions.   Under the guidance of Joseph E. Flanagan, president of the Flanagan & Biedenweg Co. of

132. Folding sample window of stained and painted glass known as *Christ Blessing Little Children*, made by The Munich Studio, c. 1912. (54⅞" x 31"). *Thomas S. Snyder*

129

LEADED SELECTED OPALESCENT and PAINTED GLASS
Rules for ordering and further description see general information page

1420. $9.70 square foot

1421. $10.00 square foot

1422. $8.60 square foot

1423. $17.25 square foot

1424. $15.00 square foot

1425. $8.50 sq. ft.

1426. $11.75 sq. ft.

Copyright by the National Ornamental Glass Manufacturers Association of the United States and Canada

133. Page from the *International Art Glass Catalogue* published by the National Ornamental Glass Manufacturers' Association, 1914. *CHS*

Chicago, Ludwig von Gerichten of Columbus, Ohio, and George Mueller of Milwaukee, the National Ornamental Glass Manufacturers' Association (later renamed the Stained Glass Association of America) was founded in July 1903. Comprised of manufacturers and craftsmen working in all aspects of decorative glass, the association elected Flanagan president and drew up a list of nine goals:

1. To eliminate existing evils.
2. To stop the cutting of prices.
3. To get an equitable price for our product.
4. To have competitions conducted honestly.
5. To encourage every one not to make work so low in artistic standard as to hurt the craft.
6. To help each other in case of strikes or other labor troubles.
7. To create the sentiment among architects to specify higher price in order to permit us to do better work.
8. To get all craftsmen acquainted with each other.
9. And any other good thing to make our profession more of a pleasure than a curse.

In 1907, when the Chicago glassworkers' strike made it apparent that association members needed to be informed of conditions in the industry, the association began to publish *The Ornamental Glass Bulletin* (later changed to *Stained Glass*) on a monthly basis. From 1909 until his death in 1928, Joseph E. Flanagan served as editor, publishing the bulletin in Chicago.

In 1909 Flanagan, Max Mueller of Schuler & Mueller, and Frank L. Linden of the Linden Glass Company conceived the idea of compiling a national catalog which would illustrate stock designs in stained glass and list their standard prices. Each association member was asked to submit twenty designs for church and domestic windows, ranging from simple to medium grade, and to note the selling price of each. From these, median prices were established and the first of a series called *International Art Glass Catalogue* was printed and distributed in quantity to manufacturers, millwork supply houses, and other wholesalers. The goal was to make it easier for builders to secure art glass, while stabilizing prices and reducing the undercutting by unscrupulous glassworkers and millworks. Editions were updated periodically and, imprinted with the company's name, often took the place of the individual catalogs previously issued by the various local firms.

Although union contracts, standardized catalogs, and the national association did much to improve the stained glass industry, it was to continue, as it remains today, half art and half business. Relying as it did on artistic talent and original effects, the product could not be standardized. Since nearly all of the work was done by hand, labor costs could not be reduced by the introduction of improved machinery. In addition, it was a seasonal business, depending upon large orders at Christmastime and large church or commercial contracts to keep the glassworkers busy. Except for those shops devoted exclusively to church work, most of the firms diversified their output to take advantage of new markets generated by the development of electric light, the automobile, and such amusement devices as player pianos, nickelodeons, and slot machines. Others expanded their scope to include the making of glass mosaics.

Art Glass Lampshades

Decorators had long considered glass shades a decorative as well as practical material for shielding the glare of oil, gas, or electric light. Subtle colors and textures came to life as light shone through the shades. Glass could be etched, enameled, or sandblasted to orchestrate the light, or pressed, engraved, or textured to achieve sculptural effects. But the most popular of the ''art shades'' were those made from leaded or bent colored glass.

Leaded art glass shades (mosaic shades) were made from the same materials and by the same methods used in constructing stained glass windows. Sheets of machine-rolled glass were purchased commercially and then ''finished'' in the local studio. This entailed cutting the sheets into the individual pieces of which the shades were composed and then fitting them together over plaster or wooden forms molded into the final shape. A cartoon of the pattern would have been drawn on the mold. The small pieces of art glass were usually held together by delicate cames of copper foil.

Mosaic shades featured the floral and geometric themes then popular in interior decorating. Conventionalized flowers predominated, with water lilies, roses, peonies, daffodils, and other familiar garden flowers blooming vigorously in opalescent glass. For those with simpler tastes and angular Mission furniture, there were chaste shades composed of simple rectangles of green, gold, or blue-green glass.

Other shades were made of several large pieces of glass which had been ''bent'' into shape by softening in a kiln. After the panels had been cut from sheets of opalescent glass, each piece was placed on a mold containing the desired shape. The heat of the kiln relaxed the glass and caused it to assume the shape of the mold. Some bent glass shades were assembled using lead; others were set into molded frames made of other metals.

Louis J. Millet, the Linden Glass Company, and Mitchel & Halbach designed and produced glass lampshades to complement interiors well before 1900 and advertised them along with their art glass windows and mosaics. By 1906 Orlando Giannini, partner in the firm of Giannini & Hilgart, had designed a series of leaded glass lampshades to be used with bases of green-glazed Teco ware made by the local

R. Williamson & Co., 1882–1929.
Founded by Richard Williamson, this firm manufactured a variety of gas, electric, and combination fixtures which it sold wholesale ''to the trade.'' By 1910 its large, colorful catalogs showed ''Fixtures in Square, Mission, and Colonial Designs'' and stated that ''Our art glass studio is complete in every detail which places us in a position to furnish artistic effects'' as well as to make ''art glass shades and domes according to designs furnished.'' Fixtures were not marked with the company name until the early 1920s.

After Richard Williamson died in 1914, the company was headed by his widow, Dora Ummach Williamson, and later by their son, Richard, until it merged with the Beardslee Chandelier Manufacturing Company of Chicago in 1929.

134. *Geranium Art Lamp* with red and green flowers on a gold opalescent ground made by R. Williamson & Co., c. 1915. (h: 24½″). *Dora Williamson White*

Gates Potteries (see page 55). Several were simple leaded domes composed of squares of glass in soft green and blue tones. A few were starkly geometric, with flaring wings of chevron-shaped glass similar to those designed by Frank Lloyd Wright; others featured a border of conventionalized fruit or flowers. These lamps were designed for use with kerosene, since many homes continued to be lit with a combination of gas and oil-burning fixtures long after the invention of the electric light bulb.

By 1910 several of the firms that manufactured and sold gas and electric fixtures wholesale had added an art glass department to produce leaded or bent glass shades. R. Williamson & Co., at the corner of Washington and Jefferson streets, advertising as "the largest manufacturers and jobbers of lighting supplies in the world," produced all types of brass and wooden lamp standards, wall fixtures, and chandeliers. They also supplied dozens of varieties of Art Dome Shades in plain, geometric, and floral patterns. Conventionalized grapes, cherry blossoms, roses, water lilies, and oak leaves formed borders for the shades of pastel opalescent glass which came in diameters from fourteen to twenty-eight inches. Those in the more severe Mission style consisted of rectangular and triangular panels of opalescent glass set into angular brass or wooden frames. Others were edged with fringes similar to those which later bordered the skirts of "flapper" dresses.

Located only a few blocks away on West Washington Street was the Moran & Hastings Manufacturing Company, which produced a similar line of lighting fixtures for distribution to department stores, mail-order houses, and other retail dealers. The leaded and bent glass shades supplied by its art glass department resembled those made by Williamson, although designs tended to be less complicated and more geometric.

Shades of opalescent glass overlaid with filigree, landscapes, and floral designs in lightweight stamped and cut-out metal were produced by the H. J. Peters Co., which advertised "exclusive lighting effects" and "classy designs." The shades were composed primarily of a metal shade backed with bent panels of milky glass in soft pastel colors. The more expensive shades incorporated two or more colors of glass. For example, one lamp featured a landscape of hills and trees rendered in amber glass with water and sky in a pleasant shade of blue. The metal parts of the shades and the lamp standards were finished in a variety of patinas, including Antique Brass, Roman Gold, Violet Gold, Japanese Bronze, or Verde Antique (a green which resembled weathered bronze).

Smaller firms such as the Colonial Art Glass Company, Edward Miller & Co., the Chicago Mosaic Shade Company, and W. H. Lau created fixtures in floral patterns or the austere Mission style and executed orders for fixtures designed by Chicago architects. For example,

135

136

135. Desk lamp with purple irises on a green field made by the Colonial Art Glass Company, 1906–14. (h: 15"). *CHS, gift of Suzanne Swift*

136. Two plates illustrating lamps from the H. J. Peters Co. catalog, c. 1920. *A. Christian Revi*

133

137. Lamp with opalescent glass
shade featuring pink flowers with
green leaves on an amber ground.
The bronze base simulates a tree
trunk. Made by The Mosaic
Shade Company, 1909–29.
(h: 27″). *CHS*

134

W. H. Lau produced light fixtures for the B. Harley Bradley house in Kankakee, Illinois, designed by Frank Lloyd Wright in 1900, and for the E. J. Mosser house in Chicago, designed by George W. Maher in 1905.

Art glass shades were also produced in small studios operated by a single artisan or a group of workers who combined glass with metalwork, ceramics, or other crafts. In his Ravenswood workshop, metalsmith George R. Trautmann produced elegant light fixtures in the Arts and Crafts style, which he sold through a salesroom he maintained in the Fine Arts Building on Michigan Avenue. The bases of Trautmann's lamps, wall sconces, and chandeliers were handcrafted from copper; the shades featured rectangles, triangles, or squares of glass set in a copper framework. Other professional metalsmiths known to have created art glass shades for their handwrought bases included Robert R. Jarvie, Christia M. Reade, and Jessie M. Preston.

Taking advantage of the Arts and Crafts Movement's emphasis on handcraftsmanship and home improvement, crafts supply shops and department stores sold lamp-making kits for home enthusiasts, while various manuals on glassworking and metalwork issued from Chicago's publishing houses. *Popular Mechanics*, founded in Chicago in 1902, often contained sections on home craftsmanship. Like mailorder catalogs and Gustav Stickley's *The Craftsman*, the magazine addressed itself to those who wanted the latest styles for the least cost. Beginning around 1910, the Popular Mechanics Press developed an entire series of small handbooks, priced at fifty cents, which supplied complete instructions for making Arts & Crafts furnishings. One was entitled *Arts-Crafts Lamps*. In this booklet, published in 1911, John C. Adams indicated how one could imitate bronze or copper leaded glass desk lamps, chandeliers, and lanterns by using cardboard, glue, colored paper, and passe-partout tape. Many of his designs bore a strong resemblance to those created by metalsmiths Jarvie, Trautmann, and Preston or by Frank Lloyd Wright, William Drummond, and other Prairie School architects.

Professional glassworkers employed by the large light fixture manufacturers, art glass studios, and similar enterprises often also produced shades in home workshops for family, friends, and occasional customers. Pullman Palace Car Company employee Theodore Scudella, for example, created Tiffany-style lamps in his home in Pullman on the city's South Side. An Italian by birth, Scudella had completed his apprenticeship in Murano before emigrating to America in 1905. Here he went to work as a glazier in the Pullman Palace Car Company factory making jeweled transoms, domes, and other glasswork for railroad cars.

In 1908, after being laid off, Scudella joined the Tiffany Studios in New York, having attracted the attention of Louis Comfort Tiffany when the latter toured the Pullman works some time earlier. Scudella's family, however, had remained in the Midwest and when the Pullman

The Mosaic Shade Co., 1909–1929.
Little is known about the lamp manufactory operated by Saviour and Laurence Vivirito. Table lamps with cast bronze or brass bases impressed with the firm's name feature floral leaded shades made from pastel and opalescent glass.

Company was able to offer him a job again seven or eight months later, he returned to Chicago. Here he continued to make intricately leaded lampshades in the famous patterns that had become so familiar to him while he was working for Tiffany, but now he marked them with his own trademark. His son William Scudella, now seventy and recently retired to Michigan, continues this family tradition, patiently leading hundreds of tiny fragments of colored glass and jewels together to create graceful domes ornamented with peonies, wisteria, or dragonflies.

Hundreds of art glass shades were turned out by the Drehobl Bros. Art Glass Company during the 1920s, although the mainstay of the firm was the production of the colorful stained glass panels which were inserted in the paneled fronts of Seeburg player pianos and nickelodeons. Manufactured in Chicago, the Seeburg instruments were decorated with landscapes, dancing girls, or geometric compositions. Drehobl Bros. was also kept busy cutting and finishing plate glass windows for that increasingly popular new vehicle—the automobile.

Glass Mosaics

The popularity of "mosaic" art glass windows and lamps was matched by renewed appreciation for pictures and decorative designs composed of tiny pieces of colored glass set in mortar. During the last quarter of the nineteenth century, walls, ceilings, pillars, fireplaces, and similar vertical surfaces began to be covered with colorful mosaic decoration, and lobbies of fashionable office buildings, theaters, hotels, clubs, and churches were elaborately and expensively bejeweled with tiny bits of sparkling colored glass. Lasting color and good light reflection, combined with the fact that they were easy to clean, made glass mosaics an attractive and practical solution to the problem of decorating large and dimly-lit interiors.

During the 1870s and 1880s, the English taste for mosaics made London the center of glass mosaic production. As of old, the actual glass continued to be made in Venice, but the cutting and fitting of the segments to create the final mosaic was done in London. It was from the latter city that the first samples of glass mosaic shown in Chicago were obtained.

In 1886 John W. Root had visited England and had prevailed on William H. Burke of Burke & Co. to come to Chicago and lay a marble mosaic pavement in the vestibule, elevator halls, and rotunda of the Rookery building, which was then under construction. This initial undertaking proved so successful that Burke decided to establish a branch in the city and arranged for an exhibit space in the Institute of Building Arts, a permanent gallery where architects, builders, and clients could view the latest in building materials. Frank L. Davis, an employee of Burnham & Root at the time, was hired as Burke's

Chicago representative.

In January 1889 Davis installed an exhibit of marble floors, wainscoting, columns and entablature, and panels of marble and glass mosaic in the city's Institute of Building Arts for Burke & Co. The glass mosaic panel, which featured a pair of sea horses, was made of thousands of enameled gold tesserae (irregular cubes). It had been designed in England, glued on paper, and shipped to Chicago, where a mosaicist from London, assisted by Davis, set it in cement encased in an iron frame. Kept by Davis as a display piece for many years, the sea horse panel was eventually set into the wall above the Madison Street entrance to the Chicago Athletic Club, where it can still be seen.

Davis later formed his own firm to supply marble, ceramic, and glass mosaic and his first customer was his former employer, John W. Root, who commissioned Venetian glass mosaics for a small building used as the entrance to the Central Market on South Water Street in Chicago. Shortly after, in 1890, Davis inlaid glass mosaics in bands on octagonal English alabaster columns in the first story of the Reliance Building at State and Washington streets, another Burnham & Root commission. The Reliance Building still stands today, but the glass mosaic disappeared long ago.

At the time of the World's Columbian Exposition two very fine glass mosaic panels dealing with Columbus's discovery of America were installed in the Columbus Memorial Building. According to Davis these had been executed by a firm known as the Company Murano. One mural showed sailors planting the flag on the soil of the New World and employed a number of techniques to depict tropical foliage, land, sky, water, sails, and the hands, faces, and garments of the soldiers. The other, using similar methods, portrayed the throne room of Queen Isabella. Set into a brick wall, the two glass mosaics were unfortunately considered part of the structure rather than art works, and during later remodeling one of the murals was walled in with brick.

Saddened by the lack of appreciation for this beautiful expression of patriotism, Davis noted bitterly in the February-March 1943 bulletin of the Illinois Society of Architects that "while trade will follow the flag and seek security beneath its billowy folds, cold-blooded commercialism will not protect art when it interferes with sales and dividends." In fact, the other mural was saved and placed in storage when the building was razed in the 1950s.

After the 1893 Fair, glass made by the Tiffany Glass & Decorating Company of New York and other American firms supplanted Venetian glass for use in mosaics. Much more vibrant than the glass produced up to that time, Tiffany's new favrile or "handmade" glass had been originally developed for use in stained glass windows. For the Columbian Exposition of 1893, however, the new glass was made in smaller pieces to create the mosaic for a small chapel designed by Louis Comfort Tiffany for his firm's exhibition. In the chapel, which was one of

he most popular exhibits at the Fair, clusters of columns supporting the canopy over the altar featured shafts that were completely covered by glass mosaic of reds, greens, and browns in random patterns. The otherwise simple altar was fronted with a white and iridescent glass mosaic. Behind the altar glowed an iridescent glass mosaic with peacocks and vine scrolls in shimmering blues and greens set in black marble. Iridescent glass, mother-of-pearl, and transparent tesserae backed with gold or metal foil were used to create this unique mosaic. Moreover, the white mortar backing reflected light through the glass, producing a subtly luminous effect. Undeniably effective, Tiffany's chapel was proof that American ingenuity could rival and even surpass anything produced abroad.

In 1895, as a result of its impressive showing at the Fair, Tiffany glass was used to execute a large glass mosaic for the fascia of the gallery in the main entrance of the Marquette Building, then under construction on the northwest corner of Adams and Dearborn streets. The decision to name the building in honor of the French priest who had accompanied Joliet on his journey up the Chicago River in 1673 had prompted architects Holabird & Roche to propose decoration of the lobby entrance with scenes of Marquette and Joliet's travels in the Illinois country.

According to Robert Koch's *Louis C. Tiffany, Rebel in Glass* (New York: Crown, 1964), the glass mosaics in the Marquette Building were the work of J. A. Holzer, chief mosaicist for the Tiffany Glass & Decorating Company, who left the firm in 1895 to set up his own studio in Chicago to execute the glass mosaics for the Marquette Building. In this building, three long pictorial panels, each separated by a narrow panel carrying a single figure, cover the gallery rail, which is hexagonal in shape and about ninety feet in length. For the mosaic, small pieces of glass were shaped to form the beads, buttons, bone, teeth, and claws which compose the colorfully detailed trappings of the American Indian. Larger pieces indicate the sweep of the birchbark canoe, the skins of the teepees, and trees in the forest.

A year later, Holzer again used favrile glass to execute the mosaic work installed in the Chicago Public Library at Michigan Avenue and Washington Street, now the library's Cultural Center. Charles Coolidge, the resident architect of the Boston-based firm of Shepley Rutan & Coolidge, devoted particular attention and care to the design of the glass mosaics to be installed in the great dome which is on the third story of the building.

A few years later, when the firm of D. Burnham & Co. designed the court in Marshall Field & Company's new retail store on the northeast corner of Washington and State streets, the architects specified a barrel-vaulted dome of favrile glass mosaics to span the court between the fifth and sixth floors. Executed by Tiffany Studios, the Field dome features elliptical mosaic panels and incorporates 1,600,000 pieces of

139

138. Grand staircase at the Chicago Public Library, 79 E. Washington Street. *Photo by Barbara Crane for the Commission on Chicago Historical and Architectural Landmarks*

139. Detail from the glass mosaic mural in the Marquette Building, 1895. *Photo by William R. Boles*

iridescent glass which, spotted irregularly over the entire field, produce an effect simulating stars twinkling in a less brilliant sky. Covering an area of 6,000 square feet, the dome took fifty men two years to produce and install. It was unveiled in September 1907 to mark the opening of the new store and remains in the south rotunda of the State Street store today. At one time yet another Tiffany glass mosaic dome and fountain were the central attractions of Marshall Field's Men's Grill Room on the sixth floor of the Store for Men, a separate building across Washington Street. This dome, together with the fountain, were later destroyed in the course of remodeling.

The local firm of Healy & Millet was also busy providing stained glass, glass mosaics, and frescoes for public buildings, churches, and private residences both in Chicago and throughout the Midwest. While much of its best work was done in conjunction with Louis Sullivan, the firm was responsible for many other important commissions as well, including the design and execution in 1895 of the vaulted glass mosaic ceiling for the main lobby of the new Fisher Building on the corner of Van Buren and Dearborn streets. Unfortunately, most of the ceiling was destroyed when the lobby was remodeled.

Since Healy & Millet were also responsible for the stained glass installed in the celebrated Auditorium Building, it is possible that the glass mosaics remaining in the lobby of the Congress Hotel, formerly the Auditorium Extension, are an example of their work. Built in 1892, the annex was originally connected to the Auditorium by a tunnel built under Congress Street and was used to house the overflow of guests.

When glass mosaics were at the height of their popularity, several Chicago firms began creating elaborate glass mosaic fireplace facings for expensive residences and private clubs. Composed of iridescent or foil-backed tesserae, the glass mosaic facings sparkled when struck by sunlight and shimmered magnificently in firelight. They were used in conjunction with art glass windows or bookcase lights, repeating theme, color, and material to further unify interiors of residences designed by architects, particularly those associated with the progressive Prairie School.

In 1900 Orlando Giannini had executed a gold enamel and glass mosaic mantel featuring "wisteria sprays and pendant blossoms," designed by a talented young Chicago artist, Blanche Ostertag. The house for which it was created was the Chicago residence of Joseph M. Husser, designed by Frank Lloyd Wright in 1899. The Ostertag mantel, described as early as June 1900 in Robert C. Spencer, Jr.'s *Architectural Review* article discussing Frank Lloyd Wright's work, may have served as a prototype for the spate of mosaic mantels which followed.

Glass mosaic fireplace facings frequently formed an integral part of the highly individualized and carefully integrated residences designed by Prairie School architect George W. Maher. In 1901 Louis J. Millet,

140. Thistle motif glass mosaic panel from the fireplace of the James A. Patten mansion, Evanston, designed by George W. Maher and executed by Louis J. Millet, 1901. (45 9/16″ x 27½″). *Mr. and Mrs. Ronald Handler*

141. View of entrance hall
fireplace faced with glass mosaic
in the Ernest J. Magerstadt
residence, designed by George
W. Maher, 1908. *HABS, Library
of Congress*

who had ended his partnership with Healy, was commissioned by
Maher to supervise the execution of the interior decoration of the
James A. Patten mansion in suburban Evanston.   One of the largest of
the residences designed in accord with Maher's "motif rhythm theory,"
the Patten house, as noted earlier, incorporated a unifying motif—in
this case the thistle—in the furniture, rugs, frescoes, portieres, and
stained glass.   Inset into the massive oak fireplace in the entrance hall
were exquisite panels of iridescent mosaic glass in which the thistle
exuberantly spread its sharp spiky leaves in shimmering tones of blue,
green, and gold.   In the windows, large stylized thistles glowed in
stained glass.   The thistle motif, wrote Maher in the August 1903 *Inland
Architect & News Record,* was chosen because it possessed "refinement of outline and a strong organic growth which could be readily
accommodated to the various materials that are employed in the
construction of the building."

Giannini & Hilgart executed a number of glass mosaics "with
ornament peculiar to Geo. W. Maher."   Among the first of these was a
brilliant blue and gold vine-encrusted fireplace facing installed in the
new game room added in 1900–1901 to the large marble mansion at 40
East Erie Street that manufacturer Lucius G. Fisher had just purchased
from its original owner, Samuel M. Nickerson.   Typical of Maher's use
of mosaic was the fireplace of the Glencoe house he designed for
Harry Rubens in 1902.   The architect used one of his favorite motifs,
the hollyhock, and expressed it in blue, green, and dull-gold ceramic
and glass mosaics to face a massive brick fireplace.

A promotional booklet put out by Giannini & Hilgart around 1918
stressed the variety of opalescent, iridescent, and metallic color effects
which could be achieved using glass mosaics and offered "to furnish
special designs in co-operation with the architects and in accordance
with their instruction."   Judging from the preface to the catalog and its
illustrations, elaborate glass mosaic fireplaces constituted a significant
percentage of the firm's business.   Among the mantels pictured was
one commissioned by architect Joseph Llewelyn for the E. K. Boisott
residence in LaGrange, Illinois.   Also illustrated was a mantel faced
with conventionalized amaranthus designed by architect W. J. Dodd
for the Ferguson house in Louisville, Kentucky, and one featuring a
sinuous grapevine with bronze stems and pearl grapes commissioned
by Myron Church for a Chicago residence.

Glass mosaic fireplace facings were similarly used in conjunction
with art glass in several large and elaborate residences designed by
Tallmadge & Watson, Howard Van Doren Shaw, W. Carbys Zimmerman
and other prominent Chicago architects prior to World War I.   During
the 1920s, however, the popularity of decorative mosaic began to wane
as architecture and interiors reflected the new taste for Colonial or
similar revival styles and glass mosaics came to be considered flashy
and old-fashioned.

The Mainstay: Memorial Windows

While domestic art glass dominated much of the market, ecclesiastical commissions remained the mainstay of many of the city's older firms and became the focus of several new ones. Churches were constantly being built, remodeled, expanded, torn down, and rebuilt, bringing hundreds of commissions to the dozen or so studios which specialized in church and memorial work. A combination of factors, including building budgets and the preferences of pastors and/or building committees, determined the final choice of windows.

Flanagan & Biedenweg's 1909 catalog advised that, in estimating costs, "church architects generally specify from 3 to 4 per cent of the total cost of the church for ordinary windows, made up in a neat design in opalescent glass, and from 5 to 6 per cent for a good grade of glass, with figure subjects in the prominent windows." Windows were generally graded according to their use. The auditorium or sanctuary contained the best or first grade of glass, the Sunday school and vestibule the second grade, and the classroom and tower windows the third, or lowest, grade.

As one of the city's largest and oldest stained glass manufacturers, Flanagan & Biedenweg advertised "fine figure windows" in "European and American styles." European-style windows tended to be medieval in inspiration and employed much paint for detail, while American-style windows were characterized by the use of opalescent glass, conventionalized landscapes, and pastel colors, with painting restricted to faces, hands, and a few details.

Windows pictured in their catalog, as well as those extant throughout Chicago, reflect Flanagan & Biedenweg's preference for American-style biblical figures and story-telling scenes bordered by swirling scrolls, foliage, or Gothic spires and crockets. Faces, hands, and other fine details were painted, while thick, ripple-textured drapery glass simulated folds in gracefully flowing garments. Clouds, sky, stones, trees, shrubbery, and architectural details were created by use of expanses of appropriately colored opalescent glass. The most common themes were familiar biblical ones such as "Christ Blessing Children," "Mary at the Tomb," "Christ in Bethany," "Gethsemane," the "Nativity," or the "Ascension," with figure groupings and facial expressions borrowed from famous works of religious art.

Ornamental windows did not include human figures and were simpler in design. They featured floral compositions, Gothic spires, or decorative medallions of religious symbols and emblems. The latter were often chosen by non-Christian groups whose teachings forbade the use of human figures or by small Christian congregations which could not afford the more elaborate pictorial windows.

Scattered among the illustrations in Flanagan & Biedenweg's catalog were letters from clergy and other satisfied customers and a

Drehobl Bros. Art Glass Co., since 1919.

In 1919, after fourteen years as a glasscutter for Flanagan & Biedenweg Co., Frank J. Drehobl (1889–1954) joined his brother Joseph to form what has become one of Chicago's oldest surviving art glass firms. Early on, the Drehobls secured a contract to supply the J. P. Seeburg Piano Company with leaded glass landscape panels for upright pianos and jukeboxes. With the help of eight employees—including a number of women—the company was soon turning out some 1500 panels a month. The firm also made plate glass for autos, stained glass for Balaban & Katz movie theaters, geometric art glass for bungalows and apartment buildings, and leaded glass lampshades.

During the Depression, a large contract for the stained glass windows for Anshe Emet Synagogue on N. Pine Grove kept the firm in business. Later ecclesiastical commissions included windows for the Immaculate Heart of Mary Church at 3834 N. Spaulding and for St. Beatrice Church in Schiller Park.

The firm has been located at 2847–51 N. Lincoln Avenue since 1926. Now owned by Frank J. Drehobl, Jr., it continues to execute and repair leaded glass windows and light fixtures for residences and churches.

142

143

142. Official award ribbon, Grand Prize for American Glass, awarded to the Flanagan & Biedenweg Co. at the St. Louis World's Fair, 1904. *John Vinci*

143. A panel from the *Magi* window, by the Flanagan & Biedenweg Co., which won the Grand Prize for American Glass at the 1904 World's Fair. Joseph E. Flanagan later donated the window to DePaul Academy, where several of his children attended school. (78½″ x 48½″). *DePaul University*

144

144. Three stained glass panels—the center a door panel—designed by Max Guler and associates for the office of Drehobl Bros. Art Glass Co., c. 1935. The panels are of pastel stained glass with painted details. (Door: 69½″ x 20¾″; panels: 54¼″ x 12¼″). *Drehobl Bros. Art Glass Co. Inc.*

145

The Munich Studio, 1903–1932.

In 1903 Max Guler, who had studied china painting in his native Munich, Germany, joined L. Holzchuh, an experienced bookkeeper, and Dennis L. Shanahan, a former salesman for Flanagan & Biedenweg, to open The Munich Studio which specialized in European-style memorial windows. Like medieval stained glass, their windows were characterized by elaborate figure groupings and an abundance of architectural forms as well as facial features and details executed in iron oxide and yellow stain.

Brochures issued by The Munich Studio between 1905 and 1925 listed over 150 churches containing examples of their work. Chicago installations include St. Agnes, 2648 W. Pershing Road (1905); St. Veronica, 330 N. Whipple Street (1905); St. Leo's, 7747 S. Emerald Avenue (1914); St. Philip's, 6232 S. Eberhart Avenue (1916); Our Lady of Sorrows, 3121 W. Jackson Boulevard (1920–24); and St. Margaret Mary, 2324 W. Chase Avenue (1924).

In 1923, when the firm was located at 111 W. Austin Street (now Hubbard Street), it employed over thirty craftsmen, seven of whom specialized in glass painting. But the Great Depression brought business to a standstill and forced the company to close. Guler and several of his key associates joined Drehobl Bros. Art Glass Company where he, Herman Schulze, and Peter Kugel continued to design and paint memorial windows while George Wieroeder and Joseph Lazar cut, fired, and leaded the stained glass into intricate patterns.

list recording the names and locations of some 240 houses of worship containing their windows. Addresses were heavily Midwestern, although a surprising number were located as far away as Pennsylvania and North Carolina. The Reverend Austin D. Crile, pastor of the local Wicker Park Evangelical Lutheran Church, wrote that the members of his congregation were very pleased with the twelve figured windows placed in their church. "We are ready to order some more. Your workmanship, price and honesty satisfies us fully," he added. "The windows placed in my new church of the Good Shepherd are not surpassed by any in the country," wrote Reverend Patrick O'Brien of Toledo, Ohio, "there is no longer reason to go to Europe for art windows when your house can give such excellent satisfaction."

Germanic baroque-style windows were the trademark of The Munich Studio, a firm founded in 1903 by Max Guler, Dennis S. Shanahan, and L. Holzchuh. Guler had been trained as a china painter in Munich, Germany, before emigrating to Chicago in 1896. Holzchuh was an experienced bookkeeper, and Shanahan an Irish glassworker who had accumulated considerable sales experience while employed by Flanagan & Biedenweg. As a result, Guler was able to devote his time to the design and execution of "pictorial windows beautifully grouped in rich, gorgeous colors." His work was characterized by dramatic contrasts of light and shadow, infinite attention to detail, asymmetrical figure groupings, and an abundance of architectural elements. He used imported antique, or hand-blown, glass in combination with iron oxide and yellow stain to create facial expressions, patterns on garments, and other detail. Iron oxide was even brushed along the sides of leadings to create sharper contrasts of light and shadow.

While most of The Munich Studio's windows depicted traditional biblical themes, a few expressed patriotic or ethnic aspirations, making them unique expressions of their culture and their time. In the years when Chicago's neighborhoods were dominated by a single ethnic group and Catholic parishes were particularly close-knit, it was not uncommon to find national patron saints or heroes among the saints portrayed in stained glass. Fine examples still remain in the church of Saints Cyril and Methodius on the corner of 50th Street and South Hermitage Avenue in the heart of an old Bohemian community. Named in honor of two Greek brothers who brought Christianity to the Slavs in the mid-ninth century, the church contains twenty-three stained glass windows executed in 1913 by The Munich Studio. Among these, four express Bohemian religious and national aspirations by recalling the stories of *SS. Cyril and Methodius Bringing the Church to the Slavic People*; *St. Wenceslaus, Ruler of Bohemia*; *St. Ludmilla and Her Young Grandson, Wenceslaus*; and *The Baptism of Borivoj*, Bohemia's first Christian duke.

Religion and patriotism were again combined in 1924 in the

145. *George Washington*, *Father Marquette*, and *Abraham Lincoln* from the school of St. Margaret Mary Church, 2324 W. Chase Avenue.   The Washington and Lincoln windows were executed by The Munich Studio, 1924. *Photo by William R. Boles*

146

147

146. Cutting and assembling
stained glass windows at the
H. M. Hooker Company, c. 1906.
Elizabeth F. Cheney

147. Artists designing stained
glass windows at the H. M.
Hooker Company, c. 1906.
Elizabeth F. Cheney

vestibule of St. Margaret Mary Church located at 2324 West Chase Avenue in the West Ridge section of Rogers Park. Here a large window, executed by The Munich Studio, portrays Father Marquette on his journey up the Chicago River. Flanking the window are stained glass portraits of George Washington and Abraham Lincoln. The Washington window was installed in memory of Private George Harles, killed during World War I; the Lincoln window honored Mr. and Mrs. John Powers. A window similar to the one depicting Father Marquette had been made at the time of the World's Fair in 1893 by McCully & Miles for St. Catherine of Genoa Church on Chicago's South Side. When the old church was replaced in 1923, the Marquette window, which was unsigned, was not reused; it may be the window that was incorporated the following year in St. Margaret Mary Church in memory of members of the Chicago Assembly, Catholic Daughters of America.

"European Style Antique Work" was also produced by the studios of the H. M. Hooker Co., a large paint and glass concern whose glass studio was under the direction of Charles H. Bradshaw. Like the windows created by The Munich Studio and Flanagan & Biedenweg, the Hooker Co.'s finest products included *St. Cecilia*, *The Great Physician*, *Christ in Gethsemane*, and other figural windows created from European glass highlighted with paint.

In addition to this European style of work, H. M. Hooker & Co. executed memorial windows in what their catalog termed a "High Art" style, employing opalescent glass in conventionalized landscape or floral settings. Extremely simple, classic ornamental versions consisted of rectangles or diamonds of opalescent glass in soft, muted colors relieved by delicate floral garlands. In Hooker & Co.'s pictorial windows both the settings and figures were more conventionalized than in windows executed by other firms and tended to be outlined by simpler frames of scrolls or Gothic spires.

Stained glass memorial windows were also produced in large quantity by the Chicago studios of Daprato, the country's largest supplier of statuary, ecclesiastical garments, altars, and other accessories required by churches and clergy. The entire top floor of the firm's multi-storied building on West Adams Street was devoted to stained glass studios. Thus clergymen and church building committees could outfit their entire structure—including pews, altar cloths, and art glass windows—without leaving the company's building.

Quite unique were the windows created by Thomas A. O'Shaughnessy, an innovative and somewhat eccentric Irishman who made his first stained glass window at the age of twelve. Disdaining paint, O'Shaughnessy employed tiny particles of brilliantly colored glass to create translucent mosaics which he termed "imprisoned light." He preferred to use a special "pot metal" glass made from an extremely fine-grained sand that he had discovered near Ottawa, Illinois. O'Shaughnessy arranged for this glass to be made under his direction

H. M. Hooker Co., 1855–1917.
H. M. Hooker Glass & Paint Co., 1918–c. 1967.
    The large paint and glass establishment operated by Henry M. Hooker (1829–1914) began as a small stock of paint and oils in the drugstore founded by Hooker and his brother Fayette in 1855. Hooker sold the drug business in 1868 to concentrate on the selling of paints, oils, varnishes, and imported glass. After 1889, when George H. Bradshaw joined the firm, H. M. Hooker Co. did an extensive business in art glass memorial windows.
    By 1918 the company had moved to a large building at 651-59 W. Washington Street where 300 employees made and sold a variety of glass, mirrors, art glass windows, floor varnish, and house paints to customers throughout the United States, Canada, and Cuba. After Hooker's death, the firm was operated by R. V. Thomas and John N., Andrew R., and Arthur Dole. It merged with the Oxford Electric Company around 1967.

Thomas A. O'Shaughnessy, c. 1914–1950.

Before establishing his reputation as a stained glass artist, Missouri-born Thomas Augustin O'Shaughnessy (1870–1956) studied at the Art Institute and worked as an artist-reporter for the *Chicago Daily News*. Some consider him responsible for the celebration of Columbus Day because of his efforts, beginning in 1894, to save the replicas of Columbus's ships—the Niña, Pinta, and Santa Maria—from being scuttled after the 1893 World's Columbian Exposition. After he staged a spectacular Columbus Day pageant on October 12, 1911, in Grant Park, Mayor Carter Harrison proclaimed Columbus Day a legal holiday for Chicago, a practice soon emulated in other parts of the country.

From his first to his final stained glass commission, O'Shaughnessy's works resembled glass recreations of medieval illuminated manuscripts. Like the borders of the Book of Kells, his colors were clear and bright, with the designs boldly executed and clearly symbolic. Indeed, his first Chicago commission, a memorial window designed in 1914 for the Henry O. Shepard Public School on S. Francisco Avenue, was described as a "translucent mosaic tablet" designed "to represent an illuminated page." The window had been commissioned by the Old-Time Printer's Association in memory of the founder of the Inland Printer Company.

During the 1930s O'Shaughnessy called his studio on W. Superior Street the Ecclesiastical Art Guild. In later years he often used the facilities of Drehobl Bros. Art Glass Company to execute his work.

Local installations of his work still to be seen include: St. Procopius Abbey, Lisle (1916); St. Luke's Church, 528 Lathrop, River Forest (1919); St. Patrick's Church, 718 W. Adams (1921); St. Stephen's Episcopal Church, 3533 N. Albany Avenue (1933); and the Madonna della Strada Chapel, Loyola University (1945–51).

at a glass factory in Kokomo, Indiana, and then used it for his windows.

O'Shaughnessy's most celebrated pot metal window was the McSwiney Memorial Window triptych representing Faith, Hope and Charity in St. Patrick's Church on the corner of West Adams and Desplaines streets. One of the city's oldest public buildings, St. Patrick's Church was built in 1856 by Irish Catholics.

In 1917, when the church was in need of renovation, O'Shaughnessy redecorated the interior by stencilling the walls and installing fifteen large windows featuring designs derived from the Book of Kells, a hand-illuminated manuscript produced by Irish monks during the Middle Ages. O'Shaughnessy had first seen the Book of Kells when he visited Ireland as a student. This experience led to his interest in early Irish art, which became the dominant influence on his work for the remainder of his life.

The large Faith window donated by the artist features a complex of symbols representative of Irish history and culture. Circles, squares, and rectangles form a luminous collage incorporating the Celtic cross; the shamrock (standing for the Trinity); St. Bridget accompanied by two angels giving the world literature, music, and art; and St. Patrick, the patron saint of Ireland. Set into frames of bronze, the decorative panels in the twenty-five-foot-high window are filled with mosaics composed of hundreds of pieces of delicately colored translucent glass, some joined with leadings as slender as a penstroke.

Reflecting his training at The Art Institute of Chicago as a student of Louis Millet, O'Shaughnessy's work was distinguished by fresh interpretations of traditional themes as well as original designs inspired by his patriotism and natural surroundings. In 1919, when he executed *The Immaculate Conception* window for St. Luke's Church on the corner of Lathrop and Lake streets in River Forest, O'Shaughnessy substituted native white morning glories for the lilies traditionally used to symbolize the purity of the Virgin Mary. Beneath the clouds supporting the Virgin he created a scene depicting dawn in the Des Plaines Valley, with the sun's fresh rays bringing life to the flora and fauna typical of Chicago at that time. Like O'Shaughnessy's other windows, it was constructed throughout of American glass.

O'Shaughnessy continued to work until he was in his eighties. His last commission, in 1945–50, was a series of windows illustrating the story of the creation for the Madonna della Strada Chapel of Loyola University on Devon Avenue at Lake Michigan. The painted details were supplied by Thomas S. Snyder, a glass painter with H. Eberhardt & Co. during the day and assistant to O'Shaughnessy in the evening. A perfectionist to the end, O'Shaughnessy worked on the windows for months. As soon as one window was totally assembled, he would examine it in the light and begin breaking out large sections, dissatisfied with the way the glass pieces harmonized or transmitted light. After months of waiting, Father James Mertz, the Jesuit priest respon-

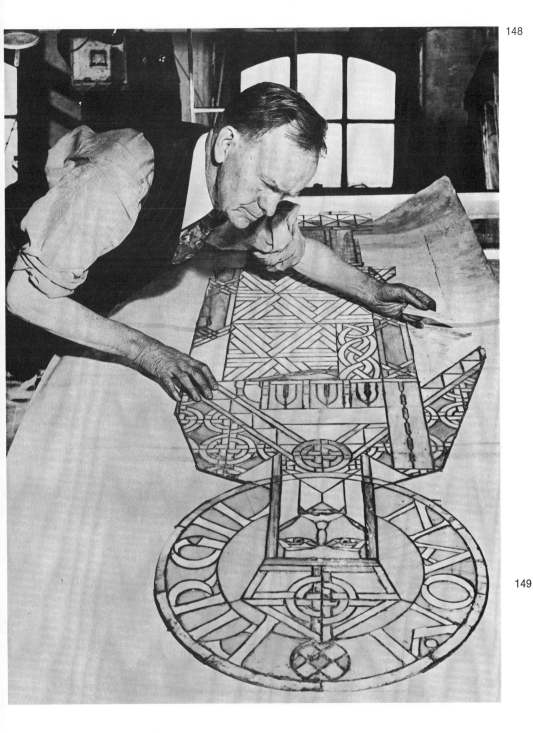

148

149

148. Thomas A. O'Shaughnessy
at work in his studio, c. 1943.
Joseph O'Shaughnessy

149. *McSwiney Memorial
Window*, designed and executed
for St. Patrick's Church by
Thomas A. O'Shaughnessy.
Joseph O'Shaughnessy

sible for the construction of the chapel, grew impatient and complained to the artist's son. Joseph O'Shaughnessy, realizing that his father would never consider the commission finished, went into the studio, removed the windows, and delivered them to the church.

World War I and After

The outbreak of war in Europe in 1914 affected most of the firms engaging in the production of memorial windows. The importation of antique glass, cut jewels, and solder from Germany, Austria, and Hungary was abruptly cut off, causing the price of English and American antique glass to rise considerably as supplies diminished. At the same time, church orders placed with European makers were indefinitely delayed, stimulating the demand for American-made windows. Glass, lead, and labor were all in short supply after the United States entered the war in 1917. Once the war was over, however, there was a flurry of activity as families and congregations sought to honor those who had died in the war by installing memorial windows. Postwar prosperity encouraged the building of new churches, while congregations whose plans had had to be postponed because of the war hurried to install long-awaited stained glass.

On the domestic scene, stained glass continued to enhance the living room windows and bookcase doors of bungalows and modest homes, but was fast becoming passé among the fashionable. To the trend setters of the 1920s, stained glass windows, like Tiffany shades and Mission furniture, symbolized the unsophisticated and somewhat garish taste of the previous generation. As the Prairie School and the Arts and Crafts movements lost their momentum, the glass associated with these styles also fell out of favor.

During these postwar years American Colonial, Tudor, Dutch Colonial, and similar historically based architectural styles became increasingly popular and colorful art glass windows were replaced by clear plate glass or tiny diamond panes. When used in fashionable homes, stained glass tended to be relegated to libraries and recreation rooms. Here tiny circles, diamonds, or rectangles of colored glass picturing knights, heraldic emblems, or literary figures were inset in diamond pane or casement windows. The functional art glass windows of the Prairie School architects were replaced by purely ornamental windows depicting religious, historical, or legendary scenes.

Although the decline in the quality of domestic art glass did not become evident until the late 1920s, it had actually begun earlier. In 1905 the well-known stained glass designer, Harry Eldredge Goodhue of Massachusetts, was already calling attention to the unfortunate effects of the widespread use of badly designed and inferior glass. "The

150. *King Arthur*, one of a series of panels executed by The Linden Company for exhibition at the Century of Progress Exposition, 1933. (23½" x 15¼"). *Frank L. Linden, Jr.*

country has been flooded with tawdry, cheap ornamental 'Art glass,' as it is called, and it is no wonder that the better class of house owners prefer to have their windows of plate glass rather than endanger the otherwise refined effect by the use of leaded glass acquired in the usual way of so much per foot," he complained in the November 1905 *Architectural Record*. But as an art glass producer, he could not help but ask "is it not to be deplored that in most of our expensive residences, where there is no need to calculate the cost of beautiful decoration, we find so little of that art which might add a finishing touch to the loveliness of the whole?"

The debate over what ailed the art glass industry continued through the 1920s. Art glass manufacturers put the blame for the declining interest in domestic glass on the architects who specified inexpensive art glass or none at all; architects in turn criticized the manufacturers for producing badly designed glass and the contractors for substituting cheaper glass than their plans specified; contractors, meanwhile, continued to install whatever the glass producers created or the client desired.

Surprisingly, stained glass was not abandoned by one of the most enterprising designer/craftsmen of the 1920s, a young man named Edgar Miller. Working in every medium from stained glass to carved wood to stone, Miller created interiors that were fresh in concept and unique in design.

In 1927, exactly ten years after he had come to Chicago from Idaho to study at the Art Institute, Miller began a collaboration that resulted in one of his most striking achievements, the exotically remodeled buildings at 155 West Burton Place and 1734 North Wells Street. That year he and portrait painter Sol Kogan began turning an old, red brick house on Burton Place into the first of nine duplex apartments rich with handcarved oak, handpainted glass, and parquet floors. Recognized as novel in their day, the courtyard apartments are now treasured as prime examples of vernacular architecture, and are recognized as the nucleus from which the Old Town artists' colony later emerged. Recalling the project in 1978, Miller explained how the apartments were completed:

> He (Kogan) got the material and I determined how to use it. Practically all of the material was reclaimed, because when a building was demolished, the good wood, tile, and marble used to be saved. So here was second-hand material that didn't cost much, but was distinguished as hell. To use it you just had to have taste and a sense of space. [Alan G. Artner, "Back in Town: Edgar Miller, Design Pioneer." Chicago Tribune, Arts & Fun, July 2, 1978.]

In the windows at the Burton Place and Wells Street apartments, Miller used obscure, rough textured glass of the type commonly

Edgar Miller, 1919–c. 1967.

During a career which began in Chicago in 1917 and extended well into the 1960s, Edgar Miller (b. 1901) worked in many media, from stained glass to carved wood and stone. Born in Idaho, he came to Chicago to study at the Art Institute in 1917. Although he did not remain there long, the Institute eventually awarded Miller three Frank G. Logan medals for his work.

Miller, who had studied china painting as a youth, often applied mineral paints to glass as well as porcelain. During the 1920s he used the facilities of the Hull-House Kilns to fire his work; later he, Taylor Poor, and Joe Faher assisted Eugene Deutch in establishing a pottery which Deutch operated until the 1950s.

Noted for his originality, Miller was frequently commissioned by Howard Van Doren Shaw, Holabird & Root, Andrew Rebori, and other Chicago architects to execute stained glass, sculpture, and murals for their buildings. He also created murals for local restaurants, taverns, and clubs, and painted portraits of many prominent Chicagoans. Two of his most celebrated residential interiors remain at 155 W. Burton Place and 1734 N. Wells Street.

"I got an enormous amount of enjoyment out of doing these things," Miller related in a July 2, 1978, *Chicago Tribune* interview, "but I have never taken them with great seriousness. They were for people who were interested in living in dramatic, charming surroundings, that's all. . . . My great desire was to communicate with others in a common language. The human being who relates to human beings is the one who achieves something."

Miller, who moved to Clearwater, Florida in the 1960s, is now living in San Francisco, California.

153

employed in glazing bathroom windows. He created bold geometric compositions accented with black painted glass and occasional tints of color. Here and there a stylized human figure or whimsical bird, fish or beast appeared, adding a lighthearted touch to the brilliant leaded glass.

Some of Miller's stained glass panels, especially those designed for churches, bear a striking similarity to woodcuts—a resemblance that is not coincidental, since many were derived from woodcut studies. To create this effect, or to give the illusion of watercolor, glass was often painted and fired in a kiln, using techniques that Miller had learned as a young boy when he studied china painting.

Miller's versatility and creativity attracted the attention of some of Chicago's best-known architects, including Howard Van Doren Shaw, Thomas E. Tallmadge, members of the firm of Holabird & Root, and Earl H. Reed, Jr. The latter was so taken with Miller's glass designs that in 1932 he wrote to H. H. Saylor, editor of *Architecture* magazine, suggesting that an article be devoted to the artist's work. After seeing the enclosed photographs Saylor replied: ''You are quite right that that man, Edgar Miller, shows a fresh new note in his glass. By all means see what you can find out.'' In the article he wrote about Miller, Reed reported:

> *True to his type, his productive moments are preceded by deliberate contemplation of the problem to be met in both its structural and decorative aspects. Few or no sketches are made unless others must be let into the secret. Then suddenly, it seems, the composition emerges full-blown, with superb finish, from the material itself. It is common for Miller to proceed boldly in lead and glass, for instance, without benefit of cartoon, matching colors and cutting forms in accordance with a vivid and compelling inner sight.* [Earl H. Reed, Jr. ''Edgar Miller, Designer-Craftsman,'' Architecture *(August 1932): 68*]

In 1925 one of Miller's stained glass panels won the Frank G. Logan Purchase Prize at the Exhibition of Modern Decorative Arts sponsored by The Art Institute of Chicago. Featuring a design of birds, it had the folk-art quality that still characterizes much of Miller's work. Believing that art should be figural rather than abstract because human beings could more readily understand the former, Miller often incorporated super-beings, large-eyed fish, quizzical cats, or similar beasts into his work.

More sophisticated were the large etched and sandblasted panels featuring classical huntresses which Miller designed in 1929–30 for the clerestory of the Diana Court Room in the Michigan Square Building at 540 North Michigan, built for real estate developer Murray Wolbach by architects Holabird & Root but later demolished. In one, Diana, goddess of the hunt, prepared to shoot her bow. Behind her

151. Panel with design of birds in blue, red, yellow, and orange stained and painted glass, designed and executed by Edgar Miller, c. 1925. (27¼″ x 18″). *The Art Institute of Chicago, Frank G. Logan Purchase Prize*

152. Pair of sandblasted and
etched plate glass panels
designed by Edgar Miller for the
clerestory of Diana Court in the
Michigan Square Building, 1929.
(49⅜" x 39⅛"). *The Art
Institute of Chicago, gift of Fred A.
and Harvey A. Goldberg*

her emblems—a star and the moon—shone over a landscape of conventionalized plants. In another panel, Diana held a falcon in her right hand, while a stag stood serenely behind her. Though designed by Miller, the panels were actually executed by a local glass shop, because the Sign and Scene Painters Union (of which Miller was not a member) prevented him from touching the work.

During the postwar years general trends in interior decorating inevitably affected the design of glass lighting fixtures. These changes reflected a new notion of the role of illumination in a modern interior. Earlier in the century designers had concentrated on turning lamps into "objets d'art," considering the design of the lamp itself as important as the way in which it provided light. By the 1920s, however, many designers believed that since the prime purpose of a lamp was to ensure a logical distribution of light, the elements of the fixture should be subordinated to its lighting function. The rays of the electric light bulb were no longer imprisoned behind spectrums of opalescent or richly colored art glass or openwork metal shades; they now were released through domes, triangles, or spheres of opaque or neutral-colored glass of white, gray, or black, or allowed to escape directly upward, where they were softened and diffused by the ceiling.

In the decoration of these new kinds of glass lampshades, the flowers and other natural motifs so highly favored during the previous decades gradually gave way to sunbursts, crescents, or zigzags. Instead of looking to the garden or surrounding prairie, designers now turned to distant places and periods for inspiration—from pre-Columbian America and ancient Egypt to eighteenth century France.

To achieve unique and integrated interiors, Chicago architects and decorators continued to design unique table lamps and lighting fixtures. Always an innovator, Frank Lloyd Wright used opaque white glass as early as 1913 for the table lamps at the Midway Gardens Restaurant. Opaque glass rectangles were used to create octagonal-shaped shades attached to a horizontal arm which could be raised or lowered on a slender, vertical stand. Alfonso Iannelli, who executed much of the modernistic sculpture in Midway Gardens, also designed lighting fixtures, creating surprisingly modern-looking lamps and wall sconces from simple panes of opaque white or subtly tinted glass. Following the lead of architects and decorators, large manufacturers such as R. Williamson & Co. added lines of streamlined modernistic fixtures.

Although visible fixtures remained, there was a new fascination with invisible lighting. As M. J. Wetzel explained in the April 1928 issue of *Lux*, a French magazine devoted to lighting, "It is an advantage to hide the light source, as the effect is more striking when one cannot see its origin. Hence the disappearance of bulbs into walls, ceilings, and behind pilasters where they are masked by diffuser screens."

Skylights, a popular form of indirect lighting which earlier would have featured conventionalized flowers by Healy & Millet or striking linear patterns by Frank Lloyd Wright, became large expanses of clear glass distinguished by texture and bold lead lines. Typical was the skylight designed in 1929 by Chicago architect Jens J. Jensen for the Howard Avenue Trust & Savings Bank (later renamed the North Shore National Bank of Chicago) on Howard Street. Wedges of clear, textured glass were leaded into kaleidoscope patterns, then fitted together to form a dramatic square surrounded by eight circular satellites. Wedge-shaped wall fixtures of opaque white glass reflected light toward the ceiling, and called attention to the silvery frieze whose abstracted landscape combined foliage, clouds, and sky against a cool green plaster wall of ever-widening zigzags.

Toward the end of the 1920s a number of factors combined to bring about the decline of the art glass industry. By then several of the leading stained glass designers had died. Louis J. Millet, who had devoted most of his later years to church commissions, had passed away in 1923. Joseph E. Flanagan, president of Flanagan & Bieden-weg, died suddenly in 1928, the next issue of the *Ornamental Glass Bulletin* unfinished on his desk. His company carried on for a few more decades but eventually dispersed most of its equipment and stock of costly antique glass among the Drehobl Bros. Art Glass Company and other firms.

Nevertheless, most of Chicago's art glass firms prospered until the Stock Market crash of 1929 and the ensuing depression, which brought virtually all building to a halt. Since they depended primarily upon the construction of new churches and new houses for their existence, several art glass companies closed down. Others continued to fill some church commissions but with sharply curtailed staffs.

While leaded art glass fixtures and windows had remained popular throughout the 1920s, they were totally out of style ten years later. Lubomyr Wandzura, now owner of the Giannini & Hilgart art glass studio, recalls how, a decade or so ago, he helped Fritz Hilgart's son, Fred, discard the hundreds of lamp molds that were still in the shop. Similarly, William Scudella, who followed in his father Theodore Scudella's footsteps as a Pullman Palace Car Company employee and today makes Tiffany-style lamps, relates that his first job at the Pullman factory was to break out the stained glass transoms of railroad cars to replace them with panes of clear plate glass.

By the time of the A Century of Progress Exposition in 1933, the decline in the importance of art glass in Chicago was apparent. Instead of the glorious displays of stained glass that had evoked awe and acclaim at the Columbian Exposition, what was to be seen was relegated to the Hall of Religion and the Illinois Host House.

In the Hall of Religion the Drehobl Bros. Art Glass Company displayed a stained glass panel depicting a young boy at prayer. Nearby was a window which had been designed, cut, and fitted together in one evening by members of the Artists Guild of Chicago in the studio of Thomas O'Shaughnessy. Consisting of over 1,000 pieces of O'Shaughnessy's special pot metal glass, the window was dominated by a Celtic cross of intricately interlaced iridescent glass. After the Fair, the window was installed in St. Stephen's Episcopal Church at 3533 North Albany Avenue, where it remains today.

O'Shaughnessy's own work at the Century of Progress was represented in the twenty-one windows he made for the Illinois Host House. He had been promised $5,000 for his work, he told a *Chicago Daily News* reporter who dropped into his studio in 1937, but was never paid a cent. Not knowing where he would get his next month's rent, the indomitable Irishman worked on, as did other stained glass workers in small shops around the city, somehow scraping a living. Their work is to be found throughout the city, waiting to be appreciated anew.

153. Detail of the skylight of clear textured glass designed for the Howard Avenue Trust & Savings Bank by architect Jens J. Jensen, 1929. *CHS, gift of the North Shore National Bank of Chicago*

154. The *Artist Guild* window made of Illinois pot-metal glass and bronze and assembled in one night in Thomas A. O'Shaughnessy's studio for the 1933 Century of Progress Exposition. *Joseph O'Shaughnessy*

(overleaf)
155. Terra cotta ornament on the Wrigley Building, 400 N. Michigan Avenue, executed by the Northwestern Terra Cotta Company, 1920–24. *Trygve Kristiansen*

159

ARCHITECTURAL TERRA COTTA

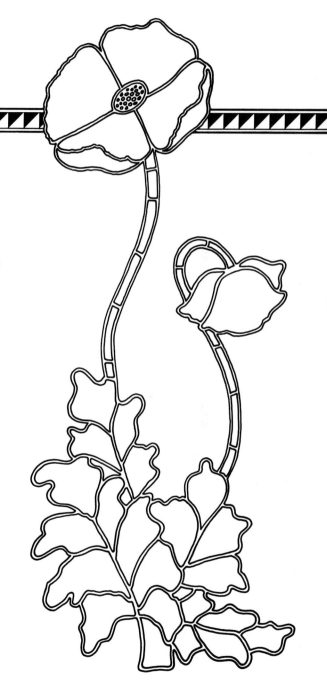

Terra cotta (Latin for "burnt earth") had been used as a building material in other parts of the world since ancient times, but it was not employed for architectural purposes in America until the early 1870s, when the country's first architectural terra cotta factory was established in Chicago. Here rapid rebuilding after the Great Fire, technological progress, and architectural innovations—the same combination of factors that encouraged the widespread use of ornamental glass in private and public buildings—also stimulated experimentation and, in time, extensive use of architectural terra cotta in the city.

Taking advantage of steam-powered machinery, nearby clay deposits, and Chicago's excellent transportation network, local terra cotta manufacturers quickly created a thriving industry. Though wide-ranging in the scope of its activities, Chicago's terra cotta industry involved only four major firms: the original Chicago Terra Cotta Company, its successor the Northwestern Terra Cotta Works, the American Terra Cotta & Ceramic Company, and the Midland Terra Cotta Company.

The Chicago Terra Cotta Company

The story of the Chicago terra cotta industry actually began in Louisville, Kentucky in 1866, when a builder named Joseph N. Glover started producing inexpensive clay imitations of the cast iron or stone urns and statuary then much in favor as embellishments for buildings and gardens.

Glover's method was relatively simple: he obtained a cast iron model of the ornament he wished to reproduce, used it to make a plaster of Paris mold, and then took a clay impression of the interior of the mold. From this process he obtained a clay copy of the iron model, identical in shape but slightly smaller because the clay shrank during firing. Finally the terra cotta piece was painted brown on the outside and coated with pitch on the inside. Now it was ready for the builder—a clay imitation of an iron imitation of a cut stone ornament.

161

Chicago Terra Cotta Company, 1868–1879.

The country's pioneer terra cotta works was founded in Chicago in 1868 by two florists and seed dealers, Albert H. Hovey and J. F. Nichols, to produce horticultural and architectural terra cotta. Before long Sanford E. Loring (of the architectural firm of Loring & Jenney) assumed direction of the Chicago Terra Cotta Company (also known as the Chicago Terra Cotta Works) and of its production of buff and red terra cotta for cornices, door and window caps, and other architectural uses.

In 1870 James Taylor, an English potter, became superintendent of the company which by then was producing tiles, vases, and artwares, as well as architectural ornamentation. A terra cotta cornice made by the firm may be seen on the Capitol in Springfield, Illinois.

Having mastered this technique in Kentucky, Glover moved to Indianapolis, Indiana, which was near a coal mining region where layers of fine quality clay were regularly excavated to get to the coal seams underneath. Here Glover's raw material was quite cheap, since it was removed as a by-product of the coal-mining process.

Glover's move to Indianapolis increased his business prospects but not his capital. When two prosperous Chicago florists and seed dealers, Albert H. Hovey and J. F. Nichols, made an offer to buy his operation in 1868, Glover sold his company but agreed to stay on as superintendent. Hovey and Nichols were anxious to expand the production of horticultural wares, but within a year they discovered that it would be more profitable to move the terra cotta factory to Chicago, their principal market. Freight rates made it cheaper to transport the raw materials—both the clay and coal for fuel—to Chicago than to export the finished terra cotta from Indianapolis.

Soon after, the works were relocated in Chicago at the corner of West 15th and Laflin streets on the city's West Side. The operation was named the Chicago Terra Cotta Company and shares were sold to finance it. Roofing manufacturer Samuel Barrett, who put up the most capital, was named president; J. F. Nichols became secretary; and Joseph Glover remained superintendent. The most important addition was Sanford E. Loring, who was installed as treasurer. A practicing architect, Loring had been a student of John M. Van Osdel (known as Chicago's first architect) and was, at the time, in partnership with William LeBaron Jenney, who later designed the first metal-framed skyscraper.

Secretary Nichols, anxious to expand the operation of the new company, traveled to Europe, where terra cotta had long been used for architectural purposes and convinced Giovanni Meli, a skillful clay modeler, to come to Chicago. In his three years at the factory Meli created numerous original designs for statues, urns, fountains, and vases, as well as window caps and trim. However, the quality of the terra cotta was rather inferior and the company soon went into debt.

But Loring remained confident that terra cotta could become an excellent construction material if only the Chicago company could improve the quality of its product. Seeking advice, he wrote to John M. Blashfield, proprietor of England's largest terra cotta works. Blashfield referred the letter to James Taylor, then superintendent of one of his works, who was already planning to emigrate to America.

In Blashfield's factory in England, James Taylor had worked on the terra cotta ornament shipped to the United States for the construction of the Museum of Fine Arts in Boston, one of the first American buildings to incorporate this material. Arriving in the United States, Taylor first tried to establish a terra cotta factory in New York but, unable to interest a backer, continued on to Chicago. In August 1870 he was appointed superintendent of Loring's terra cotta works.

Under Taylor's supervision the old open-fire kilns were replaced with English muffle kilns and new methods were introduced in the preparation of clay and the manufacture of finished stock. These changes, combined with expanded facilities, soon enabled the works to produce architectural terra cotta comparable in quality to the English product. One of the few commercial concerns to escape the Chicago Fire of 1871, the Chicago Terra Cotta Company received several large orders for terra cotta as the city began to rebuild its commercial and residential areas after the catastrophe. Because of the great post-Fire demand, Loring gave up his architectural practice in the spring of 1872 and became president of the expanding company.

The greatest demand at the time was for terra cotta building cornices, which had important cost and weight advantages over the more customary galvanized iron or stone cornices. Although a single piece of terra cotta cost about the same as a comparable piece of sandstone or limestone, the cost of the terra cotta product was greatly reduced when a number of identical pieces were required. Moreover, terra cotta weighed less than stone so that walls and foundations could be made lighter, which facilitated construction and reduced the cost of the building. By 1877 the cost differential had become so great that John C. Cochrane, architect of the Illinois State Capitol, testifying before a Senate committee considering the approval of the Chicago Terra Cotta Company's contract for supplying a terra cotta cornice for the Capitol, stated: "I suppose a cornice that cost $10 a foot in terra cotta would cost $100 in stone, so that you will see that no man could afford a stone cornice unless it was very plain." The result was that Illinois's Capitol received a terra cotta cornice.

During the 1870s active competition among terra cotta, iron, and stone for use as architectural embellishment encouraged Loring to develop a variety of products that could be made more cheaply than their iron or stone equivalents. But he also had to persuade builders to use the new material. "In those days it was necessary to convert the architect and hypnotize the owner in order to get a contract," Harry J. Lucas, a pioneer of Chicago's terra cotta industry, told historian Walter Geer. Loring must have done just that, for the factory was seldom short of work.

Within a short time after the Fire, Chicago Terra Cotta had developed a number of stock patterns, particularly window and door caps, and was producing large quantities of hand- and machine-pressed ornamental tiles. Porous terra cotta blocks for fireproofing cast iron columns were made using a process patented by Loring. The firm also made glazed brick, trimmings, hip-rolls, crestings for large buildings, and red chimney groups. The demand for chimney tops was particularly brisk and constant, requiring the company to keep a special wagon on the road equipped with ladders and scaffolding. The factory also continued to cast garden ornaments

156

157

156. Page illustrating terra cotta window caps from an 1874 Chicago Terra Cotta Company catalog. *Trygve Kristiansen*

157. Section of a terra cotta spandrel executed by the Northwestern Terra Cotta Company for the Irwin Building designed by Cyrus P. Thomas, 1880. *Mr. and Mrs. Timothy Samuelson*

and statuary and, in addition, produced redware vases, water coolers, and tablewares.

By 1876 the Chicago Terra Cotta Company included a department for throwing redware, facilities for grinding the materials to be mixed with the clay, a modeling room or studio, coal sheds, a 15 h.p. steam engine, a small experimental glazing kiln, and a work force of more than seventy-five. While most of the work could be performed by semi- or unskilled laborers, the modeler who created the original clay model had to have considerable artistic skill. In 1876, when superintendent James Taylor described the works in the December issue of the *American Architect*, the company's chief modelers were James Legge, a former stonecarver, and Isaac E. Scott, an architect and woodcarver. Taylor characterized the two men as "adepts in the modern Gothic school."

Manufacturing Terra Cotta, 1876

While manufacturers used molds and some labor-saving machinery, the early terra cotta products were essentially handmade. At the Chicago Terra Cotta works, both architectural and horticultural wares were made from buff or red-colored clays obtained from Indiana. To minimize shrinkage, ensure even drying, and give added strength to architectural terra cotta, pure sand and "grog" (pulverized terra cotta) were added to the clay. In the making of statuary and other art wares boiled slip (liquid clay) was used because it created a fine smooth surface and produced uniform coloration.

The clay and mineral components were first ground to a powder in crushers which resembled coffee mills. The powder was then dumped on the floor and water added. Workers mixed the powder and water to the proper consistency by tramping on the mixture with their bare feet. Full-size clay models were made to shrinkage scale (12¾" to one foot) for each different shape, and the plaster molds were made using these models. Next, clay was pressed into the mold to a thickness of about one inch and clay partitions were inserted so that the final product would be a terra cotta block, hollow except for an interior grillwork. The blocks were kept small to prevent the material from twisting during firing. Thus a large ornament would often consist of several small blocks fitted together. For overhanging ornaments, such as a cornice, small holes were left in the interior partitions of the blocks for the insertion of the metal fittings used to anchor the terra cotta blocks to the building.

After the clay stiffened it was removed from the mold, retouched, and allowed to dry. Exposed surfaces were coated with a liquid slip, which, during the subsequent firing process, developed into a thin protective glaze. For the firing, the clay pieces were placed in

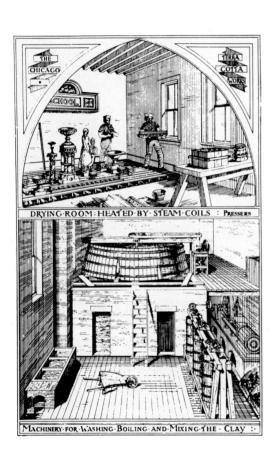

DRYING·ROOM·HEATED·BY·STEAM·COILS : PRESSERS

MACHINERY·FOR·WASHING·BOILING·AND·MIXING·THE·CLAY

158. Woodcut showing workrooms at the Chicago Terra Cotta Works from the December 30, 1876, *American Architect*. Ryerson and Burnham Libraries, The Art Institute of Chicago

164

a huge, beehive-shaped muffle kiln and subjected to temperatures gradually raised to 2,000 degrees Fahrenheit or more, depending upon the particular type of clay and glaze used.

After the firing, the kiln was allowed to cool slowly, a process which took several days. The terra cotta was then laid out like pieces of a puzzle and location numbers were painted on each segment to indicate its position on the building for which it was intended. Where required, the joints were squared or cut to proper alignment and size since an exact fit was essential to ensure that moisture did not seep between the blocks.

For transportation to the building site the terra cotta was securely packed in hay and braced to prevent shifting. At the site the terra cotta blocks were piled on wooden runners according to their destined location on the building. To ensure accurate setting and effective pointing of the mortar joints, the Chicago Terra Cotta Company employed its own staff of skilled masons to erect the terra cotta.

By 1876 the now thriving terra cotta firm was supplying large quantities of terra cotta for local building and was shipping even larger quantities to locations outside of Chicago, to clients as far away as Massachusetts, Utah, and Texas. A year later, in 1877, Loring took advantage of a large contract to supply terra cotta for two residences and a high school in Boston to expand his business.

Finding it impractical to ship the material from Chicago, Loring decided to establish a branch of his terra cotta factory in Boston. He was able to lease a part of the Boston Fire Brick Company, to which he moved men, tools, and materials from Chicago. His brother, Edward Loring, stayed behind to supervise the Chicago works. James Taylor, who had retired to New Jersey earlier that year, was persuaded to oversee the Boston branch. Under his supervision the Boston works succeeded in producing an excellent gray terra cotta for the school. Shortly afterward the firm received several large contracts to produce terra cotta for a dormitory at Brown University and for the Hotel Dorrance—both in Providence, Rhode Island—as well as for the Morse Building in New York.

Although the Boston enterprise started out well, a dispute over money between Loring and the Boston Fire Brick Company ended in the closing of the Boston works. Partly as a result of the financial losses incurred by the Boston operation and partly, according to a contemporary, "due to an unfortunate blow he had received on the head," Loring's business dealings became a tangle of broken promises and unpaid debts. In 1879 the Chicago Terra Cotta Company was liquidated. Loring resumed his architectural practice but, except for writing a series of articles on fireproof construction, had little more to do with the terra cotta business from then on. Nevertheless, he had, to quote his contemporary, Harry J. Lucas, "lifted the craft to a point where rapid development was possible."

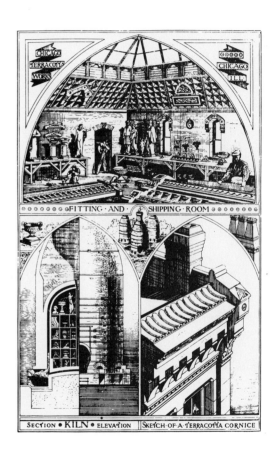

159. The Chicago Terra Cotta Works as depicted in the December 30, 1876, *American Architect. Ryerson and Burnham Libraries, The Art Institute of Chicago*

160

161

160. Loading the tunnel kiln at
the Northwestern Terra Cotta
Company, c. 1925. *Trygve
Kristiansen*

161. Grinding the edges of terra
cotta blocks to ensure a perfect
fit at the Northwestern Terra Cotta
Company, c. 1925. *Trygve
Kristiansen*

163

162. The modeling room at the Northwestern Terra Cotta Company, c. 1925. John Sand, who worked for the firm until it closed, is the fourth modeler from the left. *Trygve Kristiansen*

163. Workmen in the fitting room at the Northwestern Terra Cotta Company hand-number pieces of terra cotta to indicate their eventual placement on a building, c. 1925. *Trygve Kristiansen*

True, Brunkhorst & Company, 1877–1886.
True, Hottinger & Company, 1886–1887.
Northwestern Terra Cotta Company, 1888–1956.

In 1877 John R. True, John Brunkhorst, Gustav Hottinger, and Henry Rohkam—all former employees of the Chicago Terra Cotta Works (officially True, Brunkhorst & Company and later True, Hottinger & Company) to produce architectural terra cotta and garden ornaments. The firm incorporated as the Northwestern Terra Cotta Company in 1888 and by 1927 had become the largest terra cotta manufacturer in the United States, with a main factory at 2525 Clybourn and branch factories in Denver, St. Louis, and Chicago Heights. Northwestern furnished the terra cotta for many important Chicago buildings, including the Rookery, the Tacoma, the Railway Exchange Building, the Wrigley Building, the Blackstone Hotel, the Merchandise Mart, and the Carbide & Carbon Building.

164. Buff terra cotta sample tile from the Northwestern Terra Cotta Works, c. 1884. (5¼″ x 4″ x ⅞″). CHS

The Northwestern Terra Cotta Works [True, Brunkhorst & Company]

In 1877 John R. True, Gustav Hottinger, John Brunkhorst, and two other employees left the Chicago Terra Cotta Company to establish the firm of True, Brunkhorst & Company, not knowing that their enterprise would shortly become the successor rather than the competitor of the first Chicago works. Establishing themselves in a two-story brick factory at the junction of Lincoln Avenue and Wells Street, the men produced a fine grade of architectural terra cotta, although the bulk of their work was horticultural ware which could easily be shipped to the many greenhouses located northwest of the plant. When Loring went out of business, True, Brunkhorst & Company found itself with calls for terra cotta in excess of its kiln capacity. The fledgling firm solved this problem by leasing the old Chicago Terra Cotta plant at the corner of West 15th and Laflin streets and hiring extra help. Calling itself the Northwestern Terra Cotta Works the new company soon found itself with a thriving business. By 1883 the company was able to build a large new factory on the corner of Clybourn Avenue and Wrightwood Avenue in the northern suburb of Lake View and to erect four large kilns using brick made on the premises.

The owners of the Northwestern Terra Cotta Works were highly aware of the importance of advertising and made the name of the company known throughout the country by means of catalogs, samples, and personal calls. An illustrated catalog which appeared in December 1884 showed dozens of stock horticultural and architectural terra cotta designs, including chimney pots, columns, coping, cornices, and decorative medallions. The firm also made up terra cotta sample tiles which it distributed to architects and prospective clients.

By May 1884 the Northwestern Terra Cotta Works was working on more than fifty contracts for such buildings as the new Chicago Board of Trade, the Royal Insurance Building, the Pullman Palace Car Company offices, and for ornament for the residences of Mrs. Catherine Price, George M. Barber, and Walter S. Peck. Terra cotta proved ideal for embellishing commercial structures and for helping create the picturesque Queen Anne look then so popular for private residences.

By 1886 the Northwestern Terra Cotta Works could send *The Inland Architect and Builder* a list of twenty-five buildings located in various places from Chicago to Minnesota for which it was making terra cotta. The company reported:

The demand for our red and brown semi-glazed terra-cotta is such this year that we were obliged to buy the works on corner West Fifteenth and Laflin streets (the old Chicago Terra Cotta Works), and build two new kilns at our works on corner Clybourn and Wrightwood avenues, giving us in all fourteen kilns, and enabling us to supply our clients with usual promptness. [The Inland Architect *VII, no. 11 (July 1886): 97*]

In January 1888, nine years after its founding, the firm finally incorporated under the name of the Northwestern Terra Cotta Company. With contracts for several major buildings in hand the firm completed its reorganization just in time to face its first major competitor, the American Terra Cotta & Ceramic Company.

The American Terra Cotta & Ceramic Company

Chicago's third major terra cotta works, the American Terra Cotta & Ceramic Company, was an outgrowth of the Spring Valley Tile Works founded in 1881 by William Day Gates in Spring Valley, McHenry County, forty-five miles northwest of Chicago. That year Gates had inherited a sizeable amount of land in that area and gave up his Chicago law practice to develop the extensive clay deposits on his property. Purchasing a nearby abandoned sawmill, he revamped and equipped it with machinery necessary to produce terra cotta drain tiles, a product much in demand. The old mill equipment was used to grind the clay, and drying rooms and kilns were erected on the site. As Gates explained in 1930:

Just because I didn't know any better and as a dam by a millsite was in no manner a Terra Cotta factory by a damsite, I remodeled it into a drain tile factory using water power, then later into the manufacture of Terra Cotta and pottery, building on largely, installing steam, and at first using the local clay. [*Lowell Albert Nye,* McHenry County, Illinois, 1832–1968 (*Woodstock: McHenry County Board of Supervisors, 1968): 795*]

Changing the name of the company from Spring Valley to Terra Cotta Tile Works and the name of the place to Terra Cotta, Gates produced tiles, brick, pottery, and architectural terra cotta. Favored by a number of circumstances, the company prospered. It enjoyed both a good location—the Chicago and Northwestern Railway crossed its property—and abundant natural resources. Moreover, Gates provided skillful management, maintaining the company's main business and sales office in Chicago where he could meet with architects and contractors and keep abreast of local building developments.

In 1887, when a fire partially destroyed the works, Gates rebuilt and enlarged the factory and renamed the company the American Terra Cotta & Ceramic Company. The new factory was equipped with steam-powered machinery for grinding and mixing clay, large modeling and drying rooms, and a laboratory for experimenting with clay bodies and glazes. An old farmhouse across the road was turned into The

Spring Valley Tile Works, 1881.
Terra Cotta Tile Works, c. 1881–1888.
American Terra Cotta & Ceramic Company, 1888–1966.
Founded by William Day Gates (1852–1935), the American Terra Cotta & Ceramic Company made sewer tiles, architectural terra cotta, and Teco art pottery at its factory in Terra Cotta (near Crystal Lake), Illinois. A family-owned concern, Gates's four sons—Ellis, Neil, Major Earl, and Paul—each of whom had attended manual training or ceramic schools, assisted in the operation of the company and its branch, the Indianapolis Terra Cotta Company, acquired in 1918. These firms produced and installed the terra cotta for a number of large buildings, including the Chicago and Northwestern Terminal, the Great Lakes Naval Station, and the Illinois Naval Armory, and for many banks, schools, and office buildings in Chicago and in St. Paul and Minneapolis, Minnesota.

During the Depression the firm was purchased by George A. Berry II, who began to use its kilns for the heat treating of steel. The last terra cotta was produced in 1966, and the factory site is now the headquarters of the American Steel Treating Company owned by George A. Berry III.

Gates Potteries (see page 55), where modelers and Gates himself created vases and other artwares between orders for architectural terra cotta. In the surrounding fields grew the hay used for packing the terra cotta for shipment. The idyllic setting was made complete by a small terra cotta chapel erected by the workers alongside a lake.

In spite of its rustic setting Gates's business—like the Northwestern Terra Cotta Company—had energetic and enterprising leadership as well as modern equipment. This put both firms in an ideal position to profit from the demand for clay products associated with attempts to fireproof buildings in the 1880s. Whereas terra cotta had initially been used for ornamental purposes only, once its potential as a plastic fireproofing material was discovered, it quickly became prized for its utilitarian qualities as well.

Fireproofing the City

Prior to the Great Chicago Fire of October 1871, stone, iron, and brick were commonly believed to be fireproof building materials. Inspection of the fire ruins, however, showed broken bricks, crumbled granite walls, and twisted iron columns which had melted and given way. From the disaster architects learned the need to protect all cast iron structural work with a sheathing of fire clay, terra cotta, or brick.

The innovative use of terra cotta as a fireproofing material has been attributed to three different men. One was George H. Johnson, who in 1852 had migrated from England to New York City, where he became manager of the Architectural Iron Works. Eight years later Johnson moved to Chicago and, in partnership with architect John M. Van Osdel, built four cast iron front buildings on Lake Street. In 1870 Johnson obtained the first of four patents on fireproof hollow tile.

When the Great Fire broke out on October 8, Johnson was in New York. Returning immediately to Chicago he surveyed the fire ruins on October 12, and soon thereafter came up with the idea of using hollow, hard burned clay as a covering for cast iron columns and beams as well as for creating a fireproof floor by putting terra cotta tiles between the beams. He also devised terra cotta tiles for partitions and for backing up exterior walls. A year later these ideas were incorporated by Van Osdel in the construction of the Kendall Building, an eight-story structure begun in 1872 at the southwest corner of Washington and Dearborn. On the interior, iron I-beams and vertical columns were encased in terra cotta tiles and elongated tiles were fitted together to form arched ceilings, partitions, and floors, inaugurating a system of fireproof construction that would become universal until the adoption of reinforced concrete around 1910.

Under Johnson's direction, fireproofing was also provided for the Cook County Jail and Court House. In 1874, when business fell off,

165. Green glazed plaque from a gatepost at the entrance to the American Terra Cotta & Ceramic Company factory in Terra Cotta, Illinois. (h: 18½″). *George A. Berry III, TC Industries, Inc.*

Johnson returned to New York City, but came back to Chicago three years later and went into partnership with George M. Moulton. In 1879 Johnson died and a year later Moulton joined with his late partner's son, Ernest V. Johnson, and A. T. Griffin to form the Pioneer Fire proof Construction Company, with offices on Clark Street and a manufactory and clay mines at Ottawa, Illinois.

The second man credited with inventing terra cotta fireproofing was Johnson's associate, John M. Van Osdel, who at the time of the 1871 Fire was supervising the construction of the Palmer House hotel. Seeing the fire approach, Van Osdel gathered his plans and record books and took them to the basement of the building. After digging a pit, he placed the documents inside and covered them with sand and a layer of damp clay. The records survived the fire and thus suggested a method of fireproofing which Van Osdel then adopted in the construction of the Kendall Building.

However, in Walter E. Geer's *The Story of Terra Cotta,* J. H. Junge and Harry J. Lucas, contemporaries of Sanford E. Loring in the terra cotta business, related that Loring conceived of fireproof construction in association with architect Peter B. Wight. But although Loring had developed and patented a process for porous terra cotta by 1876, his scheme for fireproofing was not publicized until 1886, when it was incorporated in the light court of the Rookery building. It was not published until the December 1887 issue of *Building & Architectural Weekly.*

While the initiator of the use of terra cotta for fireproofing remains in dispute, there is little doubt that the tremendous expansion of the terra cotta industry during the 1880s and 1890s was intimately linked with the development of metal frame or ''Chicago construction.'' In 1884–85, in the Home Insurance Building, Chicago architect William LeBaron Jenney had demonstrated how a metal frame could be used to construct tall buildings. Jenney's success led to a boom in sky-scraper construction which in turn gave a strong stimulus to the terra cotta industry, since this material could supply the insulation required by iron and steel members.

In 1886 the passage of a city ordinance requiring all buildings in Chicago over ninety feet high to be absolutely fireproof further stimulated the expansion of the terra cotta industry. Primitive fire fighting equipment, combined with the growing numbers of tall buildings, had prompted revision of the building codes for public safety.

While both the Northwestern Terra Cotta Works and the American Terra Cotta & Ceramic Company made porous tiles of the type used in fireproofing, several other firms devoted themselves exclusively to producing this particular type of insulation. Among the most important were the Wight Fireproofing Company, organized in 1879 by architect Peter B. Wight, and the Illinois Terra Cotta Lumber Company, founded in 1884 in the town of Pullman.

166. Advertisement for the Pioneer Fire proof Construction Co. from the April 1885 *Inland Architect & Builder. CHS*

Terra Cotta Skyscrapers

Beginning in the 1880s the local use of terra cotta increased more rapidly than that of any other building material. This was because architects of what became known as the Chicago School of Architecture specified that it be used to sheathe the steel or iron construction frame carrying the exterior walls of the tall buildings which began to dominate the city's business district. Terra cotta tiles were used to fireproof the building's interior structural members, while the exteriors of the "skyscrapers" tended to be faced with pressed brick and blocks of terra cotta rather than the more traditional marble, iron, or stone.

Builders of skyscrapers found terra cotta an attractive medium because of its lightness, durability, and potential for decorative uses—attributes which stemmed from the nature of the material. Since terra cotta blocks had to be made hollow and only moderately thick to facilitate firing, a given bulk of terra cotta weighed only half as much as a piece of stone of the same size. Secondly, terra cotta retained its handsome surface and crisp details longer than other building materials. But, above all, its plastic qualities enabled architects to use terra cotta to embellish their structures with artistic and highly original ornament. Thus economy, safety, and appearance—important considerations in skyscraper construction—suggested the use of terra cotta as an ideal building material.

Burnham & Root had first used terra cotta in combination with brick in 1880 in the Grannis Block, a seven-story office building housing a bank above a row of storefronts on North Dearborn Street. "Here our originality began to show," Daniel Burnham told his biographer Charles Moore, "we made the front of the building all red, the terra-cotta exactly matching the brick. It was a wonder. Everybody went to see it, and the town was proud of it."

The Montauk Block, also designed by Burnham & Root and erected in 1881–82 on West Monroe Street, was the first building to be called a "skyscraper." It was fireproofed internally with hollow terra cotta tile and its red brick exterior incorporated bands of terra cotta and decorative iron work which divided the stories into four layers. Within five years several other skyscrapers were completed, including the Mallers Building (John J. Flanders, 1884); the Pullman Building (Solon S. Beman, 1884); the Home Insurance Building (William LeBaron Jenney, 1885); the Insurance Exchange (Burnham & Root, 1885); the Rookery (Burnham & Root, 1885); and the Tacoma (Holabird & Roche, 1889). The Rookery was the first to incorporate highly glazed terra cotta in its inner light court, the result of considerable experimentation with clay bodies and glazes by the Northwestern Terra Cotta Works.

The first all-steel framed skyscraper, the ten-story Rand McNally Building designed by Burnham & Root in 1888 and completed in 1890, was also the first building to use all terra cotta façades on the street

167. The Mallers Building, 1884.
CHS

172

169

168. Terra cotta ornamenting the facade of the Rookery, 209 S. LaSalle St., executed by the Northwestern Terra Cotta Company, 1885. *The Richard Nickel Committee*

169. Detail of terra cotta executed for the light court of the Rookery by the Northwestern Terra Cotta Company, 1885. *Photo by William R. Boles*

173

170. Entrance to the Rand
McNally Building showing terra
cotta executed by the Northwestern Terra Cotta Company, 1890.
Trygve Kristiansen

174

ronts, a practice quickly adopted by other builders. Located on West Adams Street, the Rand McNally Building, since razed, must have been particularly attractive to passersby for, according to Root's biographer Donald Hoffman, its four small entrances were emphasized by terra cotta "foliation particularly exquisite at the capitals, where the forms seemed in the very process of bubbling forth from the material."

By 1900 the Loop was dominated by steel-framed structures sheathed in glazed brick and terra cotta. Several buildings now considered landmarks of the Chicago School were particularly rich in terra cotta ornamentation. These included the previously mentioned Rookery; the Manhattan (William LeBaron Jenney, 1890); the Woman's Temple (Burnham & Root, 1892); the Schiller Theatre (Adler & Sullivan, 1892); the Venetian (Holabird & Roche, 1892); the Masonic Temple (Burnham & Root, 1892); the Chicago Stock Exchange, (Adler & Sullivan, 1894); the Reliance (D. H. Burnham & Co., 1890, 1895); the Marquette (Holabird & Roche, 1895); and the Fisher Building (D. H. Burnham & Co., 1896). The terra cotta used in the Venetian Building was supplied by the American Terra Cotta & Ceramic Company; the terra cotta used for all the others was produced by the Northwestern Terra Cotta Company.

When terra cotta was used for tall office buildings in the early 1880s, it was often in the form of a crest of large, heavy ornament along the roof-line in shades of buff or brick red. By 1890, however, architects tended to sheathe entire buildings in terra cotta of one color, particularly white or cream. In many cases, as can be seen from the illustrations on the following pages, a terra cotta skin followed the contours of the steel frame and a large percentage of the skyscraper's exterior was filled in with glass.

When D. H. Burnham & Co. recommended terra cotta as a practical and economical façade for the Reliance Building—a columnar skyscraper decorated with French Gothic details—the reaction of the Economist (August 1894) was highly favorable. "This is an innovation. It is indestructible and as hard and as smooth as any porcelain ware. It will be washed by every rainstorm and may if necessary be scrubbed like a dinner plate." The January 1895 Architectural Record also commented on the Reliance's glossy façade, predicting that "if it stands the test of Chicago's severe winters and changeable climate, there can be no possible doubt but what as a material for exterior construction it will be largely used in such cities as are afflicted with a smoky, sooty atmosphere."

Two years later, in 1896, D. H. Burnham & Co. again chose terra cotta for a similar skyscraper designed for manufacturer Lucius G. Fisher. Inspired by the owner's name, the architects selected a pale salmon terra cotta for the façade and created gargoyle-like sea monsters and exotic fishes to enhance its richly modeled Gothic details.

In 1904 D. H. Burnham & Co. and the Northwestern Terra Cotta

172

174

171

171. Terra cotta on the exterior of the Marquette Building, executed by the Northwestern Terra Cotta Company, 1895. *Photo by Barbara Crane for the Commission on Chicago Historical and Architectural Landmarks*

172. Terra cotta ornamentation on the Fisher Building, 343 S. Dearborn Street, executed by the Northwestern Terra Cotta Company, 1896. *Photo by Barbara Crane for the Chicago Commission on Historical and Architectural Landmarks*

173. Entrance to the Manhattan Building, 423–39 S. Dearborn Street, as it appeared in 1947. *CHS*

174. Red terra cotta trim on the Germania Club building, 108 W. Germania Place, executed by the Northwestern Terra Cotta Company, 1889. *Photo by William R. Boles*

173

175. The Reliance Building, 32
N. State Street, 1890–95. *CHS,
gift of Albert L. Straus*

176. The Studebaker Building,
c. 1895. Designed by Solon S.
Beman, its terra cotta trim was
executed by the Northwestern
Terra Cotta Company. *CHS*

177

179

180

177. Bas relief figure in the lobby of the Railway Exchange Building. *Photo by William R. Boles*

178. The city office of the Northwestern Terra Cotta Company in the Railway Exchange Building as pictured in Northwestern's catalog, c. 1910. *CHS, gift of Robert A. Furhoff*

179. White glazed terra cotta lobby of the Railway Exchange Building. *Photo by William R. Boles*

180. The Railway Exchange Building, 80 E. Jackson Street, executed by the Northwestern Terra Cotta Company, 1904. *CHS*

Company introduced yet another use of terra cotta by employing it on the interior as well as the exterior of the new Railway Exchange Building, erected to house the business offices of most of the railroads centered in Chicago. Here Burnham took advantage of the easy maintenance and excellent light-reflecting qualities of terra cotta. Highly glazed light cream terra cotta covered the simple crenelated façade of the seventeen-story building, the top floor of which featured a band of large round windows. Inside, a vestibule enhanced by bas-relief figures of Art, Science, and Industry led to a spacious rotunda, white in finish and cooly attractive. The floor and wide staircase were of marble, but the wall and ornamental balustrades were of cream terra cotta. Rising above this, the walls of the light court were constructed of highly glazed enameled brick, making the interior offices light and cheerful. Upstairs, on the fourteenth floor, enameled tiles in tones of green, cream, wine, and tan brightened the walls of the downtown office of the Northwestern Terra Cotta Company.

A few years earlier, in 1897, the American Terra Cotta & Ceramic Company had produced enameled terra cotta details for the interior of the new Illinois Central underground station on Van Buren Street. Terra cotta newel posts and signs guided passengers into a waiting room whose elaborate columns were encased in glossy terra cotta. Enameled terra cotta was soon being widely promoted for use in hospitals, indoor swimming pools, gymnasiums, breweries, and restaurants because it was so easy to clean.

During the 1890s terra cotta was widely used to ornament houses and especially to give modest structures a more impressive appearance. It was occasionally used as a substitute for brick and stone in the construction of private residences. The expense of building an entire house of terra cotta tended to limit their ownership to officers of terra cotta companies. In 1892 William D. Gates, president of the American Terra Cotta & Ceramic Company, impressed contemporaries by moving his family into an all terra cotta residence in suburban Hinsdale. Designed by Jenney & Mundie, the large two-story house featured elaborately trimmed windows and an exotically ornamented colonnaded porch. Four years later Nathan Herzog, treasurer of the company, erected a similar Jenney & Mundie home on West Adams Street near fashionable Garfield Park. Gustav Hottinger, Fritz Wagner, and Adolph F. Hottinger, president, vice-president, and secretary-treasurer, respectively, of the Northwestern Terra Cotta Company, walked to work from impressive terra cotta-encrusted residences on Oakdale Avenue. On Wellington Avenue stood the elegant terra cotta home of one of the firm's original founders, John R. True.

Quite apart from its growing importance as a building material, terra cotta continued to be used for vases, garden pottery, decorative plaques, and statuary. An outstanding example of the latter was a bust of John Brunkhorst, one of the Northwestern Terra Cotta Company

181. Terra cotta house built by William Day Gates in suburban Hinsdale, 1892. *Family of William Day Gates*

179

182

183

182. Buff terra cotta bust of John Brunkhorst (1850–1886) executed at the Northwestern Terra Cotta Company by Frederick Almenraeder, 1886. (h: 27″). *CHS, gift of Mrs. Frieda Brunkhorst Hahne and Mrs. Alma Brunkhorst Piggot*

183. The Northwestern Terra Cotta Company's display at the 1893 World's Columbian Exposition. *CHS, gift of Mrs. Frieda Brunkhorst Hahne*

founders. Executed by a company modeler, the bust stood at the entrance of the elaborate terra cotta pavilion erected by the firm at the 1893 World's Columbian Exposition. In reviewing the prize-winning exhibit, the *American Architect and Building News* commented

> *One very charming little exhibit was that made by the North-western Terra-cotta Company. The exhibit was in the form of a small Gothic structure, consisting of eight arches and eight dividing columns, on which rested an open-work ribbed roof.... The result was most satisfactory because well done. Above each column small Gothic arches were introduced, in the niches of which stood little figures quite in keeping with the spirit of the whole, each bearing in his arms some ornamental bit of terra cotta, a vase, a small bust, an architectural ornament, or what not.* [American Architect and Building News *(November 11, 1893): 73-74*]

By 1893 terra cotta had made such an impact on Chicago's architectural and business communities that terra cotta and white were chosen as the official colors for the decorations at the Columbian Exposition. Some Chicagoans, of course, criticized the selection, calling it a "liver and lard" color scheme befitting the "hog butcher of the world." But, predictably, the editor of *The Clay Record,* organ of the brick and tile industries, found it a most appropriate choice. Terra cotta, he declared, was "symbolical of commercial enterprise and of culture, of brick skyscrapers and of fashionable gloves."

While Chicago's terra cotta-blushed skyline may have "symbolized" commercial enterprise and culture, it directly reflected the work of architects like William LeBaron Jenney and Henry Ives Cobb and firms such as Holabird & Roche, Burnham & Root, and Adler & Sullivan. Under the guidance of Daniel Burnham (who had started his career in the office of Loring & Jenney) and John Wellborn Root (a brilliant designer who had worked for Peter B. Wight) the firm of Burnham & Root could claim responsibility for many of the massive brick and terra cotta skyscrapers which dominated Chicago's Loop. However, it is with the firm of Adler & Sullivan that the use of terra cotta is now most often associated.

During a productive fifteen-year association, lasting from 1880 through 1895, Dankmar Adler became known for his technical ingenuity while Louis H. Sullivan earned praise for his imaginative decorative designs. During the mid-1880s when Adler & Sullivan were establishing their architectural practice, the buildings they designed often featured terra cotta ornament. Sullivan, who was primarily responsible for the ornamentation, favored conventionalized motifs derived from botanical forms. For example, the deep red terra cotta spandrels of the Troescher Building on South Market Street (demolished 1978), and the trim of the Ruben Rubel house on South Ashland

Avenue—both designed in 1884—displayed angular floral abstractions, incorporating shells and snake-like spirals. But in the course of the next few years Sullivan's botanical motifs gradually became more natural and luxuriant, taking the form of elongated buds, sinuous tendrils, and sharply pointed leaves.

A further evolution of Sullivan's style of terra cotta ornamentation became evident in the early 1890s as geometrical forms began to supplement the botanical motifs. For example, the Schiller Theatre Building (later renamed the Garrick), designed in 1892 to house Chicago's German Opera Company, featured large geometrical forms intertwined with small clusters of curly leaves in light brown terra cotta. The building was topped by a soaring tower encircled by a decorative terra cotta frieze ornamented with heads of heroes from German folklore. At street level, an arcade embellished by busts of German poets, artists, and philosophers drew attention to the theater entrance.

Geometrical patterns predominated in the warm yellow-gray terra cotta which framed the simple arched entrance to the Chicago Stock Exchange designed by Adler & Sullivan in 1893. A two-story terra cotta arcade ornamented with low relief signaled the location of the Trading Room. The heavy, projecting cornice harmonized with the ornamental motifs on the body of the building. Some years later, similar geometric shapes softened by organic motifs appeared in the sea-green terra cotta blocks Sullivan used to ornament the exterior of the large country house he designed in 1907 for Chicagoan Henry B. Babson in Riverside, Illinois.

Between 1907 and 1919, when Sullivan's commissions consisted primarily of banks in small Midwestern towns, his buildings continued to be individually designed. Without exception they were profusely ornamented with richly colored terra cotta which combined foliate and geometric forms. Similarly, in 1922, an elegant medallion of lustrous pale green terra cotta crowned Sullivan's last structure, the William P. Krause Music Store and residence at 4611 North Lincoln Avenue, designed in association with one of his former draftsmen, William C. Presto.

Much of Sullivan's terra cotta ornament had been modeled by Kristian Schneider, a Norwegian-born sculptor whom Sullivan personally had trained to execute his designs. Sullivan knew Schneider when the latter was a plaster modeler on the Auditorium Building, as well as at the Northwestern Terra Cotta Company, the firm which since 1880 had supplied terra cotta for Adler & Sullivan's buildings. After 1906, however, when Schneider became chief modeler for William D. Gates's American Terra Cotta & Ceramic Company, many of Sullivan's commissions were executed by that firm. As a result of the association Sullivan and Gates developed a strong friendship which lasted until the architect's death. During Sullivan's last years, when he had few commissions because his architectural style had

184

185

184. Red terra cotta block from an ornamental band on the Ruben Rubel residence, designed by Adler & Sullivan and executed by the Northwestern Terra Cotta Company, 1884. (9¼″ x 16″ x 3½″). *Mr. and Mrs. Timothy Samuelson*

185. Red terra cotta pier capitol from the Henry Stern residence, designed by Adler & Sullivan, 1885. Because this piece did not repeat on the building, it was hand-sculpted by the modeler at the Northwestern Terra Cotta Company. (11½″ x 17″ x 16¾″). *Mr. and Mrs. Timothy Samuelson*

181

187

188

189

186

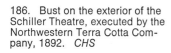

186. Bust on the exterior of the Schiller Theatre, executed by the Northwestern Terra Cotta Company, 1892. *CHS*

187. Terra cotta ornamentation on the Schiller Theatre. *The Richard Nickel Committee*

188. Entrance to the Chicago Stock Exchange, executed by the Northwestern Terra Cotta Company, 1894. *The Richard Nickel Committee*

189. Elaborate green glazed terra cotta blocks ornamented the brick exterior of the Henry B. Babson residence, Riverside. *The Richard Nickel Committee*

190. The Krause music store and residence, 4611 N. Lincoln Avenue, 1922. *Northwest Architectural Archives, University of Minnesota*

fallen out of fashion, Gates remained a loyal friend. As one of Sullivan's biographers recounted:

It was now that industry, like art, came to his aid. So many, many years had Sullivan made use, in his lavish decorations, of terra cotta in all its forms, that he had created for this material a fashion which had gone far to enrich its manufacturers. Christian Schneider (sic), of the staff of the American Terracotta Company, had long been the modeler for Sullivan's designs. So fruitfully had the architect and his modeler collaborated that the Company, whenever Sullivan had modeling to be done in materials other than clay, such as iron casting or sawed wood, were in the habit of lending Schneider to the Sullivan office. The long association had led to firm friendship between Sullivan and the President of the Terracotta Company, C. D. Gates (sic).

Gates was a long, lean angular Yankee whose deepest qualities were kindness and humor. He was a man whose absorption in commerce did not dull his sense of justice. To enable Sullivan still to say he had an "office," Gates and his colleague Albert Sheffield—a dark square-built man who was secretary to the firm and as amiable as his supervisor—invited the champion of terra cotta to move his desk and table into a corner of a large room in the quarters of the company. [*Willard Connelly,* Louis Sullivan As He Lived *(New York: Horizon Press, 1960): 284–85*]

Long before Sullivan's death in 1924 the influence of his masterful style of terra cotta ornamentation was discernible in the work of other Chicago architects. Although Frank Lloyd Wright, a former employee of Sullivan's, later became known for his own distinctive style, he was clearly influenced by Sullivan in his early work. The most obvious example was the pattern on the large tan-colored terra cotta blocks with an overlapping circle motif which surfaced the ground floor of the four-story Francis Apartments, designed by Wright and erected at 4304 South Forrestville Avenue in 1895 (later demolished). Later, in his Prairie houses, Wright rarely used terra cotta except for decorative sculpture, as in the Susan Lawrence Dana house in Springfield, Illinois.

The work of George Grant Elmslie, Sullivan's chief draftsman for sixteen years, also showed a strong Sullivan influence. In 1912 Babson Brothers, a phonograph distributing company, commissioned the architectural firm of Purcell, Feick, and Elmslie to create a new showroom and executive offices for them. The result—a combination of crisp vertical brick piers, foliate terra cotta ornament, and broad recessed panes of glass—was one of the most attractive small commercial buildings of the day.

Purcell and Elmslie, who remained partners until 1922, became known for their designs for relatively small-scale buildings intended for

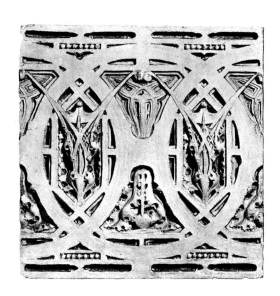

191. Buff terra cotta block from the frieze on the Francis Apartments designed by Frank Lloyd Wright, 1895–96. (17⅞" x 17 7/16" x 4"). *Mr. and Mrs. Timothy Samuelson*

184

public use such as courthouses, town halls, churches, and banks. All of these were richly embellished with exuberant and distinctive terra cotta ornament. While Purcell and Elmslie designed several local residences, the majority of their commissions were executed in various small Midwestern towns rather than in Chicago.

The Terra Cotta Industry Organizes and Advertises

The adaptability of terra cotta to steel frame construction—which became widespread after 1890—revolutionized the terra cotta industry and caused it to expand rapidly. To meet the demand for huge amounts of terra cotta of uniform quality, manufacturers introduced mass-production methods into their factories and employed ceramic engineers to improve the quality of the clay and glazes used. Nationwide, the production of architectural terra cotta doubled between 1890 and 1900; during the following twelve years it quadrupled.

By 1900 the Northwestern Terra Cotta Company had become the nation's largest terra cotta producer, employing 750 workmen in a plant covering twenty-four acres. Along with the younger American Terra Cotta & Ceramic Company, it dominated the Midwestern market. Companies founded in New York, New Jersey, and Pennsylvania during the previous decade supplied the Eastern seaboard, while California's Gladding, McBean & Co. made terra cotta for the West Coast.

This rapid expansion brought competition and price cutting as companies attempted to secure the most profitable and prestigious contracts. And, in their attempt to meet the flood of orders, some firms produced inferior terra cotta. This led to lawsuits by architects and building owners who found themselves saddled with terra cotta that had chipped, crazed, or cracked. Realizing that rampant competition and poor quality work could rapidly ruin the industry, officers of the leading terra cotta companies met in Chicago in December 1911 to organize a National Terra Cotta Society.

Electing Fritz Wagner (general manager of the Northwestern Terra Cotta Company) as president, and William D. Gates (of the American Terra Cotta & Ceramic Company) as secretary, the National Terra Cotta Society pledged to encourage high and uniform standards of work; to promote the use of terra cotta through advertising and publications; and to cooperate in technical matters that would benefit the entire industry. Uniform contract and estimate forms and a code of ethics were adopted and work was begun on a uniform weight schedule. The Society launched a national advertising campaign aimed at architects and draftsmen and published two editions of *Architectural Terra Cotta Standard Construction* devoted to general construction techniques and shop practice. These were followed by a series of brochures, *The*

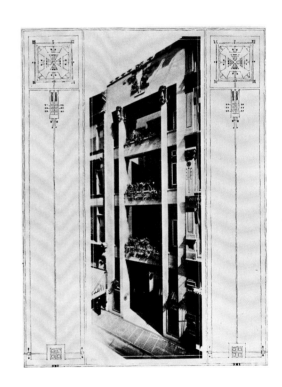

192. The Babson Brothers' Edison Shop, showing terra cotta ornamentation executed by the American Terra Cotta & Ceramic Company, 1912. *Northwest Architectural Archives, University of Minnesota*

School, The Store, The Bank and *The Garage*, which were distributed free to architects' offices and the general public.

To solve some of the technical and scientific problems encountered in terra cotta production, the Society financed two fellowships in the Bureau of Standards, where unbiased experiments in the production of ceramics were conducted under United States government supervision. As a means of acquainting architects and builders with the range and quality of their products, terra cotta manufacturers joined with brick, tile, and pottery producers to sponsor a Clay Products Show in Chicago in 1912.

The National Terra Cotta Society also cooperated with the American Ceramic Society, whose organization in 1899 had been encouraged by terra cotta producing members of the National Brick Manufacturers Association. The founding of the American Ceramic Society in turn led to the establishment of ceramic departments in several state universities, where the training of ceramic engineers did much to further the scientific development and improvement of glazes and clay bodies. In the Midwest, Ohio State University was the first to open a ceramic department—in 1894; the University of Illinois at Champaign-Urbana opened its department of ceramics in 1905.

After the turn of the century, rapid technological advances, combined with the strong demand for terra cotta, led to mechanization and standardization within the terra cotta industry. By 1920 electrical and steam-powered machinery crushed, ground, mixed, and moved the clay. Glaze formulae numbered in the tens of thousands, while colors ranged from cream to glittering ceramic gold.

One important technological change was the invention of a machine capable of extruding unadorned terra cotta blocks known as ashlars in a variety of sizes. Yet another innovation was the glaze "gun" which used compressed air to apply an even coat of glaze to the terra cotta blocks. Finally, newly developed gas-fired tunnel kilns baked the terra cotta blocks which, after being loaded on flatbed cars, were pushed through a temperature-controlled, four-hundred-foot tunnel over a seven-day period by a hydraulic mechanism.

In spite of these innovations, however, most pieces still had to be modeled, pressed, and finished by hand, for the basic procedures required in manufacturing architectural terra cotta were still the same as those followed by the Chicago Terra Cotta works in 1876. Thus the terra cotta industry remained labor intensive, requiring large numbers of workers to manufacture the product and large and profitable contracts to justify substantial overhead expenses.

For modest buildings, architects and builders often minimized the expense of terra cotta by employing "stock" designs kept on hand at the manufactory. These were uniformly sized and pre-priced, allowing the contractor to determine not only the scale but the total price of the completed ornament. They also came in myriad sizes, shapes, and colors, so that pieces could be used alone, repeated in bands, or clustered in groups. Builders who ordered stock designs did not, however, get immediate delivery, since the terra cotta producers kept on hand only the molds and not the finished pieces. Nevertheless, since stock items did not require the services of a modeler they could be more quickly—and therefore more cheaply—manufactured than specially designed items.

The Midland Terra Cotta Company

Although both Northwestern and American offered some stock designs, they were most often associated with the Midland Terra Cotta Company, a new firm organized in December 1910 by William G. Krieg, formerly a city architect, and Alfred Brunkhorst, son of one of the founders of the Northwestern Terra Cotta Company. In its modern plant at West 16th Street and South 54th Avenue in Cicero, the Midland Terra Cotta Company kept in stock hundreds of molds for terra cotta coping, pilasters, columns, and medallions, as well as interchangeable pieces which, when assembled, created entire facades for stores, banks, or garages.

Terra cotta was particularly favored for ornamenting small country banks and Midland's catalog provided intricately detailed plans for four versions of "neat and attractive" bank fronts developed entirely from stock molds. Symbolic of the economic well-being of the community, the bank was a prominent architectural feature of every Midwestern town. It was "the temple to the God of Money, as modern temples go," according to Frank Lloyd Wright, who himself submitted a terra cotta-ornamented design for "A Village Bank" in a contest sponsored by *The Brickbuilder* in 1901.

Many of Midland's stock molds imitated the foliate terra cotta designed by architect Louis H. Sullivan and his protégé George Grant Elmslie. Flattened adaptations of Sullivan's luxurious foliage combined with simplified rectangular devices can still be seen on hundreds of structures ranging from large office buildings to small garages in many Chicago neighborhoods and Midwestern towns. Sullivanesque ornament, like most of Midland's stock terra cotta, featured a glossy white or yellowish-tan glaze, although the company's catalog stated that any color or finish could be supplied on request.

After 1900 the use of terra cotta—particularly stock ornament—on commercial and industrial structures became increasingly widespread as architects and their clients lavished attention on the interiors rather than the exteriors of buildings. As construction techniques became more standardized and modest structures looked more and more like boxes, architects and builders resorted to terra cotta ornament to add an individual touch to an otherwise undistinguished building. This

Midland Terra Cotta Company, 1910–c. 1939.
  Located at W. 16th Street and 54th Avenue in Cicero, the Midland Terra Cotta Company furnished terra cotta for buildings throughout the Midwest. Its major installations in Chicago included Municipal (now Navy) Pier, the Medinah Temple, and the Engineers' Club Building as well as numerous movie theaters.

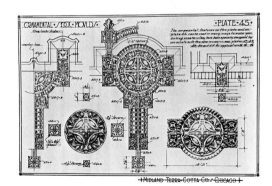

193. Examples of stock terra cotta available from the Midland Terra Cotta Company, c. 1925. *Ryerson and Burnham Libraries, The Art Institute of Chicago*

might take the form of crisp white terra cotta coping, a T-shaped Sullivanesque medallion, a pair of rampant lions, or flower-filled urns.

Terra cotta trim was also used to improve the appearance of apartment buildings, store buildings, and factories. Used in conjunction with brick, light-colored terra cotta effectively lightened the building's façade, accented its entrance, and contributed to a clean, well-kept appearance. Logos, trademarks, nameplates, and ornate entranceways were all easily created in this plastic medium, offering yet another opportunity for architects and businessmen to express their individuality or pretensions while drawing attention to a place or product. In the October 1920 issue of *Common Clay*—which was devoted entirely to a discussion of the artistic use of terra cotta on factory buildings— William D. Gates pointed to the benefits of an aesthetically pleasing working environment: "The man working in an attractive building has more self-respect than the man working in a shack. The man who has self-respect does better work than the man who hasn't," he wrote. Appropriate and attractive trim repaid "a thousand fold the time, labor and brains spent on it." The returns—for architect, client, and worker—were "large and permanent."

Chicago architects would soon find even more spectacular uses for terra cotta as they designed apartments, commercial buildings, and places of entertainment to suit the tastes of a new decade.

Fantasies of the 1920s

Released from the grim realities of World War I, Americans of the 1920s allowed free play to their fantasies during a free-spending decade. In architecture and design this produced a variety of styles best characterized as eclectic historicism.

Eagles, gnomes, and giant owls peered down from the cornices of banks and office buildings, while Indian chiefs, Egyptian pharoahs, and assorted deities guarded auto repair shops, dimestores, warehouses, and other temples of Midwestern commerce. From northern Rogers Park to southern Hyde Park, from elegant lakeside apartment buildings to the Central Manufacturing District, the city sprouted thousands of terra cotta-laden buildings recalling the splendors of the past or crystallizing a flight of imagination. And in the Loop skyscrapers resembling richly iced wedding cakes sprang up next to movie theaters emulating exotic East Indian palaces.

One of the earliest and most celebrated buildings to embody the new architectural mood was the opulent skyscraper erected between 1919 and 1921 at Michigan Avenue and the Chicago River to house the chewing gum empire founded by William Wrigley, Jr. The exterior of the Wrigley Building, designed by Graham, Anderson, Probst and White, was covered entirely with glossy cream-colored terra cotta

194. The Wrigley Building at night. *CHS*

188

ornamented with details suggested by the Giralda Tower of Seville Cathedral, a work dating from the Spanish Renaissance. At night, over 200 floodlights illuminated its Michigan Avenue façade. The intensity of the light, like the various shades of white in the terra cotta sheathing, was graded to provide increasing brilliance of reflected light from sidewalk to searchlight, transforming the building into a dazzling spire that could be seen for miles.

In 1924–25 the passion for skyscrapers embellished with derivative details reached new heights with the construction of the Jewelers Building at 35 East Wacker Drive. Discussing this "recklessly extravagant work" designed primarily by the local firm of Thielbar and Fugard, architectural historian Carl W. Condit noted:

Terra-cotta has never been used more lavishly for strictly orna-mental ends: the entire surface of the twenty-four-story main block and the seventeen-story tower above it is covered with molded tile in the thickly encrusted manner of certain kinds of Baroque architecture. At each corner of the lower volume stands a typically classical embellishment in the form of a colonnaded drum surmounted by a little dome, and a fifth, much larger in size, tops the tower. The four smaller of these belve-deres conceal water tanks, and that at the top is a mechanical penthouse. [*Carl W. Condit,* Chicago, 1910–29, *(Chicago: The University of Chicago Press, 1973): 114–15*]

Originally designed for the jewelry trade, the building was renamed the Pure Oil Building in 1926 when that company became its principal tenant. Later, following another shift in corporate headquarters, it became the North American Life Building.

Another white terra cotta skyscraper impressive in size and clas-sical detail was the Insurance Exchange, the largest office building in Chicago until the 1960s. The building was originally begun by D. H. Burnham and Company in 1911–12; an addition in 1927–28 by Graham, Anderson, Probst and White expanded the structure to cover the entire block bounded by Jackson, Sherman, Van Buren, and Wells streets.

Providing a startling contrast to the pale terra cotta outlined against the sky was the boldly colored Carbide and Carbon Building erected in 1928–29 at 230 North Michigan Avenue. Designed by the firm of Burnham Brothers, successors to D. H. Burnham and Co., the slender ziggurat-shaped skyscraper featured black marble with bronze trim at the entranceway. The first four stories were faced with polished black marble and the remaining thirty-six with smooth bottle green terra cotta. Trimming the soaring fifty-foot campanile and the parapet at the roof level were blocks of gleaming gold terra cotta. The result of an expensive two-fire process, the gold-surfaced blocks had liquid gold incorporated into the glaze.

195. The Jewelers Building (later the Pure Oil Building), 35 E. Wacker Drive, executed by the Northwestern Terra Cotta Com-pany, 1924–25. *David R. Phillips, Chicago Architectural Photographing Co.*

196. The terra cotta façade of
the Marbro Theatre, executed by
the Midland Terra Cotta Company,
1927. *Theatre Historical Society*

197. The Granada Theatre, 6427
N. Sheridan Road, executed by
the Midland Terra Cotta Company,
1926. *CHS*

The gold and green terra cotta used on the Carbide and Carbon Building, as well as the terra cotta sheathing the Wrigley Building, the Jewelers (Pure Oil) Building, and the Insurance Exchange were all produced by the Northwestern Terra Cotta Company. Northwestern, the oldest and largest terra cotta firm in the area, still captured many of the most prestigious contracts within the city. Yet Chicago's two smaller companies, the American Terra Cotta & Ceramic Company and the Midland Terra Cotta Company, were also kept busy manufacturing terra cotta for hundreds of structures throughout the central United States. Between 1920 and 1929, for example, American and Midland together received over 3,800 orders, averaging approximately a contract a day, according to records at the University of Minnesota. Among these were commissions for schools, apartment buildings, department stores, gas stations, factories, banks, railroad stations, automobile showrooms, hospitals, and movie theaters.

Of all the terra cotta buildings, a series of magnificent movie theaters was undeniably among the most imaginative. During the 1920s Chicagoans flocked to the celluloid extravaganzas known as "moving pictures" while movie theater moguls such as Barney Balaban and Sam Katz, Lubliner & Trinz, and the Marks Brothers competed to build opulent terra cotta palaces filled with foliate columns, sweeping staircases, great chandeliers, and elegant fountains. Interior decorative schemes ranged from Moorish to East Indian, while exterior ornamentation ranged from simple marquees highlighted with musical instruments and Greek masks to highly ornate façades heavily encrusted with figures and classical detail.

Memorable theaters in the Loop included the Roosevelt, the Woods, the Chicago, and the Oriental. The West Side had the Central Park, the Paradise, and the Marbro, while the South Side boasted the Avalon, the Tivoli, the South Town, and the Picadilly. Popular North Side houses included the Uptown, the Granada, the Norshore, and the Howard.

According to a 1924 Northwestern Company brochure, an attractive "moving picture facade" of terra cotta was "the best and most permanent advertisement of the entertainment offered." Tactile, fireproof, and economical, terra cotta proved ideal for executing ornate exteriors and throughout the Roaring Twenties all three Chicago terra cotta companies filled dozens of orders for movie theaters. The Rialto, the Plaisance, the Bishop, the Chicago, the Oriental, the Norshore, and the Howard were all executed by the Northwestern Terra Cotta Company. The Central Park and the Woods were the work of the American Terra Cotta & Ceramic Company. Paul F. Larson, a ceramic engineer for the Midland Terra Cotta Company from 1924 through 1928, remembered that his firm supplied the terra cotta for the Marbro, the Granada, the Paradise, the Picadilly, and the South Town. "For the Marbro and [the] Granada we used the same plaster of Paris molds and saved the

198. The Chicago Theatre, 175 N. State Street, designed by Rapp & Rapp and executed by the Northwestern Terra Cotta Company, 1921. *CHS*

200

199

201

202

204

203

205

199. The Chinese City Hall, Wentworth Avenue and 22nd Street, as it appeared in 1949. *CHS*

200. Terra cotta roof detail on the gate to Chinatown, Wentworth and Cermak avenues. *Photo by William R. Boles*

201–204. Details from the white terra cotta façade of the former Hyde Park Chevrolet salesroom, 55th St. and Lake Park Avenue. *Photo by William R. Boles*

205. Polychrome terra cotta logo advertising Peter Hand beer, 1623 N. Sheffield Avenue. *Photo by William R. Boles*

192

206

207

208

209

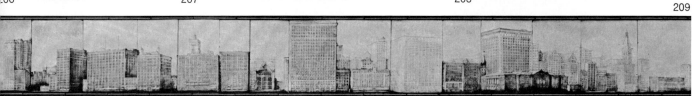

210

211

206. Polychrome Indian head, 4629 N. Broadway. *Photo by William R. Boles*

207. Polychrome terra cotta ornament on a former garage, 5006 N. Clark Street. *Photo by William R. Boles*

208. Detail from the Chinese Club House, designed by Michaelsen & Rognstad and executed by the American Terra Cotta & Ceramic Company, 1929. *Northwest Architectural Archives, University of Minnesota*

209. Chicago's terra cotta skyline captured in a polychrome frieze on a small commercial building at 6560–64 N. Sheridan Road. *Photo by William R. Boles*

210. Buff terra cotta arches at the entrance to St. Thomas the Apostle School, 5467 S. Woodlawn Avenue, designed by Shattuck & Layer and executed by the Northwestern Terra Cotta Company. *Photo by William R. Boles*

211. Winged auto tire in polychrome terra cotta, 3640 N. Halsted Street. *Photo by William R. Boles*

Marx Bros. (sic) considerable money,'' Larson noted.

Automobile showrooms and garages were considerably smaller and less elaborate than movie theaters, but they too incorporated special features. Both required designs featuring very large windows or entrances as well as a large space on a level with the street. Gasoline fumes made it imperative that the buildings be fireproof and thoroughly ventilated.

In Chicago, as elsewhere, the parts and attributes of the automobile tended to inspire rather than to inhibit design, while the limitless adaptability and economy of terra cotta allowed the whimsies of the architect or owner to become reality. On some garages, winged automobile tires or exotic heads wearing earrings of nuts and bolts hovered over the entrance. More conservative shops were decorated with terra cotta floral sprays or bowls of fruit.

A small but elegant Egyptian temple displayed Marmon-Hupmobiles on North Sheridan Road, while Gothic arches richly framed the big display windows of a showroom (now the Broadway Bank) on the corner of North Broadway and West Elmdale. Fanciest of all was the Hyde Park Chevrolet showroom and parking garage on the corner of 55th Street and Lake Park Avenue. Here classy convertibles raced across the white terra cotta building in concert with bas-relief crankshafts, stop lights, tires, dashboards, drive chains, and six-cylinder engines. The ornamentation of the façade for this showroom, built by M. Louis Kreman in 1929, expressed the decade's fascination with speed.

While moviegoers swooned over Rudolph Valentino in the Granada Theatre and mechanics repaired autos under the eyes of mythological gods, other Chicagoans danced away their evenings in the Spanish-Moorish terra cotta-frosted Aragon Ballroom or ate chop suey across from the colorful terra cotta Chinese City Hall on Wentworth Street. Young couples rented courtyard apartments in the gleaming Spanish-style Casa Bonita on North Ridge Avenue, and deposited their paychecks in the Laramie State Bank on Chicago Avenue. Here the bright terra cotta exterior depicted such symbols of prosperity as men hoisting bags of money, families gathering around brimming baskets of fruit, and columns of bubbling coins. Students attending the school attached to St. Thomas the Apostle Catholic Church on South Woodlawn Avenue entered the building under buff-colored terra cotta arches decorated with zigzags and sunbursts, while nearby three seven-foot-high terra cotta angels guarded the entrance to the church itself.

By 1923 the increasing prosperity and upward mobility of the city's population had enabled the moving firm of W. C. Reebie & Brother to erect an expensive Egyptian-style building on North Clark Street to house its general offices and expand its warehouse facilities. Founder William Reebie had originally envisioned a Greek temple, but his brother John, who had been to Egypt, convinced him that an Egyptian

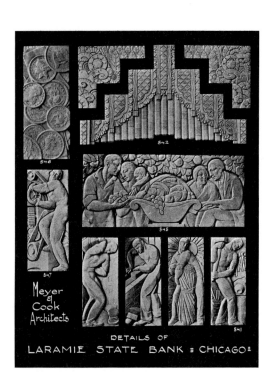

212. Details from the Laramie State Bank (now Citizens National Bank), 5200 W. Chicago Avenue, from *Modern Architectural Ornament*, the Northwestern Terra Cotta Company, c. 1930. *Ryerson and Burnham Libraries, The Art Institute of Chicago*

194

motif was more suitable to the moving and storage business. The discovery of King Tutankhamen's tomb in 1922 reinforced John's argument and inspired the brothers to adopt as their motto: "If old King Tut were alive today, he'd store his goods the Reebie way."

Designed by Chicago architect George S. Kingsley, the W. C. Reebie & Brother building at 2325 North Clark Street displays a variety of colorful Egyptian motifs. Papyrus and lotus, symbols of Upper and Lower Egypt, decorate five sturdy columns beneath a cornice ornamented with a motif featuring green serpents and a sun disk flanked by brilliant blue falcon wings. Two large figures representing Pharoah Rameses II, who conquered the Hittites and built the temples at Abu Simbel, guard the door. To suggest the sun-drenched atmosphere of Egypt the interior of the building was decorated in soft pink, blue, green, yellow, and turquoise plaster accented with gold. Lily and papyrus motifs appear again in the stained glass and on the walls, where colorful inset panels portray the daily journey of the Sun and the transportation of cargo on the Nile—symbolic of the services rendered by the Reebie brothers.

Executed by the Northwestern Terra Cotta Company, the terra cotta for the Reebie warehouse was modeled by Fritz Albert, a self-taught Egyptophile who incorporated hieroglyphics he had himself invented into the terra cotta work. On the base of each pharoah, for example, the name *Reebie Brother* appears in pseudo-hieroglyphics. One pharoah pledges "Forever I work for all of your regions in daylight and darkness," while the other assures "I give protection to your furniture thereby." Albert was so intrigued by the Egyptian style that he went on to create several pairs of terra cotta bookends featuring various gods and hieroglyphic inscriptions with as yet undeciphered references to former Chicago mayor William Hale Thompson.

As Chicago's cityscape attested, terra cotta could be made to assume almost any form, size, color, or texture envisioned by an architect or his client. This was largely due to the plastic nature of the clay combined with a manufacturing process, which created buildings "hand-tailored" to express an architectural idea. The soft clay permitted an ornamental motif to be developed to the most minute detail, while the necessity for a full-scale model allowed the architect to examine, improve, or redesign—a luxury unobtainable in any other masonry material.

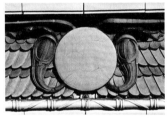

214

215

213. Entrance to the W. C. Reebie & Brother warehouse, 2325 N. Clark Street, executed by the Northwestern Terra Cotta Company, 1923. *Photo by Roberta Stadler*

214. One of the twin pharoahs flanking the entrance to the Reebie warehouse. *Photo by Roberta Stadler*

215. "Reebie brother" in hiero-glyphics devised by Northwestern Terra Cotta Company modeler Fritz Albert. *Photo by Roberta Stadler*

216. Interior of the W. C. Reebie & Brother warehouse, showing stained glass and plaster orna-mentation. *Photo by Roberta Stadler*

217. Polychrome ornament on the Reebie warehouse. *Photo by William R. Boles*

From Blueprints to Buildings

Architects and terra cotta producers spent many hours in collaboration to produce the complex and often fanciful terra cotta ornament and facades that graced many buildings in Chicago and other places throughout the Midwest. Indeed, the labor of hundreds of workers involved in all stages of production intervened between the initial architect's sketch and delivery of the finished terra cotta to the construction site. Actual manufacture of the terra cotta—which began with the pressing of the clay into the mold—could not take place until the preliminary stages involving shop drawings, model and mold production, and clay and glaze selection and preparation had been completed.

Once the decision to use terra cotta had been made by the architect and his client, complete scale drawings and plans for steel framing were supplied to the manufacturer. Draftsmen employed by the terra cotta firm then made shop drawings showing full size details as well as the jointing and construction of the terra cotta. Before the manufacturer proceeded with the work, the drawings were submitted to the architect for approval.

The smallest building required several shop drawings while major structures such as a multi-storied office building required as many as 100 to 200 drawings. Trygve Kristiansen, former president of the Northwestern Terra Cotta Company, recalled that when he joined the firm as a designer in 1924 approximately fifty men worked in the drafting room using ink to hand-draw the designs for the terra cotta pieces on large sheets of linen. Kristiansen, who had studied architecture in Germany, served for many years as a liaison between the Northwestern Terra Cotta Company and the architectural firms.

Once approved by the architect, shop drawings were sent to the factory's modeling room where full size clay or plaster models were made according to the specifications. Photographs of the models were then sent to the architect for further approval. In many cases the architect would come to the factory to check the models before the next stage of production—the making of the molds used to create the finished ornament.

Although some of the country's finest architects designed terra cotta ornamentation, the final product owed its form to the skill and experience of the sculptors who executed the clay models used in the manufacture of the terra cotta. While the names of the modelers who worked in the 1880s and 1890s are unknown, we do know more about the later ones.

Three of the most celebrated modelers employed by the Chicago terra cotta manufacturers early in the twentieth century were Kristian Schneider, Fritz Albert, and Fernand Moreau. Like most of the modelers they had been trained as sculptors before emigrating to America. Fritz Albert, born in Berlin, and Fernand Moreau, a Parisian, had both

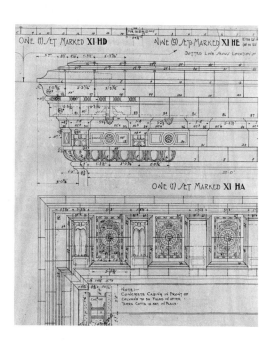

218. Section of scale drawing prepared at the Northwestern Terra Cotta Company detailing the ornamentation for the Rothschild & Co. building (now Goldblatts), State and Van Buren streets, designed by Holabird & Roche, 1912. *Edward and Allen Mertes*

come to Chicago to work on their country's pavilions for the 1893 World's Columbian Exposition. After the Fair, both stayed in the city and eventually went to work for the American Terra Cotta & Ceramic Company, where they modeled Teco pottery as well as architectural ornament for William D. Gates.

By 1906 the two men had joined the Northwestern Terra Cotta Company, replacing Kristian Schneider, a talented Norwegian sculptor who had left to become chief modeler for William Gates. Best remembered for his masterful execution of Louis H. Sullivan's intricate ornament, Schneider acquired an enviable reputation among Chicago artisans. Sullivan, for example, would permit only Schneider to model his ornament, as J. R. Wheeler, president of the Farmers' & Merchants' Union Bank in Columbus, Wisconsin, discovered in 1919. According to one of Sullivan's biographers, Wheeler recalled that:

> The terra cotta ornament seemed very expensive, and no one was good enough to model it, according to Sullivan, but this man Schneider. Finally I went to see Gates, the head of the terra cotta company, and questioned him about his price—rather bluntly, I'm afraid. He told me in no uncertain terms how lucky I was, that he was making no money on the contract, and that for anyone but Louis Sullivan it would be much higher. Gradually I came to realize what I was getting. [John Szarkowski, The Idea of Louis Sullivan (Minneapolis: University of Minnesota Press, 1956): 10]

Schneider remained at the American Terra Cotta & Ceramic Company until 1930, when he joined the Midland Terra Cotta Company. When he died five years later, a young modeler named John Sand was sent over from the Northwestern Terra Cotta Company to complete the ornament he was working on at the time of his death.

John Sand had been a modeler at Northwestern since May 1920, when he arrived with his family from Luxembourg at the age of seventeen. Having attended art school in Europe, Sand was so sure of his modeling aptitude that when he applied for the job he asked permission to complete the normal five-year apprenticeship in three. "In two years I was better than most," he claimed in an interview. Since he spoke German and French, he had no difficulty communicating with the other modelers, most of whom were also immigrants speaking one of those languages.

When John Sand joined the Northwestern Terra Cotta Company, the firm was in the midst of executing the Wrigley Building and Fritz Albert was foreman of the modeling room. Northwestern was at the peak of its production, maintaining 30 modelers and 800 employees. The modeling shop was so busy, Sand recalled, that they worked ten hours a day, seven days a week, with Christmas Day their only day off.

The work was demanding, but modelers were well paid. During

219

219. Polychrome terra cotta detail on the Belle Shore Apartment Hotel, 1062 W. Bryn Mawr Avenue. *Photo by William R. Boles*

220. Polychrome ornamentation at the top of the building at 10 W. Elm Street, executed by the Northwestern Terra Cotta Company, 1928. *Photo by William R. Boles*

the mid-1920s, according to Paul F. Larson, a former Midland Terra Cotta Company employee, modelers received $2.00 an hour—a high wage at a time when the other workers were paid about 60¢ per hour. This differential was due in part to the high degree of skill required to be a modeler and in part to the fact that the modelers had a strong union while the other workers were not organized.

In 1927 officers of the Northwestern Terra Cotta Company brought over six French sculptors. There were several reasons for this. Chief among them was that enactment of the 1924 immigration law had diminished the supply of European artisans in all fields, while the level of skill attained by American-trained craftsmen did not meet the company's standards. But the choice of French rather than German modelers was no accident. On the one hand the management did not want to strengthen the predominantly German modelers' union and on the other it wanted to be the first to introduce the new decorative styles developing in France. French leadership in the decorative arts had been conclusively demonstrated two years earlier in the dazzling display at the 1925 Paris Exposition Internationale des Arts Decoratifs et Industriels Modernes. According to Trygve Kristiansen of the Northwestern Terra Cotta Company, his firm was among the first to manufacture flat "Modern French" terra cotta ornament in the United States. Using motifs inspired by designs in the large exposition catalogs they had brought with them from Paris, the six modelers quickly convinced local architects of the merits of the new "Art Deco" or "Moderne" designs. Soon colorful stylized flowers, dancing zigzags, plump birds, and exotic maidens began to make their debut in Chicago architecture. Unlike the prevailing historically inspired styles, these motifs represented an architectural style that looked to the future.

One of the most talented of the new French modelers was Edouard Chassaing, a young Parisian sculptor who had won two gold medals at the 1925 Paris exposition. At the Northwestern Company Chassaing developed distinctive schemes for ornamentation in the French style for numerous Chicago buildings. In 1928, for example, he helped Chicago architect B. Leo Steif create the motifs for a new apartment building at 10 West Elm. Here fanciful neo-classical figures and geometric forms in shades of blue, peach, coral, and indigo danced above the first floor and below its brightly-hued gables, creating a "Skyscraper in Rainbow Hues" or a "Tall Symphony in Blue" according to contemporary newspapers.

As interpreted in terra cotta by Chassaing and his colleagues, nature was reduced to its basic geometric forms. Flowers and leaves became flattened circles and triangles, while the lines and patterns within these became evenly spaced rays or chevrons. Other favorite forms were volutes, arcs, and rays; bubbles, symmetrical ripples, and fountains; and the stepped form known as the ziggurat. Stylized American Indians, Mayans, Incas, Aztecs, and Egyptians occasionally

appeared, but floral forms tended to predominate. These and Moderne ornament were particularly suitable for multicolored terra cotta, for the interplay of colors helped to emphasize the dramatic forms of the design while making the low-relief ornament more distinct.

In addition to the modelers employed by the terra cotta manufacturers, architects occasionally engaged well-known local artists to execute clay or plaster models for their ornament. For example, Chicago sculptor Richard W. Bock, who had been employed by Northwestern in the late 1880s, later executed clay models for the distinctive stylized ornament on the now demolished Devoe Building (1913) and for the Tree Studio addition (1914) on East Ohio Street, as well as the terra cotta statuette and fountain designed by Frank Lloyd Wright for the Springfield, Illinois, residence of Susan Lawrence Dana. Chicagoans Alfonso Iannelli, Edgar Miller, Eugene Romeo, and Edward Kemeys were also known to have sculpted ornamental models for local terra cotta firms.

While the optimism and energy of the 1920s were reflected in the activities and products of Chicago's terra cotta industry, this mood ended swiftly with the stock market crash of October 29, 1929.

1929 and After

The crash of 1929 created a wave of financial panic which plunged the country into the Great Depression. In common with most other handcraft industries the terra cotta manufactories went into a decline from which they never recovered.

At the time of the crash all three Chicago companies had large building contracts for which the terra cotta had been completed, but for which they had not been paid. Some clients paid in bonds, but these soon became worthless. One by one, contractors, businesses, industries, and even banks failed. By 1932 construction in Chicago had stopped completely. Workers at the terra cotta companies were laid off and production came to an end.

In 1932 William Day Gates, then eighty years old, was forced to give up the American Terra Cotta & Ceramic Company. The firm was taken over by his attorney, George Berry II, and reorganized as the American Terra Cotta Corporation. That same year the Northwestern Terra Cotta Company went into receivership and closed its plant down for a short period. Meanwhile, in an effort to provide jobs for the large numbers of unemployed, the Works Progress Administration, funded by the federal government, commissioned the construction of public buildings throughout the country. The specifications for many of these buildings called for terra cotta and before long the Northwestern Terra Cotta Company reopened and rehired many of its workers.

But changing architectural styles called for a different kind of terra cotta. By the mid-1930s the elaborate terra cotta façades of pre-Depression days had given way to plain, smooth fronts of terra cotta wall ashlars. Extruded from dies in standard shapes and resembling large tiles, the wall ashlars featured solid backs scored for bonding to plaster, brick, or tile. Economically priced and easy to clean, they were recommended for use in the construction of small, low-cost buildings as well as for quite a variety of industrial and institutional structures, such as gas stations, restaurants, laundries, subways, hospitals, schools, and fire stations. In the design of such buildings the dictates of economy and utility inevitably overshadowed artistic considerations.

When building activity resumed in Chicago following World War II, architectural tastes had changed and the city's skyline reflected the influence of the International style. As epitomized by the work of German emigré Ludwig Mies van der Rohe, the new style featured sparse columns of steel and glass distinguished by an absence of ornamental details. Young architects—growing increasingly fascinated with new applications of steel, brick, and glass—limited the use of terra cotta to interior fireproofing or ceramic tiles, employing it for functional rather than decorative purposes.

Post-World War II architectural styles reduced the economic advantage of terra cotta. While it had been a relatively inexpensive material when used for ornamentation, it offered no particular savings when used as pure construction material, since terra cotta ashlars were no cheaper than glass, brick, or marble. As new construction materials became available, terra cotta became increasingly less competitive.

Moreover, by the 1940s terra cotta had begun to lose its reputation as an easy to maintain, non-destructible material. Improper tuck-pointing and inadequate maintainance on the part of building owners had allowed moisture to seep into the joints between the terra cotta blocks on older structures. When Chicago's harsh winters turned the water to ice, the terra cotta cracked and crumbled, requiring expensive replacements and repairs. Supposedly rust-proof metal supports securing heavy terra cotta cornices and ornaments rusted and gave way, releasing mammoth pieces of terra cotta to career into the street. Moreover, much of the newer terra cotta lacked the strength of the earlier product because as the old clay beds ran out manufacturers were forced to rely on inferior clays.

Victimized by high overhead costs, cut-throat competition, and a declining market, the Northwestern Terra Cotta Company closed its doors in 1956. Trygve Kristiansen, president of the company since the early 1950s, took over management of the firm's Colorado subsidiary, the Denver Terra Cotta Company, until it closed in 1960. Modeler John Sand and several other of the remaining Northwestern employees joined the American Terra Cotta Corporation, whose factory continued to produce architectural terra cotta and garden pottery on a small scale until 1966. In that year the company discontinued the manufacture of terra cotta altogether. In the 1940s it had begun to use some of its kiln capacity for the heat treatment of steel; when terra cotta production became unprofitable the firm decided to convert completely to working with steel.

Now, just over 100 years after the birth of America's terra cotta industry, the large factories have vanished and only a few architects and former employees remain to convey the excitement and recall the activity which characterized terra cotta's finest hours. Yet thousands of structures throughout the city and the Midwest serve as testimony to the significant contributions of architectural terra cotta to the American landscape.

221. Polychrome terra cotta logo for the Clearing Industrial District executed by the American Terra Cotta & Ceramic Company. (21" x 20" x 6"). *George A. Berry III, TC Industries, Inc.*

OTHER SHOPS & CRAFTWORKERS

In addition to the individuals and shops whose work forms the basis of this study, numerous other Chicago craftsmen and shops were engaged in the production and sale of locally made ceramics and glass beginning in the 1840s. Little is known about most of these firms and individuals, many of whom remained in business for only a few years.

The following list—compiled from entries in the Chicago city directories, exhibition catalogs, and periodicals—suggests the scope and variety of activity which has made Chicago an important center of ceramics and glass production. The list includes members of the two major china painting clubs, the Atlan Ceramic Art Club (ACAC) and the Chicago Ceramic Art Association (CCAA).

Abbey, David, & Co. Advertised stoneware in the city directory, 1856.

Abercrombie, A. A. CCAA, 1907.

Abercrombie, Mrs. C. B. ACAC, 1907–10.

Adams, Eva. ACAC, 1898–1900.

Alden, Mary A. CCAA, 1899; ACAC, 1906–07.

Allfree, Esther. ACAC, 1916–18.

American Cut Glass Company. Founded about 1897 by William C. Anderson, this firm was in business until about 1920.

Anderson, Irene. CCAA, 1917–19.

Armstrong, Anna. CCAA, 1899.

Ashcraft, Charleta P. Exhibited ceramics at the 1909 and 1910 Art-Crafts exhibitions at The Art Institute of Chicago.

Atchison, Grace. ACAC, 1904. Resident of Evanston, Illinois.

Ayer, Mrs. A. C. ACAC, 1917–21.

Baler, Matilda. Exhibited ceramics in the 1905 Art-Crafts exhibition at The Art Institute of Chicago.

Band [or Bund], Minnie. CCAA, 1914; ACAC, 1918–21.

Beachey, Mrs. Evelyn. Instructor of china painting in the Department of Applied Design at The Art Institute of Chicago, 1904–11. Shared studio at 113 Auditorium Building with Estelle McBride and Augusta B. Waters, 1905–06.

Bell, Mrs. N. G. (Edith). CCAA, 1901–15.

Bentzien, Henry. Stained glass manufacturer, 1891–1902.

Bergen, Lulu C. CCAA, 1901–06.

Berglund, Mrs. A. ACAC, 1914–21.

Bergstrom, Mrs. M. G. CCAA, 1900–1901.

Blaser, William and **Roman Blaser.** Operated a pottery on the North Branch of the Chicago River, 1859–64.

Blodgett, Caroline. ACAC, 1908–11.

Bohmann, Marie. CCAA, 1912–19.

Boudinet, Blanche Van Court Schneider. Instructor in watercolor and china painting at 816 Marshall Field Building in 1906.

Boyd, Susie M. CCAA, 1900–1901.

Brandt, C. Exhibited thirteen pieces of decorated china and nine pieces of painted glass in the 1894 Chicago Architecture Club exhibition.

Brown, Mrs. Anne T. CCAA, 1914–21. Exhibited luster glass and china at The Art Institute of Chicago in 1923. Had won honorable mention for pottery in 1919.

Brown, Frederick. Operated a pottery at 145 Liberty Street, 1860-c. 1885.

Brune-Mayer, May E. CCAA, 1907. Resident of Aurora, Illinois.

Buettgen, Peter. Listed as a glass and china decorator in the city directories, 1900–1905.

Burdette, Mrs. Helen M. Clark. Taught classes in china and watercolor painting at a studio in the Auditorium Building, 1905–07.

Burgeon, Adelbert J. Listed as a china decorator in the city directory, 1896.

Burkland, August P. Listed as a china decorator in the city directory, 1907.

Bush, Mrs. Grace. CCAA, 1916–19. Awarded Burley & Co. prize, 1917; Haegar Pottery Co. prize for best design, 1919; D. H. Abbott and Co. prize for most appropriate design for tableware, 1919.

Butcher, Mrs. L. C. CCAA, 1901.

Cahill, Louise Ripley. CCAA, 1900–1901.

Carlsson & Rorabeck Co. Listed as china decorators in the city directory, 1910.

Carlsson, Olaf A. & Co. Listed as china decorators in the city directory, 1910.

Carlyle China Art Co. Listed as china decorators in the city directory, 1910.

Cawthorne, William. Stained glass manufacturer, 1901–14.

Central Cut Glass Company. Glass cutting firm founded in 1906 by Herman T. Roseen and Andrew Swanson; name changed to Roseen & Collins around 1925. The company closed in 1932.

Ceramic Art Guild. Listed as china decorators in the city directory, 1905.

Chicago Art Glass Co. Manufacturers of stained and ornamental glass, 1887–99. Founded by George H. Bradshaw (1857–1925).

Chicago Art Glass Studio. Advertised as "artists to the trade" in the *Ornamental Glass Bulletin*, 1918–24.

Chicago Ornamental Glass Works. Stained glass manufacturers, 1901–14.

Chicago Pottery Co. Manufacturer of ceramic sanitary fixtures.

Childs, Grace. Listed as a china decorator in the city directory, 1910.

Childs, Minnie. CCAA, 1901–07.

Clark, Mrs. Helen. CCAA, 1899; studio in the Auditorium Building.

Clark, Mrs. H. H. ACAC, 1910.

Classen, John S. Operated a pottery at 214 Blue Island Avenue, 1864–65.

Climax Ceramic Co. Listed in the city directories, 1909–12.

Clinton Glass Co. Stained glass manufactory operated by Louis Osterdorp, 1899–c. 1930.

Cole, Lillie E. ACAC, 1898–1906.

Colonial Art Glass Co. Advertised stained glass and "art lampshades," 1906–14.

Colson, Clarice L. CCAA, 1908.

Cooper, Helen A. ACAC, 1909. Resident of Austin, Illinois.

Cornish, Mrs. Anne. CCAA, 1912–15.

Coulter, Mary L. CCAA, 1905–06; ACAC, 1906–09. Exhibited in Art-Crafts exhibitions at The Art Institute of Chicago, 1905–13.

Cox, Mrs. Augie. Exhibited ceramics in the 1905 Art-Crafts exhibition at The Art Institute of Chicago.

Crane, Mrs. Anna Brauer. CCAA, 1899.

Dahinten, F. X. Art glass stainer, 1888–99.

Daily, Mrs. C. T. ACAC, 1909.

Davis, Mrs. S. E. CCAA, 1901.

Dawes, Effie. CCAA, 1899.

Decorative Glass Mfg. Co. Stained glass manufacturer, 1885–1911.

Dennett, Mrs. Jane S. China decorator. Graduated from the Department of Decorative Design of The Art Institute of Chicago before 1907.

Dudgeon, Edith. ACAC, 1904.

Dunne, Mrs. George. ACAC, 1912–15. Resident of La Grange, Illinois.

Duschek, Emanuel (Samuel). Operated a pottery (flower pots) at 5340 S. Campbell, 1896–1911.

Eastman, Mrs. T. S. CCAA, 1901.

Eberhardt, Hugo & Co. Stained glass manufacturers, 1891 to mid-1950s. Founded by Hugo Eberhardt (1849–1926), the firm was later operated by his son, Max Eberhardt.

Ebert, William O. Stained glass manufacturer, 1891–1907.

Edwards, Amanda. Exhibited ceramics at the 1905 and 1907 Art-Crafts exhibitions at The Art Institute of Chicago; CCAA, 1908–16.

Emmons, Mrs. G. E. ACAC, 1913; CCAA, 1916–19. Won CCAA prize for best individual exhibit in 1919.

Ennis, Sue. CCAA, 1899.

Estabrooks, Gertrude. China decorator who advertised in *Keramic Studio*, c. 1900–c. 1910.

Farrington, Mary. CCAA, 1906–14.

Foster, Lillian. CCAA, 1911–12.

Frazer, Mrs. Beulah L. ACAC, 1900–1906.

Freeman, Helen. CCAA, 1899.

Freytag, Mrs. Harry. ACAC, 1918–19.

Galback, Charles. Operated a pottery at the corner of 16th and Loomis, 1871–80.

Gale, Grace (Mrs. C. A.). ACAC, 1914–21.

Giles, Ada. Listed as china decorator in the city directory, 1905.

Goodman, Mrs. Helen Hastings. Advertised "Lustre, Art-Craft, and Mission China" and offered instruction in "keramics" and watercolor in the July 1906 *Sketch Book*.

Green, Anna Armstrong. CCAA, 1899.

Hadden, Mrs. Herbert T. ACAC, 1910–16.

Haines, Helen M. CCAA, 1907–11.

Hall, Mrs. S. M. ACAC, 1915.

Hamill, Helen A. Exhibited ceramics at The Art Institute of Chicago in 1906.

Hanauer, Nettie Spoor. Instructor in china decoration, 1910.

Harder, William C., Jr. Stained glass manufacturer at 2842 Union Avenue, 1896–1913.

Harver, Elsa Secrest (Mrs. Geo.) ACAC, 1913–17. Resident of Berwyn, Illinois.

Harris, H. B. Exhibited ceramics and glass at the 1916 Art-Crafts exhibition at The Art Institute of Chicago.

Hasburg, John W., Co. Ceramic laboratory founded by china decorator John W. Hasburg (1866–1931).

Heidelmeier Art Glass Works. Stained glass manufactory operated by John Heidelmeier at 4613 N. Clark Street, 1896–c. 1920.

Heinz Brothers. See: Monarch Cut Glass Company.

Helmerich, W. H., Co. Stained glass manufacturer, 1908–23.

Henderson, Mittie. Listed as china decorator in the city directories, 1905–10.

Hess, Emma. ACAC, 1904.

Heuerman, Magda. CCAA, 1900–1901.

Heuermann, Dorothy. Craftsworker specializing in pottery, bookbinding, and needlework. Member of the Chicago Artists Guild.

Heyn, Edward. Listed as china decorator at W. 22nd Street in the city directories, 1905–10.

Hill Art Glass & Decorative Co. Art glass manufacturers, 1896–99.

Hipple, Mary. CCAA, 1912–19. Resident of Elgin, Illinois.

Hoelscher, Mrs. Paul. ACAC, 1909–19.

Holabird Mnfg. Co. Manufacturer of glass advertising signs, c. 1908–10.

Howser, Mrs. F. G. CCAA, 1899.

Hrudka, John.   Operated a pottery on Herndon Avenue, 1896–1911.

Humphrey, Mrs. Edward L.   ACAC, 1898–1914.

Hutchinson, Mrs. Emma.   CCAA, 1914; ACAC, 1915–18.

Illinois Pottery Company.   Pottery operated by Joseph Kuhles at 785 N. Halsted Street 1876–77. Advertised in Chicago city directory as "Manufacturers of Earthenware, Vases, Spittoons, Hanging Baskets, fancy and decorated. Also, plain Flower Pots, Boston Bean Pots, etc."

Ingerson, Charles Frand.   Taught china painting and pyrography in the studio of Jeanne Stewart from 1901 until 1908, when he opened a studio in San Francisco, California.

Inglehart, M. Ellen.   CCAA, 1899–1915.

International Art Studios.   Listed at 2035 Giddings in city directories, 1910–11.

Jack, Mrs. Edna.   ACAC, 1909.

Jenkins, Victoria.   CCAA, 1900–1906.

Johnson, Olive.   CCAA, 1915–17.

Johnson-Carlson Cut Glass Company.   Glass cutting firm operated by Oscar W. Johnson and John Carlson, 1906–c. 1932.

Jones, Mrs. Edwin.   ACAC, 1907–15.

Jones, Mrs. R. A.   ACAC, 1917.

Kalmbach, Jessie.   Designer of stained glass windows and lampshades, 1905–08; graduate of the School of The Art Institute of Chicago.

Kavanaugh, Brideen.   CCAA, 1906.

Keith, Albert.   CCAA, 1902.

Keller, Alexander S.   China decorator listed in the city directory, 1905.

Keller, George, Pottery Co.   Manufacturer of flower pots since 1896. Now located at 2618 N. Lakewood Avenue.

Kerchoff, Florence.   CCAA, 1918–19.

Key, Blanche.   CCAA, 1915.

Kinsella & Haywood.   Painted and leaded glass manufacturers, 1882–84. Succeeded by F. D. Kinsella & Co.

Kinsella, F. D., & Co.   Stained glass manufacturers, 1884–1908.

Kinsella, John J., Co.   Art glass manufacturer, c. 1894–1908.

Kissinger, Isabel.   CCAA, 1911–17.

Klemm, Matilda.   Prominent china decorator who taught classes in Chicago's North Side and Lake View areas, 1890–97. Moved to 18 St. James Place in 1897.

Klipfel, Henry F.   Operated a pottery on W. 14th Street, 1896–1913.

Kohr, August F.   Operated a pottery on N. Leavitt, 1899–1911.

Krendell, Mrs. Edith.   CCAA, 1911–14.

Kulp, Mrs. Eda.   ACAC, 1917–18.

Labhart, Gustav.   Manufacturer of flower pots and cookware on W. Chicago Avenue, 1867–85.

Labhart, John Martin and Julia.   Operated a pottery on W. Chicago Avenue, c. 1846–66.

LaBryn, Harriett.   ACAC, 1915–17.

Langer, Albert.   Stained glass manufacturer, 1896–1909.

Lanyon, Fannie May Beck (Mrs. Charles Henry), (1889–1941).   Decorator of china and lampshades.

Lathrop, W. W.   ACAC, 1917–21. Resident of Aurora, Illinois.

Lawrence, Charlotte.   ACAC, 1904–06. Resident of Rockford, Illinois.

Lawrence, Emma L.   China decorator listed in the city directories, 1905–19.

Lawson, Mrs. Adde.   ACAC, 1898.

Letz, Mrs. Frank.   ACAC, 1917–21. Resident of Hammond, Indiana.

Leyendecker, Adolph A.   Stained glass manufacturer, 1908–16.

Lidberg, Myrtle E.   CCAA, 1907–15.

Liebolt, A.   ACAC, 1911–17.

Liebscher, Wilhelm.   Operated a pottery at 87 Ward Street, 1885.

Lockwood, Bertha.   CCAA, 1911–13.

Lofquist, Andrew J.   Operated a pottery on W. Winona, 1896–99.

Long, Mrs. J. C.   CCAA, 1899.

Lowry, Mrs. Raymond G.   ACAC, 1916.

Luken, Minnie.   China decorator listed in the city directories, 1905–09.

Lyster, Adelaide L.   China decorator listed in the city directories, 1905–07.

Maher, Mrs. Hubert.   ACAC, 1906–07.

Mahoney, Margaret.   ACAC, 1912–17.

Maxson, Mrs. Melina.   ACAC, 1917–21.

McBride, Estella.   Advertised as a china painter in July 1906 Sketch Book.

McConnell, Sarah.   ACAC, 1904.

McCrystal, Mrs. J. B.   ACAC, 1900–1906.

McCully & Miles Co.   Stained glass manufacturers, c. 1876–1913.

McDonald, Mrs. H. C.   ACAC, 1915–16. Resident of La Grange, Illinois.

McWhinney, Mrs. Elgin.   ACAC, 1919.

Mechwart, William.   Took over the pottery owned by F. Brown at 145 Liberty in 1884, which he operated with the help of his sons, Frank and William, Jr., until 1911.

Menzel, Paul.   CCAA, 1899.

Middleton, Matilda.   ACAC, 1900–1915.

Minister, Grace.   CCAA, 1916–18.

Misch, George A., & Brothers.   Stained glass manufacturer, 1860–c. 1903.

Monarch Cut Glass Company.   Glass cutting firm founded in 1901 by Richard, Emil, and Otto Heinz and Herman and Frank Kotwitz. Name changed to Heinz Brothers in 1902. Factory moved to St. Charles, Illinois in 1905, where it closed in 1927.

Myers, Mrs. Maude. CCAA, 1912–14.

Nash & Renning. China decorators listed in the city directories, 1905–1910.

Nye, Mrs. Laura. ACAC, 1906–07.

Park, Mrs. Ralph. CCAA, 1913; ACAC, 1914–19.

Parker, Edythe. ACAC, 1904.

Peck, Grace. ACAC, 1898.

Perlbock, Mrs. M. S. CCAA, 1899.

Peterson, Helga Mae. CCAA, 1908; ACAC, 1912–17.

Petterson, Mrs. Rena. CCAA, 1913–16.

Phelps, Mrs. E. T. CCAA, 1917–19; first prize for best individual piece in CCAA's 1918 exhibition.

Phillips, Joseph, & Co. China decorating firm operated by Joseph and William Phillips, 1881–?

Phillips, Mary A. ACAC, 1898.

Polglase, Grace. CCAA, 1901.

Porter, Alice S. ACAC, 1906.

Pruden, Elizabeth M. ACAC, 1916–18.

Punsch, H. O. CCAA, 1900–1901.

Randall, Cora A. CCAA, 1899–1907.

Rawson & Evans. Manufacturers of ornamental glass and advertising signs, c. 1880–c. 1944.

Ricks, Anna M. ACAC, 1916–17.

Rintoul, Mrs. Robert. ACAC, 1906–07.

Rood, Mrs. Marguerite. CCAA, 1912–17.

Roseen Brothers Cut Glass Company. Founded in 1904 by Herman T. and Joseph Roseen, who sold the firm to the United States Cut Glass Company in 1905.

Ruse, Mrs. Ray Estep. Advertised lessons in china and watercolor painting and metalwork in July 1906 Sketch Book.

Russell, Alice. CCAA, 1902.

Ryan, Mrs. Almira Brewster. CCAA, 1900–1906.

Sanford, Mrs. F. E. ACAC, 1917.

Schaffer, Andrew. Operated a pottery on the Western Plank Road, 1859–60.

Scheck, M. E., & Company. Small glass cutting shop operated by Max E. Scheck, 1907–08.

Schneider, Blanche Van Court. See: Boudinet, Blanche Van Court.

Schuler Art Glass Co. Stained glass manufactory, 1910–c. 1925.

Schuler-Mueller Co. Stained glass manufactory founded by Abram J. Schuler and Max A. Mueller, 1896–c. 1920.

Schwartz, Franz. CCAA, 1901.

Schweizer, John. Listed as a potter in the city directory, 1876.

Secrest, Madge. ACAC, 1904.

Senge, Mrs. Anna. ACAC, 1911–21.

Sessions, Mrs. F. M. ACAC, 1898–1919.

Seugenberger, Mrs. Nellie. CCAA, 1917–19.

Seuss Ornamental Glass Co. Stained and ornamental glass manufactory founded and operated by Max Seuss, 1886–1909.

Sevedahl, Edith. ACAC, 1915–19.

Sexton, Mrs. S. W. ACAC, 1906–21. Resident of Peoria, Illinois.

Shaw, Jessie. China decorator. Exhibited at the 1911 Art-Crafts exhibition at The Art Institute of Chicago.

Smith, Allen M. (1861–1918). Stained glass artist who, according to the October 1918 Stained Glass, was the "best known artist in the West," having created a style of work known as "The Smith designs."

Smith, Mrs. C. C. ACAC, 1915–17.

Smith, Teresa. Exhibited ceramics at the 1905 Art-Crafts exhibition at The Art Institute of Chicago.

Sower, Mrs. Frances. ACAC, 1917–21.

Sparks, Mrs. Mollie. ACAC, 1912–17. Resident of Valparaiso, Indiana.

Standish, Grace M. CCAA, 1899.

Starr, Mrs. Laura. CCAA, 1902–06.

Steele, Mrs. Fred M. ACAC, 1898.

Steinbach, Henry. Operated a pottery on Milwaukee Avenue, 1860–62.

Stewart, Jeanne M. China decorator with studio in Marshall Field Building, 1899. CCAA, 1899–1907. Moved to Portland, Oregon in 1911.

Stoddard, Laura. Instructor in ceramics at The Art Institute of Chicago, 1912–20.

Strong, Charlotte. CCAA, 1901.

Temple Art Glass Company. Art glass manufactory operated by Joseph J. Vogel (1869–1922) and Henry J. Neithart between 1903 and 1933.

Thrash, Mary. CCAA, 1917–19.

Trent, George W. & Co. Manufacturer of stained and ornamental glass, 1889–c. 1900

Trepte, Otto. China decorator. Awarded third prize for naturalistic decoration at the Burley & Co. exhibition, 1913.

Truka, Anton K. Potter, 1901–11.

Tyler, Carolyn. CCAA, 1899.

United States Cut Glass Company. Glass cutting firm in business from about 1905 to 1914, when the name was changed to the Western Cut Glass Company.

Van Hise, Maude. CCAA, 1899.

VanOven, Johanna. ACAC, 1906.

Vesey, Mrs. Belle. CCAA, 1901; officer of the National League of Mineral Painters, 1907

Walker, Abbie Pope. Instructor of ceramic painting at The Art Institute of Chicago, 1911–15.

Walker, Emma I. CCAA, 1900–1912.

Wallace, Helen. Taught china decoration at the Art Institute of Chicago in 1912.

Ward, Mrs. Ada. ACAC, 1917–21.

Warner, Mrs. George. ACAC, 1917–21. Resident of Aurora, Illinois.

Webb, Judson T. Taught pottery at The Art Institute of Chicago, 1903.

Webster, Cora. ACAC, 1915.

Wells, Mrs. Katherine. CCAA, 1900–1901.

Wells, W. H., & Brothers. Stained glass manufacturer, 1870–99.

West, Mary. Taught pottery at The Art Institute of Chicago, 1916.

Western Cut Glass Company. Glass cutting firm operated by Herman and Frank Kotwitz, c. 1914–18.

Western Pottery Company. Manufacturer of flower pots, c. 1923.

White, Ella. Exhibited luster glass at the 1915 Art-Crafts exhibition at The Art Institute of Chicago.

White, Wilomene. CCAA, 1900–1901.

Wight, Blanche. CCAA, 1901.

Willets, Florence. ACAC, 1904.

Williams, Walter. Designer for Faenza Pottery, 1921.

Williamson, Jacob. China decorator listed in the city directories, 1905–10.

Wilson, Mrs. Grover. ACAC, 1917.

Wilt, E. May Johnson. Graduate of the Department of Decorative Design of The Art Institute of Chicago. Employed as a painter by the Pickard China Studio, 1894–95.

Wolf, Mrs. Helen. ACAC, 1915–17.

Wright, Mrs. E. Scofield. CCAA, 1899; ACAC, 1906.

Wright, Mrs. Henry T. Instructor in china painting at Chicago Female College, 1878. Moved to Minneapolis in 1893 and from there to Colorado.

Wright, John. Potter, 1863–66.

Wyeth, Lucy. ACAC, 1914–16.

Yeomans, Marguerite. ACAC, 1898.

Zettler, F. X., Stained Glass Studios. Chicago representative of a stained glass manufacturer based in Munich, Germany.

Zeublin, Mrs. J. E. ACAC, 1898.

SOURCES

▼▼

In the research for this exhibit and publication a variety of sources was used. Often the search began with an object that needed identification. Once a designer, artisan, or manufacturer was identified, it became possible to find other objects made by them or their contemporaries and eventually to discover how these products related to one another and to the larger artistic, economic, and cultural developments of which they were a part. One of the challenges was to trace the histories of undocumented, ephemeral one-person studios; another was to wade through the plethora of materials generated by huge industrial establishments like the terra cotta manufactories.

Once the local significance of an individual or firm's achievement had been assessed, it was necessary to determine the place of that accomplishment in the national or, in some cases, international context. These industries were so much in the mainstream of the city's commercial and cultural life, so much taken for granted, that no particular effort had been made to record their histories. Their very nature gave many of them a short life span. A craftsman could move from one firm to another, set up his or her own shop, go out of business, and retire or move on. When a product became unfashionable it was no longer made and firms diversified and changed their output.

The sources include such standard reference materials as city directories, manufacturers' catalogs, newspapers and periodicals (from the collections of the Chicago Historical Society, The Newberry Library, the Ryerson and Burnham Libraries of The Art Institute of Chicago, and The Center for Research Libraries), and the objects themselves. Among the most helpful sources were the reminiscences of individuals who had been involved in various aspects of these industries or, in other cases, the materials preserved by their descendants out of love and respect for family tradition.

Handpainted China

The most important sources for the study of china painting were the instruction manuals written by Mary Louise McLaughlin, Susan S. Frackelton, Dominick M. Campana, and other painters between the mid-1870s and 1920. The pages of *Keramic Studio* (published in Syracuse, New York, from 1899 to 1924) are filled with information concerning techniques, designs, and exhibitions as well as illustrations of works created by prominent painters. Other useful material was found in *Art for America* (1892–1900), *Brush and Pencil* (1897–1907), *Fine Arts Journal* (1899–1919), and *The Sketch Book* (1902–07), all published in Chicago, and *Arts & Decoration* (1910–42), published in New York. Katharine Morrison McClinton's article, "American Hand-Painted China," in *Spinning Wheel* XXIII (April 1967) is a significant pioneering effort to trace the history of this once flourishing art industry.

Materials on the Atlan Ceramic Art Club include a history written by the club's founder Florence Pratt Steward (Mrs. LeRoy T. Steward), covering the years 1893 to 1902 (in the Chicago Historical Society library); exhibition catalogs (available at The Art Institute of Chicago); and a feature article on the "Ceramic Work of Mrs. Steward" in *Arts & Decoration* 1 (1910–11), which discusses the founding of the club. Biographical information on Ellen Lovgren was provided by her niece Carlyn Whitehand, while a collection of sketches, photographs, and memorabilia donated to the Chicago Historical Society by Mrs. Clifford A. Nolan, Sr., sheds light on the career of Helen F. Frazee.

The Story of Pickard China (Hanover, Pa.: Everybody's Press, 1970) by W. A. Pickard's daughter, Dorothy Pickard Platt, chronicles the history of the company and identifies artists, styles, and marks. Biographical information on other china painters was obtained from Richard J. Donath, grandson of Edward W. Donath; Mrs. William J. Love, niece of John W. Hasburg; and Elsa B. Seidel and Walter E. Seidel, children of Erhardt Seidel.

Art Pottery

In recent years, several exhibitions and their accompanying publications have generated much interest in American art pottery and its makers. Of special help were *The Arts and Crafts Movement in America, 1876–1916* (Princeton, N.J.: Princeton University Press, 1972) edited by Robert Judson Clark; *The Ladies, God Bless 'Em*, an exhibition catalog (Cincinnati: Cincinnati Art Museum, 1976); and *American Art Pottery 1875–1930* by Kirsten Hoving Keen (Wilmington: Delaware Art Museum, 1978). *Art Pottery of the United States: An Encyclopedia of Producers and Their Marks* by Paul Evans (New York: Charles Scribner's Sons, 1974) includes excellent summaries of several Chicago potteries.

Abundant information on Teco ware and the products of The Gates Potteries was found in *The Clay Worker* (1910–15), to which W. D. Gates was a leading contributor; in catalogs issued by The Gates Potteries, 1904–10; and in numerous articles including Charles Crosby, "How Teco Came to Be," *Arts & Decoration* I (March 1911); William Harold Edgar, "The Teco Pottery," *International Studio* 36 (November 1908); Susan Stuart Frackelton, "Our American Potteries," *The Sketch Book* V (September and October 1905); "Gates and His Pottery," *The Clay Worker* LVII (February 1912); Walter Ellsworth Gray, "Latter-Day Developments in American Pottery," *Brush and Pencil* IX (February 1902); Elmer C. Mitchell, "The Art Industries of America: The Making of Pottery," *Brush and Pencil* XV (April 1905); "A New Uplift to American Pottery," *The World's Work Advertiser* VIII (August 1904); Jonathan A. Rawson, Jr., "Teco and Robineau Pottery," *House Beautiful* 33 (April 1913); Evelyn Marie Stuart, "Teco Pottery and Faience Tile," *Fine Arts Journal* XXV (August 1911); and "Teco Potteries," *Pottery Collectors Newsletter* 1 (December 1971). Information on Fritz Albert was provided by Roberta Stadler, Charles R. Steers, and John Sand, while materials on Fernand Moreau were supplied by his daughter, Valentine Moreau Epstein, and his granddaughter, Mary Claire Hersh.

The work of Susan S. Frackelton is the subject of Anne Warrington's "Something New in Pottery," *The Sketch Book* III (September 1903) and, more recently, George A. Weedon, Jr.'s *Susan S. Frackelton and the American Arts and Crafts Movement* (Milwaukee: BOOX Press, 1975). The biographical files of the Evanston Historical Society yielded the transcript of an interview with Mrs. Duane Albery, who operated the Albery Novelty Pottery in partnership with her husband.

Cut & Engraved Glass

Readers with an interest in American cut glass are advised to consult two excellent surveys, Albert Christian Revi's *American Cut and Engraved Glass* (New York: Thomas Nelson Inc., 1965) and Bill and Louise Boggess's *American Brilliant Cut Glass* (New York: Crown Publishers, Inc., 1977). "The Manufacture of Cut Glass" by Edward L. Prentiss, *Brush and Pencil* XVI (November 1905), and "The Story of Cut and Engraved Glass" by Henry Tilden, *Brush and Pencil* XVIII (November 1906) also were useful for this study.

Catalogs of the glass produced by Pitkin & Brooks and other manufactories proved most helpful in comparing the product lines sold by the various firms. Among the most important sources on individual makers are Edward R. Schauble's manuscript about his grandfather, "Edward F. Koch, Manufacturer of Rich Cut Glass" (on deposit at the Chicago Historical Society) and Donald and Russell Parsche, who supplied information about their grandfather, F. X. Parsche.

Stained & Ornamental Glass

General background material on stained glass has been drawn from many sources, of which the most important are *Industrial Chicago: The Building Interests*, vols. 1 and 2 (Chicago: Goodspeed Publishing Company, 1891–96); J. Seymour Currey, *Manufacturing and Wholesale Industries of Chicago*, 3 vols. (Chicago: Thomas B. Poole Company, 1918); Alastair Duncan, *Art Nouveau and Art Deco Lighting* (New York: Simon & Schuster, 1978); Robert Koch, *Louis Comfort Tiffany: Rebel in Glass* (New York: Crown Publishers, 1964); John Gilbert Lloyd, *Stained Glass* (Jenkintown, Pa.: Foundation Books, 1963); and Albert Christian Revi, *American Art Nouveau Glass* (Camden, N. J.: Thomas Nelson Inc., 1968).

The *Ornamental Glass Bulletin* (now *Stained Glass*), first published in Chicago in 1907, contains a wealth of material on local glass producers. Other references appear in *House Beautiful*, *Brush and Pencil*, and *International Studio* as well as *The Inland Architect* (Chicago), *Architectural Record* (New York), and *American Architect and Building News* and *Architectural Review* (both published in Boston). *The Glass Worker*, published in Chicago by the Amalgamated Glass Workers' International Association of America between 1902 and 1915 contains an invaluable record of union activity in this art industry.

Several studies have been devoted to the work of individual art glass designers and craftsmen including David A. Hanks's *The Decorative Designs of Frank Lloyd Wright* (New York: E. P. Dutton, 1979) and T. Donham Wray's "The Stained Glass of Frank Lloyd Wright" in *Glass* 6 (October 1978); *The Second Presbyterian Church of Chicago* by Erne R. and Florence Frueh (Chicago: Second Presbyterian Church, 1978) which mentions a number of local firms; and the Fruehs' article, "Munich Studio Windows at Chicago's SS. Cyril and Methodius Church," which appeared in the Summer 1979 issue of *Stained Glass*.

Relatives and descendants of the art glass makers provided much useful information. Among those interviewed were Marianne Flanagan Zeman, granddaughter of Joseph E. Flanagan; Elizabeth F. Cheney, granddaughter of H. M. Hooker; Frank L. Linden, Jr., son of the founder of the Linden Glass Company; R. J. Pyne, owner of the Western Sandblast Mfg. Co. (formerly Western Sand Blast Mfg. Co.) which bought out Rawson & Evans in the early 1940s; Frank J. Drehobl, Jr., whose father and uncle founded the Drehobl Bros. Art Glass Co.; Thomas S. Snyder, who has worked for several Chicago art glass firms; Robert Williamson, grandson of the founder of R. Williamson & Co.; Arthur Hilgart, son of the former owner of Giannini & Hilgart, and Lubomyr Wandzura, the firm's present owner; Joseph O'Shaughnessy, son of Thomas A. O'Shaughnessy; and artist Edgar Miller, his sons David and Ladd, and his brother Frank.

Architectural Terra Cotta

Information on the manufacture and use of this important Chicago product may be found in several general histories including Frank A. Randall's *History of the Development of Building Construction in Chicago* (Urbana: University of Illinois Press, 1949; reprinted by Arno Press, 1972); Thomas Eddy Tallmadge, *Architecture in Old Chicago* (Chicago: University of Chicago Press, 1941); *Industrial Chicago: The Building Interests* vols. 1 and 2 (Chicago: The Goodspeed Publishing Company, 1891–96); and Walter Geer, *The Story of Terra Cotta* (New York: Tobias A. Wright, 1920), which contains a section on Chicago companies. Chicago Terra Cotta Company superintendent James Taylor's "The Manufacture of Terra Cotta in Chicago," *American Architect* 1 (December 30, 1876) is an important early reference.

Of special significance to this study is the collection of drawings and photographs of the major commissions of the American Terra Cotta & Ceramic Company on deposit at the Northwest Architectural Archives at the University of Minnesota. The collection is described in *The American Terra Cotta Index* compiled by Statler Gilfillen (Palos Park, Illinois: The Prairie School Press, 1973).

Several catalogs of Chicago's major terra cotta companies have been preserved by the libraries of the Chicago Historical Society and of The Art Institute of Chicago. Also basic were the various periodicals on file at The Center for Research Libraries: *Brick and Clay Record* (Chicago, 1892–1910), *Brickbuilder* (Boston, 1892–1916), *Clay Worker* (Indianapolis, 1884–1933), and *Common Clay*, the house organ of the

American Terra Cotta & Ceramic Company edited by William Day Gates. Notes on individual buildings, articles on new uses of terra cotta, and advertisements for various producers abound in the pages of *The Inland Architect*, *American Architect*, *Architectural Record*, and *Western Architect*.

Among those interviewed in association with the history of the various firms were former Northwestern Terra Cotta Company president Trygve Kristiansen; Edward and Allen Mertes of the Mertes Contracting Co., where the records of the Northwestern Terra Cotta Company are now deposited; modeler John Sand, who was employed by Northwestern from 1920 to 1956 and by the American Terra Cotta & Ceramic Co. from 1956 until 1966; Valentine Moreau Epstein and Mary Claire Hersh, the daughter and granddaughter of modeler Fernand Moreau; and Charles Steers and Roberta Stadler, who have been engaged in research on Fritz Albert (see Roberta Stadler's "Reebie Warehouse: King Tut on Clark Street," in the March 1977 *Inland Architect*). The author also corresponded with former Midland Terra Cotta Co. employee Paul F. Larson.

George A. Berry III, the last owner of the American Terra Cotta & Ceramic Co., supplied much valuable material concerning the company's founder, William Day Gates, as did Gates's daughter, the late Mrs. Price Williams, and his grandchildren, Ora Gates and Mrs. John T. Cochrane, Jr.

Of the individual architects who influenced the design and use of terra cotta, Louis H. Sullivan continues to arouse much interest. Paul E. Sprague's *The Drawings of Louis Henry Sullivan* (Princeton: Princeton University Press, 1979) and the efforts of the Richard Nickel Committee of Chicago to assemble a forthcoming catalog of Sullivan's work are important new contributions to the literature on his ornamental design. In *The Architecture of John Wellborn Root* (Baltimore: The Johns Hopkins University Press, 1973), Donald Hoffman discusses the imaginative use of terra cotta by another major figure of the Chicago School.

INDEX

Abbot & Co., A. H., 15, 51
Abel, Elizabeth J., 116
Adams, Eva E., biog. 18
Adams, John C., 135
Addams, Jane, 77, biog. 79
Adler, Dankmar, 180
Adler & Sullivan, 105, 108, 175, 180–1,
    fig. 110 (p. 107), *114* (p. 113), *184–5*
    (p. 181). *See also* Sullivan, Louis H.
Adoration of the Angels, 102
Albert, Fritz, 62, 72, 195, 198–9; *figs. 70–1*
    (p. 63), *78* (p. 68), *82* (p. 72)
Albery, Duane F. and Frances Huxtable, 72;
    biog. 73
Albery Novelty Pottery, 72; biog. 73; *fig. 83*
    (p. 73)
Alhambra Ceramic Works, 74, 80
All Saints Catholic Church, *fig. 104* (p. 103)
Almenraeder, Frederick, *fig. 182* (p. 180)
Almini, Peter, 101
Amalgamated Glass Workers International
    Association (A.G.W.I.A.), 128–9; *fig. 131*
    (p. 128)
American Ceramic Society, 67, 186
American Cut Glass Company, 89, 92
American Ecclesiastical Studio, 129
American Luxfer Prism Company, 114
American Steel Treating Company, biog. 169
American Terra Cotta & Ceramic Company,
    54, 62, 72, 161, 169–71, 175, 179, 181,
    184, 185, 191, 199; biog. 169; *figs. 59*
    (p. 55), *73* (p. 65), *76* (p. 66), *165*
    (p. 170), *192* (p. 185), *208* (p. 193), *221*
    (p. 204). *See also* Gates Potteries
American Terra Cotta Corporation, 203, 204
Anderson, Louise, biog. 18
Anderson, William C., 89
Androvette & Co., George E., 110, 115
Anshe Emet Synagogue, biog. 143
Antique Chinese Enamels pattern, 36
Aragon Ballroom, 194
Architectural Review, 59
Armour, Philip D., 109
Art Amateur, 10
Art-Crafts Exhibition, 58
Art Deco, 44, 199
Art Institute of Chicago, The, 15, 18, 27, 77
    Department of Decorative Design, 15,
    17; biog. 105
    School of, 17, 41, 104; *figs. 86–7* (p. 77)
Art Nouveau, 62, 116

Artists Guild (window), *fig. 154* (p. 159)
Artists Guild of Chicago, 158
The Arts, 15
Arts and Crafts Movement, 10, 27, 66, 75
Arts and Crafts Society, 54
Arts and Decoration, 17, 41
Arts-Crafts Lamps, 135
Arts for America, 12, 14; *figs. 8–9* (pp. 14–5)
Athenaeum Building, 54
Atkins, Anna Pickard, 31; *fig. 32* (p. 31)
Atlan Ceramic Art Club, 12, 14, 15, 17–8, 20,
    26, 27, 41, 74; biog. 18
Auditorium, The, 11, 26, 108, 140; biog. 105;
    fig. 107 (p. 106)
Aulich, Emil, 31
Aulich, Franz Bertram, 12, 14, 43, 44; *fig. 7*
    (p. 13)
Aura Argenta Linear pattern, 36; *fig. 42*
    (p. 35)
Avalon Theatre, 191

Babson, Henry B., 181; *fig. 189* (p. 182)
Babson Brothers, 184
Bailey, Joseph, Sr., 52, 54
Balaban (Barney) and Katz (Sam), 191;
    biog. 143
Baptism of Borivoj (window), 146
Barber, Edwin Atlee, 15
Barber, George M., 168
Barnet Pottery, 74–5, 80
Barnsdale house, Aline, 123
Barothy, Frances (Mrs. A. M.), 41; biog. 18
Barrett, Samuel, 162
Beachey, Evelyn B., 27, 41
Beardslee Chandelier Manufacturing
    Company, biog. 131
Beggs, Helen W. and Stephen J., 75
Beggs Shop, 75
Belle Shore Apartment Hotel, *fig. 219* (p. 200)
Beman, Solon S., 109, 172; *fig. 176* (p. 177)
Bennett, Bessie, 17, 27
Bennett, John, 51
Berglund, Mrs. A., *figs. 18–20* (p. 23)
Bernhardt, Sarah, 51
Berry & Co., James, 103
Berry, George, II, 199; biog. 169
Biedenweg, William E., 110; biog. 115
    See also Flanagan & Biedenweg Co.
Bigelow, Daniel F. and Folger A., 54
Bishop Theater, 191
Blackstone Hotel, biog. 168
Blashfield, John M., 162

Board of Trade, Chicago, 104, 168
Bock, Richard W., 59, 199
Boggess, Bill and Louise, biog. 85
Boisett, E. K., 142
Bordure Antique pattern, 36
Boston Fire Brick Company, 165
Boston Museum of Fine Arts, 162
Boston Society of Arts and Crafts, 26
Bradley house, B. Harley, 120, 135
Bradshaw, Charles H., 149
Bradshaw, George H., 110, 129; biog. 149
Brauer Art Studio (Julius H.), 81
Brooks, Jonathan William, biog. 85. *See
    also* Pitkin & Brooks
Brown, Charles Francis, 70
Brown University, 165
Brunkhorst, Alfred, 187
Brunkhorst, John, 168, 179–80; biog. 168;
    fig. 182 (p. 180). *See also* Northwestern
    Terra Cotta Company
Brush and Pencil, 18, 27, 58; biog. 79
Buckley, H. H., 89
Bulger, William, 77; biog. 79
Burke & Co. (William H.), 136, 137
Burley & Tyrrell, 8, 14, 15, 29, 41, 43, 51, 87,
    89; biog. 90; *fig. 3* (p. 8)
Burnham, Daniel H., 172, 180
Burnham & Co., D. H. (later Burnham
    Brothers), 139, 175, 187
Burnham & Root, 136, 137, 172, 175, 180
Bust of a Child, The, 72

Cady, J. K., 59
Campana, Dominick M., 29, 31, 37, 39, 44;
    fig. 45 (p. 37)
Carbide and Carbon Building, 187, 191;
    biog. 168
Carder, Frederick, 92
Carlsson & Rorabeck Company, 41
Carlyle China Art Company, 39, 41
Carse & Co., W. S., 101
Casa Bonita, 194
Cayuga pattern, 87; *fig. 97* (p. 88)
Centennial Exposition, Philadelphia, 47, 49
Central Art Association, 15, 17, 54
Central Cut Glass Company, 89, 92
Central Park Theatre, 191
Century of Progress Exposition, 44, 157–8
Ceramic Association, Chicago, 11, 27
Ceramic Decoration, 20
Challinor, Edward Stafford, 29, 31, 36; biog.
    29; *figs. 29* (p. 28), *31* (p. 31)

Chapin & Gore, biog. 87
Chassaing, Edouard, 199
Chelsea Keramic Art Works, 49, *fig. 53* (p. 49)
Chicago Architectural Sketch Club, 55, 58
Chicago Art Glass Company, 110, 129
Chicago Athletic Club, 137
Chicago Board of Trade, 104, 168
Chicago Ceramic Art Association, 11, 14, 15, 18, 26
Chicago China Decorating Works, 41
Christ Blessing Little Children, 116; *fig. 132* (p. 129)
Christ in Gethsemane, 149
Church, Myron, 142
Citizens National Bank, 194; *fig. 212* (p. 194)
Clark, Susan H., 8
Clarke, N. L., 59; *fig. 64* (p. 60)
Clay Products Show, 70
Clay Record, 11, 50, 111, 179, 180
Clearing Industrial District, *fig. 221* (p. 204)
Clinton Glass Co., 128
Cobb, Henry Ives, 180
Cochrane, John C., 163
Cole, Lillie E., biog. 18
Colonial Art Glass Company, 128, 133; *fig. 135* (p. 133)
Columbia Theatre, 109
Columbian Ceramic Association, 14
Columbian Exposition, World's, 11, 12, 14, 62, 80, 85, 115–6, 137, 180
Columbus Memorial Building, 116, 137
Common Clay, 64, 187
Company Murano, 137
Condit, Carl W., 187
Congress Hotel, 140; *fig. 119* (p. 118)
Convent of the Sacred Heart, 27
conventional design, 15–17, 18, 27, 29, 36, 42, 44, 58–9, 104–5
Conversational Set in Historic Ornament, 20; *fig. 14* (p. 21)
Cook County Jail and Court House, 170
Coolidge, Charles, 137
Coonley house, Avery, 122; biog. 121; *fig. 125* (p. 124)
Chicago Commerce, 81
Chicago Crucible Company, 72; biog. 70; *fig. 80* (p. 71)
Chicago Fire of 1871, 101, 163, 170, 171
Chicago Flint & Lime Glass Company, 85
Chicago Illustrated, 101
Chicago Millwork Supply Company, 127

Chicago Mosaic Shade Company, 133; biog. 135
Chicago Normal College, 77
Chicago and Northwestern Railroad Terminal, biog. 169
Chicago Opera House, 109
Chicago Pottery Club, 52; *fig. 54* (p. 50)
Chicago Public Library, 139; biog. 105; *fig. 138* (p. 138)
Chicago School of Architecture, 171, 172, 175; biog. 105
Chicago Society of Decorative Art, 10
Chicago Stained Glass Works, 102, 110
Chicago Stock Exchange, 175, 181; biog. 105; *fig. 188* (p. 182)
Chicago Terra Cotta Company, 47, 49, 161–4, 165, 168, 186; biog. 162; *figs. 52* (p. 48), *156* (p. 163), *158–9* (p. 164)
Chicago Theatre, 191; *fig. 198* (p. 191)
China Decorator, 10
china painting, 7–8, 10–11, 12, 14
China Painting: A Manual for the Use of Amateurs in the Decoration of Hand Porcelain, 8; *fig. 4* (p. 8)
Chinese City Hall, 194; *figs. 199–200* (p. 192)
Chinese Club House, *fig. 208* (p. 193)
Chinese Peacock (vase), *fig. 39* (p. 34)
Cooper, Helen G., biog. 18
Coover Studio, 42
Corday Co., James, biog. 120
Cornflower Conventional pattern, 36
Coufall, Tony, *fig. 38* (p. 33)
Craftsman, The, 64, 77, 135
Crane, Richard T., 109
Crile, Reverend Austin D., 146
Crittenden, Mrs. F. A., 12
Cross, Nellie Agnes, Charles William, and Richard Watson, 74
Crossware Pottery, 74
Crucible Gold, 14
Cut Glass Products Company, 89

Dahinten (D. X.), Feulner, & Scott, 110
Dahlquist, Edward and Elizabeth, 75
Dana House, Susan Lawrence, 59, 120, 123, 184, 199; biog. 121; *figs. 122, 124* (p. 124)
Daprato Studios, 149
Davis, Frank L., 136–7
Dawes, Effie, *fig. 5* (p. 9)
Dean, George R., 126
Decorative Art, Chicago Society of, 10

DeLee, Joseph B., 126
Denver Terra Cotta Company, 203
Deserted Garden pattern, 36
Design. See Keramic Studio
Deutch, Eugene, biog. 153
Devoe Building, 199
Diana Court Room (Michigan Square Building), 154, 156; *fig. 152* (p. 155)
Dibble, Mabel C., 12, 20, 26, 44; biog. 18; *fig. 13* (p. 20)
Dodd, William J., 59, 142; *figs. 62* (p. 58), *78* (p. 68)
Dole, Arthur, Andrew R. and John N., biog. 149
Donath, Edward W., 14, 39, 43; *fig. 46* (p. 38)
Doulton ware, 49
Drehobl, Frank J., 128
Drehobl Bros. Art Glass Company, 128, 136, 157; biogs. 143, 146, 151; *figs. 129* (p. 126), *144* (p. 145)
Drummond, William, 135
Dunning, Max, 59; *figs. 66* (p. 60), *78* (p. 67)
Dutch Decoration pattern, 36; *fig. 34* (p. 33)

Easter Lily (plate), *fig. 36* (p. 37)
Eastlake, Charles L., 7, 49, 74
Eberhardt & Co., Hugo, 110, 150
Ecclesiastical Art Guild, biog. 151
Edgerton Art Studio. *See Pickard, Inc.*
Edison Shop, *fig. 192* (p. 185)
Edson, Mira Carr, 17
Elmslie, George Grant, 184–5, 187; *fig. 128* (p. 125)
Empire Cut Glass Company, 89
Encrusted Linear, 36
Engineers' Club Building, biog. 187
Erminie pattern, 85
Exhibit of Applied Arts, Annual, 15

Faenza Pottery, 80
Faher, Joe, biog. 153
faience tiles, 49, 67, 70
favrile glass, 139, 140
Fellows house, William K., 59; biog. 105; *fig. 67* (p. 60)
Ferguson house, 142
Feulner, John, 110
Fire of 1871, Chicago, 101, 163, 170, 171
Fine Arts, The, 26
Fine Arts Building, 26, 27, 74, 75; *fig. 28* (p. 26)
Fine Arts Journal, 67, 70

First Congregational Church, 102
Fisher, Lucius G., 108, 142
Fisher Building, 108, 140, 175; *figs. 106* (p. 106), *172* (p. 176)
Flanagan, James R., Thomas C., and William C., biog. 115
Flanagan, Joseph E., 110, 129, 130, 157; *figs. 117* (p. 118), *143* (p. 144)
Flanagan & Biedenweg Co., 110, 115, 116, 126, 127, 128, 143, 146; *figs. 115–7* (pp. 116–7), *142–3* (p. 144)
Flanders, John J., 172
Flat Enamel Decoration on China, 20
Flood, Minnie Verna (Mrs. Wilder Pickard), 29
Flower in a Crannied Wall, 59
Ford Bros., 128
Foster, Belle, biog. 18
Frackelton, Susan Stuart G., 12, 66, 75; biog. 76; *figs. 84–5* (pp. 75–6)
Francis Apartments, 184; *fig. 191* (p. 184)
Frank house, Louis, *fig. 110* (p. 107)
Frazee, Helen Fenton (Mrs. A. A.), 17, 26, 27, 41, 44; biog. 18; *figs. 2* (p. 6), *6* (p. 11), *9* (p. 15), *11* (p. 17), *15–6* (p. 22), *21* (p. 24), *27–8* (pp. 25–6)
French, Myrtle Merritt, 77, 80; biog. 79
Fry, Laura, 52
Fullerton Memorial Hall (Art Institute), biog. 105

Garden, Hugh M. G., 59; *fig. 63* (p. 59)
Garrick Theatre. *See* Schiller Theatre
Gates, Ellis and Paul, 55; biog. 169
Gates, Major Earl and Neal, 70, biog. 169
Gates, William D.,
  art pottery and Teco ware, 54–5, 58, 59, 62, 64, 66, 70; biog, 57; *figs. 58* (p. 54), *61* (p. 57), *73, 75* (p. 65), *78* (p. 68)
  terra cotta, 169–70, 179, 181, 184, 185, 187, 799; biog. 169; *fig. 181* (p. 179)
Gates Potteries, The, 54–5, 58, 67, 133, 170; biog. 57; *figs. 58* (p. 54), *74* (p. 65). *See also* American Terra Cotta & Ceramic Company
Geer, Walter E., 163, 171
Geranium Art Lamp, fig. 134 (p. 132)
Gerard Company, 41
Gerichten, Ludwig von, 130
Giannini, Joseph R., biog. 120
Giannini, Orlando, 59, 62, 111, 130, 140; biog. 120; *fig. 73* (p. 65)

Giannini & Hilgart, 59, 111, 120, 126, 142, 157; biog. 120; *figs. 119–20* (pp. 118, 121), *127* (p. 125)
Gladding, McBean, & Co., 185
Glass Worker, The, 129; *fig. 131* (p. 128)
Glessner, John J. and Mrs., 49; *fig. 53* (p. 49)
Glover, Joseph N., 161–2
Goldblatts Building, *fig. 218* (p. 198)
Good Shepherd, Church of the (Toledo, Ohio), 146
Goodell, Mrs., 8
Goodhue, Harry Eldredge, 152–3
Graham, Anderson, Probst & White, 187
Granada Theatre, 191; *fig. 197* (p. 190)
Grand Central Station, 109
Grand Pacific Hotel, 103
Grannis Block, 172
Gray, Walter Ellsworth, 55, 58
Great Lakes Naval Station, biog. 169
Great Physician (window), 149
Greenleaf, Mrs. Walter, biog. 18
Griffin, A. T., 171
Groton, Elmer, 55
Grueby pottery, 55, 66, 72
Grunewald, Frederick L., 7, 14, 15
Guler, Max, 128, 146; biog. 146; *fig. 144* (p. 145)

Haegar Potteries, 43
Haenisch, Fran, biog. 87
Halbach, J. Frederick, 109. *See also* Mitchel & Halbach
Hall of Religion, 157–8
Hand Book to the Bric-a-brac Collection, 47
Hand Brewery, Peter, *fig. 205* (p. 192)
Harles, George, 149
Hasburg, John W., 14, 15, 18, 43, 44; *fig. 8* (p. 14)
Harrison, Annie Pratt, 11
Harrison, Carter, biog. 151
Haviland & Co., 49
Havlin Theatre, 109
Hazenplug, Frank, biog. 79
Healy, George Louis, 104; biog. 105
Healy & Millet, 17, 104–5, 108, 115, 116, 140, 142, 157; biog. 105; *figs. 105* (p. 104), *107–8* (p. 106)
Heart pattern, biog. 87
Heine Chimney Company, H., 81
Heinz Brothers (Emil, Otto, and Richard), 89, 93. *See also* Monarch Cut Glass Company

Heller home, Isidore, 120
Herndl, Marie, 116
Herrick Designs Co., 42
Herzog, Nathan, 179
Hilgart, Fred, 157; biog. 120
Hilgart, Fritz, 110–1; biog. 120. *See also* Giannini & Hilgart
Historic Ornament, 17
Hobstar and Wreath pattern, biog. 90
Ho Ho Shop, 75
Holabird & Roche, 139, 175, 180; *fig. 218* (p. 198)
Holabird & Root, 154, 156; biog. 153. *See also* Root, John Wellborn
Holloway, Charles, biog., 105
Holy Name, Cathedral of the, 102
Holzchuh, L., 146; biog. 146
Holzer, J. A. 116, 139
Home Insurance Building, 171, 172
Hooker Company, Henry M., 110, 129, 149; biog. 149; *figs. 146–7* (p. 148)
Hooley's Theatre, 109
Hotel Dorrance, 165
Hottinger, Adolph F., 179
Hottinger, Gustav, 179; biog. 168
House Beautiful, 18, 64; *fig. 116* (p. 117)
Hovey, Albert H., 162
How to Use Enamels on China, 126
Howard Avenue Trust & Savings Bank, 157; *fig. 153* (p. 158)
Howard Theatre, 191
Hull-House Kilns/Shops, 77, 80; biog. 79; *figs. 88–90* (pp. 78–80)
Humphrey, Mrs. Edward L., biog. 18
Hunt Glass Company, biog. 90
Husser house, Joseph M., 140
Hyde Park Chevrolet, 194; *figs. 201–4* (p. 192)

Iannelli, Alfonso, 156, 199
Illinois Central Railroad Station, 179
Illinois Host House, 158
Illinois Naval Armory, biog. 169
Illlinois State Capitol, 163; biog. 162
Illinois Terra Cotta Lumber Company, 171
Immaculate Conception window, 150
Immaculate Heart of Mary Catholic Church, biog. 143
Indianapolis Terra Cotta Company, biog. 169
Inland Architect, The, 101, 108, 110, 111, 112, 115, 168; *fig. 166* (p. 171)
Institute of Building Arts, 136–7

Insurance Exchange Building, 172, 187, 191
International Art Glass Catalogue, fig. 133
   (p. 130)
Inter-State Exposition Souvenir, 103
Interstate Industrial Exposition, 47, 102
Irwin Building, *fig. 157* (p. 163)
Italian Garden pattern, 36; *fig. 29* (p. 28)

Jacobus, Oscar I., 29, 52
Jacobus, Pauline Bogart, 51–2; biog. 52
   See also Pauline Pottery
Jann, Adolf, 8
Jarvie, Lillian Gray, 74
Jarvie, Robert R., 135
Jarvie Shop, 74, 75
Jeffrey, Mrs. John B., 52
Jenkins, Victorine B., 12, 50, 52, 54
Jenney, William LeBaron, 58, 162, 171, 172,
   175, 180
Jenney & Mundie, 179
Jensen, Jens J., 157; *fig. 153* (p. 158)
Jevne & Co., Otto, 101–2
Jewelers Building, 187, 191; *fig. 195* (p. 189)
Johnson, Ernest V., 171
Johnson, George H., 170
Johnson, Mae, 29
Johnson-Carlson Cut Glass Company, 89, 93
Jones mansion, W. S., biog. 121
Journal of the American Ceramic Society, 92
Juarez, Miguel, *fig. 88* (p. 78)
Junge, J. H., 171

Kammermayer, Fred B., 81
Katz, Sam, 191
Kay Bee China Works, Inc., 80, 81
Kemeys, Edward, 199
Kendall Building, 170, 171
Kenwood Studios, 41
Keramic Studio, 10, 16, 20, 27, 29, 39, 43–4,
   74; *fig. 10* (p. 16)
King, Mrs. Philo, 52
King Arthur (panel), *fig. 150* (p. 152)
Kingsley, George S., 195
Kinsella, John D., 110
Kittredge, Emma, biog. 18
Klipphahn, Max, *figs. 33, 35* (p. 33)
Koch, Edward John, 89; biog. 87
Koch, Robert, 90, 139
Koch Cut Glass Company, 89–90, 92, 93;
   biog. 90; *figs. 98–100* (pp. 91–3)
Koehler, Florence, 17, 18, 27
Kogan, Sol, 153
Kotwitz, Frank, 89

Kotwitz, Herman E., 90, 92
Krause, William P., 181
Krause Music Store and residence, *fig. 190*
   (p. 183)
Krayle Workshop, The, 116
Kreman, M. Louis, 194
Krieg, William G., 187
Kristiansen, Trygve, 198, 199, 203
Kugel, Peter, biog. 146

Labor Museum, biog. 79
Ladies Home Journal, The, 10, 64
LaFarge, John, 104, 105
lampshades, art glass, 131, 156
Laramie State Bank, 194; *fig. 212* (p. 194)
Larson, Paul F., 191, 194, 199
Last Ray, The (vase), 37
Lau & Co., Willy H., 128, 135
Lazar, Joseph, biog. 146
LeBaron, Francis, 111
Legge, James, 164
Leistnner, Oscar, 81
LeVeau (sculptor), 74
Lewis Institute, 77
Libbey Glass Company, 80, 89
Light of the World, 116
Limoges ware, 49, 51
Lincoln window, Abraham, 149; *fig. 145*
   (p. 147)
Linden, Frank Louis, 104, 109, 120, 130;
   biog. 121
Linden Glass Company, 109, 120, 122, 130;
   biog. 121; *figs. 122, 124* (p. 124), *150*
   (p. 152)
Linderoth, Sven, 72, 74, 80
Linderoth Ceramic Company, 74
Linstedt, Mrs. D. B., biog. 18
Little house, F. W., 120
Llewlyn, Joseph, 142
Loring, Edward, 165
Loring, Sanford E., 162, 163, 165, 168, 171;
   fig. 52 (p. 48)
Lovgren, Ellen, 26; *figs. 12* (p. 19), *22–6*
   (pp. 24–5)
Loyola University, 150, 152
Lubliner & Trinz, 191
Lucas, Harry J., 163, 165, 171
luster ware, 26–7
Lutwyche Glass Co., 128
Luxheim, Joseph A., biog. 115
Lyceum, 109
Lyster, Adelaide, 8

McArthur house, Warren, 120; *fig. 120*
   (p. 121)
McCall, Thomas, *fig. 123* (p. 124)
McCrystal, May (Mrs. J. B.), biog. 18
McCully (John) & Miles, 102, 104, 110, 115,
   116, 149
McGarn, Augusta Barton, biog. 18
McIntyre, Lettie, biog. 18
McKee Glass Company, 92
McLaughlin, Mary Louise, 8, 10–11, 49–50;
   52; *fig. 4* (p. 8)
McLennan, Teanna, 27
McSwiney Memorial Window, 150; *fig. 148*
   (p. 151)
McVicker's Theatre, biog. 105
Madonna della Strada Chapel (Loyola
   University), 151–2; biog. 150
Magerstadt house, Ernest J., 123; biog. 121;
   figs. 121 (p. 123), *141* (p. 141)
Magi (window), *fig. 143* (p. 144)
Maher, George W., 123, 126, 135, 140, 142;
   biogs. 105, 121; *figs. 121* (p. 123), *126*
   (p. 125), *140–1* (pp. 141–2)
Mallers Building, 172; *figs. 167* (p. 172)
Mann, Cornie, H., biog. 18
Maratta, Hardesty Gilmore, 67; *fig. 73* (p. 65)
Marbro Theatre, 191; *fig. 196* (p. 190)
Marker, Curtis, 36; *figs. 37* (p. 33), *39* (p. 34)
Marks Brothers, 191, 194
Marquette Building, 116, 139, 175; *figs. 139*
   (p. 139), *171* (p. 176)
Marquette window, 149
Marsh, Mrs. John W., 8, 12
Marshall Field, 109
Marshall Field & Company, 11, 20, 29, 52, 87,
   92, 116, 139–40; biog. 29; *figs. 96–7*
   (pp. 86, 88)
Martin house, Darwin D., biog. 121
Masonic Temple, 175
Mathews, Gertrude Singleton, 75
Meat Course Set, 20
Medinah Temple, biog. 187
Meli, Giovanni, 162
Merchandise Mart, biog. 168
Mertz, Father James, 150, 152
Michaelson & Rognstad, *fig. 208* (p. 193)
Michigan Square Building, 154, 156; *fig. 152*
   (p. 155)
Middleton, Matilda, biog. 18; *fig. 17* (p. 22)
Midland Cut Glass Company. *See* Koch Cut
   Glass Company

Midland Terra Cotta Company, 161, 187, 191, 199; biog. 187; *figs. 193* (p. 187), *196–7* (p. 190)
Midway Gardens, 122, 156; biog. 121
Mies van der Rohe, Ludwig, 203
Miller, Edgar, 153–4, 199; biogs. 112, 153; *figs. 151–2* (pp. 154–5)
Miller & Co., Edward, 133
Millet, Louis J., 17, 18, 104–5, 130, 140, 150, 157; biog. 105; *figs. 109* (p. 107), *140* (p. 141). *See also* Healy & Millet
Mineral Painters, National League of, 12, 14, 15, 27, 74; biogs. 18, 76
Minton tiles, 49, 51
Misch, Adolph, 102
Misch & Bro., George, 102, 104; biog. 115; *fig. 103* (p. 102)
Mitchel & Halbach, 104, 108, 109, 131
Modern Decorative Arts, Exhibition of, 154
Moderne, 44, 199
Monarch Cut Glass Company, 89
Montauk Block, 172
Moon Children, The (sculpture), 59
Moran & Hastings Manufacturing Company, 133
Moreau, Fernand, 62, 72, 198–9; *figs. 51* (p. 46), *69* (p. 62), *78* (p. 68), *82* (p. 72), *101* (p. 99)
Morgan Company, 127
Morris, William, 7, 58, 74
Morse Building, 165
Mosser house, E. J., 135
Moulton, George M., 171; biog. 121
Mt. Washington Glass Company, 89
Mucha, Alphonse, 116
Mueller, George, 131
Mueller, Max A., 110, 114, 126, 130
Mundie, W. B., 58; *figs. 68* (p. 61), *73* (p.65)
Munich Studio, The, 128, 146, 149; biog. 146; *figs. 132* (p. 129), *145* (p. 147)
Munich windows, 109
Municipal Pier, biog. 187
Musée des Arts Décoratifs, 105
Museum of Fine Arts, Boston, 162
Musical Afternoon (plate), 39

National League of Mineral Painters, 12, 14, 15, 27, 74; biogs. 18, 76
National Ornamental Glass Manufacturers' Association (Stained Glass Association of America), 130; biog. 115; *fig. 133* (p. 130)
National Terra Cotta Society, 185–6

naturalistic design, 15–7, 18, 27, 29, 31, 42, 90
Navy Pier, biog. 187
Nichols, J. F., 162
Nichols, Maria Longworth, 49
Nickerson, Samuel M., 142
Nimmons, George C., 59
Norshore Theatre, 191
North American Life Building (Pure Oil Building; Jewelers Building), 187
North Shore National Bank of Chicago, 157
Northwestern Terra Cotta Company, 62, 70, 161, 168–9, 171, 172, 175, 179, 181, 185, 191, 195, 198, 199–203; biogs. 70, 168; *figs. 79, 81–2* (pp. 71–2), *155* (p. 160), *157* (p. 163), *160–4* (pp. 166–8), *168–73* (pp. 173–6)
Norweta ware, 70; biog. 70; *figs. 79, 81* (p. 71)

O'Brien, Reverend Patrick, 146
O'Brien's Art Gallery, 51
Ohio State University, 186
Old Time Printer's Association, biog. 151
Olsen, Olivia, 8
Oriental Theatre, 191
Ornamental Glass Bulletin, The (Stained Glass), 130; biog. 115
O'Shaughnessy, Joseph, 152
O'Shaughnessy, Thomas Augustin, 149, 150, 152, 158; biog. 151; *figs. 148–9* (p. 151), *154* (p. 159)
Ostertag, Blanche, 59, 140
Our Lady of Sorrows Catholic Church, biog. 146
Owasco pattern, 87
Oxford Electric Company, biog. 149

P & B grade, 85
Paist, Henrietta Barclay, 43–4
Palmer House, 103
Paradise Theatre, 191
Paris Exposition of 1889, 105
Paris Exposition of 1900, 18
Parsche, Donald C., 93; biog. 87
Parsche, Frank C., biog. 87; *fig. 92* (p. 84)
Parsche & Son Company, F(ranz) X., 85, 87, 92; biogs. 87, 90; *figs. 92* (p. 84), *97* (p. 88)
Partridge mansion, Edwin, biog. 121
Patience, Persistence, and Progress (Atlan Club motto), 12

Patten house, James A., 123, 140, 142; biog. 105; *fig. 140* (p. 141)
patterns, cut glass, 85, 87, 89, 90, 92; biogs. 87, 90; *fig. 91* (p. 82). *See also* names of individual patterns
Pauline Pottery, 29, 31, 52; biogs. 52, 54; *figs. 55–7* (p. 53). *See also* Edgerton Pottery
Peacock Alley (Congress Hotel), *fig. 119* (p. 118)
Peck, Grace H., biog. 18
Peck, Walter S., 168
Peters Co., H. J., 133; *fig. 136* (p. 133)
Peterson, Helga M., biog. 18
Picadilly Theatre, 191
Pickard, Henry Austin, Jr., biog. 29
Pickard (Wilder Austin) Inc. (formerly Pickard China Studio; Edgerton Art Studio), 29, 31, 36, 37, 39, 41, 43, 44, 80, 81; biog. 29; *figs. 31–45* (pp. 31, 33–5)
Pink Enamel Flowers pattern, 36
Pinwheel pattern, biog. 87
Pioneer Fire Proof Construction Company, 171; *fig. 166* (p. 171)
Pinto pattern, 85
Pitkin (Edward Hand) & Brooks, 85, 87, 89, 92; biog. 85; *figs. 91* (p. 82), *93–5* (pp. 85–6)
Plaisance Theater, 191
Plymouth pattern, 85
Pompeiian Room (Auditorium Annex), 64; *fig. 75* (p. 65)
Poor, Taylor, biog. 153
Popular Mechanics, 135
poster art windows, 116
Pottery Decoration Under the Glaze, 49
Powers, Mr. and Mrs. John, 149
Prairie School of Architecture, 58, 59, 123, 126, 135, 140, 152
Praying Mohammedan pattern, 36
Presto, William C., 181
Preston, Jessie M., 135
Preuszner, Roxanna Beecher, 8, 12, 50–1, 54; biog. 18
Price, Catherine, 168
Pullman, Mrs. George M., biog. 105
Pullman Building, 172
Pullman Palace Car Company, 41, 114–5, 135, 157, 168
Pullman residence, biog. 121
Punsch, H. O., 14

Purcell, Feick, and Elmslie, 184–5
Pure Oil Building, 187, 191; *fig. 195* (p. 189)
Pyne, R. J., biog. 112
Pyrographic Glass Company, 109–10
Pyrus Flocks (plaque), 37

Queen of the Elves, The (window), 116
Queen Louise Descending, 39

Rand McNally Building, 172, 175; *fig. 170*
   (p. 174)
Rapp & Rapp, *fig. 198* (p. 191)
Rawson & Evans, 111–2, 115
Reade, Christia M., 15, 17, 116, 135; biog. 105
Rebori, Andrew, biog. 153
Reebie & Brother, W. C., 194–5; *figs. 213–7*
   (p. 197)
Reed, Earl H., Jr., 154
Reliance Building, 137, 175; *fig. 175* (p. 177)
Revi, Albert Christian, biog. 85
Rialto Theater, 191
Richards, Agnes Gertrude, 26
Richter, Adolph, *figs. 34* (p. 33), *42* (p. 35)
Roberts, E. L., 127
Robertson, Hugh C., 49
Robie house, Frederick G., biog. 121
Robineau, Adelaide Alsop, 10, 16
Rockford College, 27
Rohkam, Henry, biog. 168
Roman Gold, 14, 31
Romeo, Eugene, 199
Rookery, 136, 171, 172, 175; biog. 168;
   figs. 168–9 (p. 173)
Rookwood Pottery, 49–50, 52, 67; biog. 52
Roosevelt Theatre, 191
Root, John Wellborn, 136, 137, 180. *See*
   also Holabird & Root
Rose Window pattern, biog. 90
Roseen, Herman T., 89
Rothschild & Co., *fig. 218* (p. 198)
Royal Doulton Pottery, 36
Royal Insurance Building, 168
Royal Society of Arts, 26
Rubel house, Ruben, 180–1; *fig. 184* (p. 181)
Rubens house, Harry, 123, 142
Ryerson Library (Art Institute), biog. 105;
   fig. 109 (p. 107)

Saint Agnes Catholic Church, biog. 146
Saint Andrew Episcopal Church, biog. 115
Saint Beatrice Catholic Church, 143

Saint Catherine of Genoa Catholic Church,
   116, 149
St. Cecilia (window), 149
Saint Ita Catholic Church, biog. 115
Saint Leo Catholic Church, biog. 146
Saint Luke Catholic Church (River Forest),
   biogs. 150, 151
Saint Margaret Mary Catholic Church, 149;
   biog. 146; *fig. 145* (p. 147)
Saint Patrick Catholic Church, 150; biog.
   151; *fig. 148* (p. 151)
Saint Philip's Lutheran Church, biog. 146
Saint Procopius Abbey, biog. 151
Saint Stephen Episcopal Church, 158; biog.
   151
Saint Thomas the Apostle Catholic Church
   and School, 194; *fig. 210* (p. 193)
Saint Veronica Catholic Church, biog. 146
Saint Vincent Catholic Church and Academy,
   biog. 115; *fig. 143* (p. 144)
St. Wenceslaus, Ruler of Bohemia, 146
*SS. Cyril and Methodius Bringing the Church
   to the Slavic People,* 149
Saints Cyril and Methodius Catholic Church,
   146
Sand, John, 199, 203–4; *fig. 162* (p. 166)
Sanger, Mrs. Mary McKibben, biog. 105
Sargeant, John, 52
Satsuma pottery, 26, 42, 43; *figs. 17* (p. 22),
   19–20 (p. 23)
Saylor, H. H., 154
Schaefer, Herwin, 105
Schiller Theatre, 175, 181; biog. 105;
   figs. 186–7 (p. 182)
Schmidt, Frederick J., 7
Schmidt Ceramic Company, 41
Schneider, Kristian, 181, 184, 198–9
Schoenfeld, E., 126
Schoner, Otto, *fig. 36* (p. 33)
School of Art, South Side, 8
Schreiber & Annas, 126
Schuler (Abrahm J.) & Mueller (Max) Co.,
   110, 114, 126
Schuler & Co., Walter A., 128
Schulze, Herman, biog. 146
Schwartz, Franz J., 14
Scott, Isaac E., 49, 54, 164; *fig. 53* (p. 49)
Scott, John, 110
Scudella, Theodore, 135–6, 157
Scudella, William, 136, 157
Second Presbyterian Church, biog. 105;
   fig. 118 (p. 118)

Sedji porcelain, 42
Seeburg Piano Company, J. P., 136; biog.
   143
Seidel, Anna, 39
Seidel, Erhardt, 31, 37, 39, 44; *figs. 47–8*
   (pp. 39–40)
Seipp, Conrad, 109
Selz residence, Morris, *fig. 108* (p. 106)
Seuss Ornamental Glass Co., *fig. 111* (p. 110)
Sessions, Mrs. F. M., biog. 18
Shanahan, Dennis S., 128, 146; biog. 146
Shattuck, W. F., biog. 105
Shaw, Howard Van Doren, 59, 123, 142, 154;
   biog. 153; *fig. 118* (p. 118)
Shawsheen Pottery, 75
Sheffield, Albert, 184
Shephard Public School, Henry O., biog. 151
Shepley, Rutan & Coolidge, 139
Sighs of the Pond (plaque), 39
Sign and Scene Painters Union, 156
Simon, Adolph G., Jr., 37
Sinai Congregation, Temple of the, 102
skyscrapers, use of terra cotta in, 172, 175,
   179, 180–1, 184–5
Sleeper, Fred L., 14, 43
Snyder, Thomas S., 151
South Side School of Art, 8
South Town Theatre, 191
Sower, The (tile), 116
Spencer, Robert C., Jr., 140
Spierling (Ernest J.) & Linden, 104, 109;
   biog. 121. *See also* Linden, Frank Louis
Spring Valley Tile Works. *See* American
   Terra Cotta & Ceramic Company
*Stained Glass (Ornamental Glass Bulletin,
   The)* 130; biog. 115
Stained Glass Association of America
   (National Ornamental Glass
   Manufacturers' Association), 129–30;
   biog. 115; *fig. 133* (p. 130)
Starr, Ellen Gates, biog. 79
Starring, L. T., 8
Steffens house, Oscar, 123
Steif, B. Leo, 199
Stern residence, Henry, *fig. 185* (p. 181)
Steward, Florence Pratt (Mrs. LeRoy T.), 17,
   18, 20; biog. 18; *fig. 14* (p. 21)
Stickley, Gustav, 135
Stone house, Foler P., *fig. 126* (p. 125)
Strauss, W. C., *fig. 86* (p. 77)
Stuart, Evelyn Marie, 67, 70, 127
Studebaker Building, *fig. 176* (p. 177)

Suggestions to China Painters, 8
Sullivan, Louis H., 105, 108, 140, 180–1, 184, 187, 199; *figs. 108* (p. 106), *114* (p. 113). *See also* Adler & Sullivan
Sunburst Globe pattern, *fig. 91* (p. 82)
Sunnybrook, biog. 87
Swanson, Andrew, 89
Swastica Shop, 75

Tacoma Building, 172; biog. 168
Tallmadge, Thomas Eddy, 59, 123, 154
Tallmadge & Watson, 142
Taylor, James, 162–3, 164, 165; biog. 162
Teacher of China Painting, The, 39
Teco Inn (Radisson Hotel), 70
Teco ware, 54–5, 58–9, 62, 64, 66–7, 130, 133; biogs. 57, 169; *figs. 51* (p. 46), *60–74* (pp. 56–65), *77–8* (pp. 66, 67)
Temple Art Glass Company, 128
Thayer & Chandler, 14, 51
Thielbar and Fugard, 187
Thomas, Cyrus P., *fig. 157* (p. 163)
Thomas, R. V., biog. 149
Thompson, William Hale, 195
Three Arts, The (painting), 116
Tiffany, Louis Comfort, 105, 135–6, 137–9
Tiffany Glass & Decorating Company, 36, 115–6, 135–6, 137, 140
Time and Energy Co., 42; *fig. 50* (p. 42)
Tivoli Theatre, 191
Topping, Helen M., biog. 18
Trautmann, George R., 135
Tree Studio, 199
Tremont Hotel, 103
Troescher Building, 180–1
True, John R., 168, 179; biog. 168
True, Brunkhorst, & Company. *See* Northwestern Terra Cotta Company
Tyrrell, Burley & Co., 8, 14, 29; biog. 90

Union Park Congregational Church, 102
United States Cut Glass Company, 90
University of Chicago, 77
University of Illinois at Champaign–Urbana, 186
Uptown Theatre, 191

Van Briggle Pottery, 67
Van Osdel, John M., 162, 170, 171; *fig. 103* (p. 102)
Venetian Building, 11, 175
Vesey, Belle Barnet, 74–5

Vestals, The (vase), 37
Vivirito, Saviour and Laurence, biog. 135
Vogel, Joseph J., 128
Vokernick, Franz, 31
Volkmar, Charles, 51

Wagner, Fritz, 179, 185
Walker, Abbie Pope, 27
Wandzura, Lubomyr, 157; biog. 120
Washington window, George, 149; *fig. 145* (p. 147)
Washburne, Marion Foster, 77, 80
Weber Sign Co., J. H., *fig. 112* (p. 111)
Wells, Julia, biog. 18
Wells & Bro., W. H., 102, 110
Wells Glass Company, 115
Western Cut Glass Company, 90, 92
Western Decorating Works, 7–8, 14, 51; *fig. 4* (p. 8)
Western Mineral Painters, 17
Western Sand Blast Mfg. Co., 112; biog. 112; *figs. 113–4* (pp. 112–3)
Wetzel, M. J., 156
Wheeler, Ione L., 26–7
Wheeler, J. R., 199
White, Albert L., 90
White, M. P., 59; *fig. 65* (p. 60)
White's Art Company, 39, 41; *fig. 49* (p. 41)
Wicker Park Evangelical Lutheran Church, 146
Wieroeder, George, biog. 146
Wight, Peter B., 171, 180
Wight Fireproofing Company, 171
Wildwood pattern, 36
Williamson & Co., Richard, 133, 156; biog. 131; *fig. 134* (p. 132)
Willits house, Ward, 122; *fig. 127* (p. 125)
Wirick, Charles Barnet and Jean Paul, 75, 80
Wolbach, Murray, 154
Woman's Building, 11, 12, 116
Woman's Temple, 175
Woods Theatre, 191
World's Columbian Exposition. *See* Columbian Exposition, World's
World's Fair of 1893, Chicago, 54
Worship of the Wise Men, The (window), 116
Wright, Frank Lloyd, 59, 62, 114, 120, 122–3, 126, 133, 135, 142, 156, 157, 184, 187; *figs. 120* (p. 121), *122, 124–5* (p. 124), *127* (p. 125), *191* (p. 184)
Wright, Mrs. J. V. D., biog. 18

Wrigley Building, 187, 191; biog. 168; *figs. 155* (p. 160), *194* (p. 188)

Yeschek, Frank, *fig. 41* (p. 34)
Yeschek, Joseph, 31

Zettler, Emil, 72
Zeublin, Mrs. J. E., biog. 18
Zimmerman, W. Carbys, 142